Forever Ambridge

Twenty-five years of The Archers

NORMAN PAINTING

BY ARRANGEMENT WITH
THE BRITISH BROADCASTING CORPORATION

SPHERE BOOKS LIMITED
30/32 Gray's Inn Road, London, WC1X 8JL

First published in Great Britain by
Michael Joseph Ltd 1975

Copyright © Norman Painting 1975

Sphere Books edition published 1976

to the one who didn't laugh

TRADE
MARK

Set in Intertype Lectura

Printed in Great Britain by
Hazell Watson & Viney Ltd
Aylesbury, Bucks

Contents

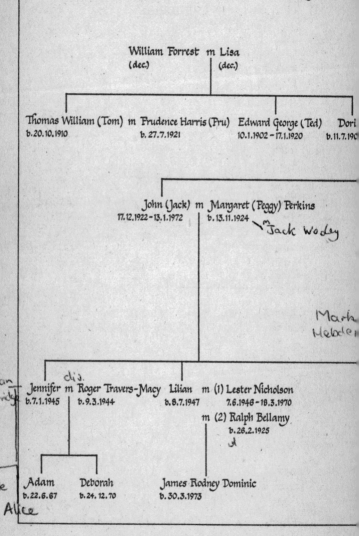

The Archer

William Forrest m Lisa
(dec.) (dec.)

Thomas William (Tom) m Prudence Harris (Pru)   Edward George (Ted)   Dori
b. 20.10.1910   b. 27.7.1921   10.1.1902 – 17.1.1920   b. 11.7.190

John (Jack) m Margaret (Peggy) Perkins
17.12.1922 – 13.1.1972   b. 13.11.1924
                              m Jack Wodey

Mark
Helder

Brian
Aldridge

Jennifer m Roger Travers-Macy   Lilian   m (1) Lester Nicholson
b. 7.1.1945   b. 9.3.1944   b. 8.7.1947   7.6.1948 – 18.3.1970
                         div.
                                      m (2) Ralph Bellamy
                                              b. 26.2.1925

Kate

Alice

Adam   Deborah   James Rodney Dominic
b. 22.6.67   b. 24.12.70   b. 30.3.1973

# of Ambridge

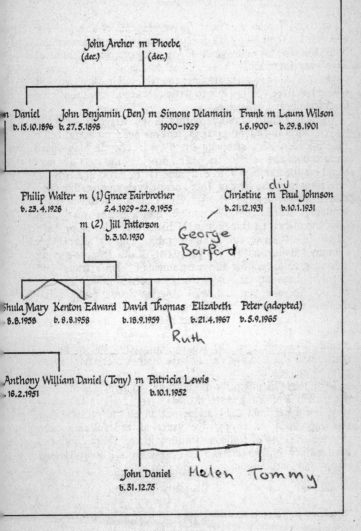

John Archer m Phoebe
(dec.)   (dec.)

|n Daniel|John Benjamin (Ben) m Simone Delamain|Frank m Laura Wilson|
|b. 15.10.1896|b. 27.5.1898   1900–1929|1.6.1900– b. 29.8.1901|

Philip Walter m (1) Grace Fairbrother   Christine m Paul Johnson
b. 23.4.1928   2.4.1929–22.9.1955   b. 21.12.1931 *div* b. 10.1.1931

m (2) Jill Patterson
b. 3.10.1930

George Barford

|Shula Mary|Kenton Edward|David Thomas|Elizabeth|Peter (adopted)|
|8.8.1958|b. 8.8.1958|b. 18.9.1959|b. 21.4.1967|b. 5.9.1965|

Ruth

Anthony William Daniel (Tony) m Patricia Lewis
. 16.2.1951   b. 10.1.1952

John Daniel   *Helen   Tommy*
b. 31.12.75

Author's Note

My grateful thanks are due to the whole team of The Archers, not only for their help with anecdotes and illustrations for this book, but also for many years of happy association. Although I have been there longer than any other member of the Cast – having played the same part since the trial run in May 1950 – it would have been impossible to write this account without help from friends and colleagues.

My dear friend and radio 'Mother' Gwen Berryman, who has played Doris since January 1951, lent me her scrapbook; while June Spencer, who, although she played Peggy in May 1950, handed over the part for ten years, provided me with her personal recollections of both early and latter days. Bob Arnold, who took over the part of Tom Forrest early in 1951 has also shared his memories with me. Anne Cullen generously made available her large collection of photographs and Alan Devereux, Chris Gittins, Edgar Harrison and Colin Skipp have all provided their accounts of memorable incidents. Miss G.I.M. ('Jimmy') Bailey, as well as being one of our longest-serving recording-engineers for the programme, is also a friend and talented photographer, whose work has been of value.

Tony Shryane and his wife Valerie, whose phenomenal memory can be called upon to confirm details of incidents that happened long ago, have offered ready help and encouragement; and Jock Gallagher, the Radio Network Editor at BBC Birmingham, has read the whole manuscript and made his mark upon the last five years of the Archer story with many valuable suggestions.

To all these friends and colleagues, and to many whom I have not named, I offer my grateful thanks. This book is not a history, but a personal celebration; not an official account, but the impression of twenty-five years of broadcasting seen through the eyes of someone who was there. Every effort has been made to ensure that the facts presented are accurate. Any errors, and all the emphases, are my own.

Foreword

by Tony Shryane

Producer of The Archers
for twenty-five years

The old adage about mighty oaks and little acorns might almost have been coined for the BBC's everyday story of countryfolk – The Archers.

Its beginnings were inauspicious enough: a low-budget regional programme produced in the Birmingham studios for a local audience that could only be counted in thousands.

It is true that most of us connected with the programme did have high hopes for it – particularly me. It was my first effort as a producer and I wasn't exactly unaware that my career prospects could be all too-closely linked with the success or failure of the new venture.

But, if we had high hopes, none of us – not even, I'm sure, Godfrey Baseley who originated the series – anticipated what was to happen when the programme was transferred to the Light Programme and broadcast to the whole country on 1 January 1951.

None of us foresaw the programme growing into one of radio's biggest audience attractions of all time; of being heard daily by more than twenty million people in Britain and many more all round the world; of creating so many myths that they're now difficult to recount and almost impossible to explain; and to becoming an almost-essential part of the British way of life.

But then everyone who has ever been associated with the programme has their own particular story to tell – some funny, some tragic, some merely actual. Add them together as Norman Painting does in tracing the history of The Archers and you get, in my opinion, twenty-five amazing years.

Introduction

Few radio programmes have generated so much love and, proportionately, so little hate as The Archers. It tells an everyday story of countryfolk, as it has done for twenty-five years; and this book is a celebration of that quarter of a century during which millions of listeners have followed the daily life of an English farming family and their friends.

When the programme began, much of English life was different from today. Only a mere handful of television sets was licensed, whereas there were over twelve million licensed radio sets – over thirty radios to every TV set. Not many families had a car; fewer still had two. Refrigerators were still regarded as luxuries, home-freezers unheard of, and washing and washing-up machines rarely found in the average home.

Many farmers milked by hand and ploughed with horses. Air-travel was for the few – and hijackings were unknown. The two great popular entertainments were the cinema and the radio, though variety theatres and music-halls continued to draw good, but diminishing, audiences.

Britain still had a complete network of steam railways. Central-heating was mainly confined to public buildings or very large private houses, and double-glazing was uncommon. Space-travel was still a dream, but austerity and food rationing a daily reality.

It was into this grey post-war world of shabbiness and shortages that The Archers entered, bringing with it a glimpse of a way of life that, although subject to the same shortages, the same restrictions and the same frustrations, seemed less daunting and more coloured with hope. The sun shone brighter there, the grass was greener.

The programme was warmly and immediately welcomed. Within weeks of its beginning it became a favourite with listeners: very soon it was more than that. For many, the characters in Ambridge were real people, and their lives more real than reality – certainly more meaningful than many of the daily lives of our listeners' own families, friends and relatives.

Letters from widows, neglected aunts or lonely people in bedsitters were posted to 'Brookfield Farm, Ambridge near

Borchester' and safely delivered. Such letters were often written as if to some understanding friend, revealing secrets and emotions that were closely hidden from real people living near at hand.

This book attempts to show at least some of the many reasons why The Archers took so quickly, and has maintained so continuously, such a hold on the affection and imagination of so many people. It is a personal account: the author has not only been actively involved in the programme both as performer and writer throughout its life, but also during the months when it was merely a suggested programme idea under consideration.

No one guessed in those days that if a programme called The Archers should eventually emerge, it would run for twenty-five years, least of all the performers, or the producer. Those of us who have played the same part from the beginning must have spent between three and a half and four years of our lives in the recording studio!

Tony Shryane who has produced most of the episodes throughout the whole run must have directed something like sixty million words of dialogue. Enough recording tape has been used to stretch from Land's End to John O'Groats and half-way back again – representing some 1,625 hours of broadcasting.

In Ambridge the cows have been milked some twenty-six thousand times, and the population has drunk more than twenty thousand cups of tea and over twelve thousand pints of beer.

The signature tune 'Barwick Green' has been played on the air over twenty-eight thousand times, and yet remains fresh. Indeed, although it must be the most frequently heard piece of music of the last quarter-century, it still found a place on a recently-issued BBC disc in a swinging arrangement by Norrie Paramor, with the Midland Radio Orchestra.

Astonishing figures like these, which allow the programme to qualify for a place in the record books, were far from our minds back in 1950 when the idea of The Archers was first being seriously considered. Even a life running into months, rather than weeks, was almost too fanciful to consider. Today some of us still find ourselves wondering whether it really is true that we have continued for so many years, for fact and fantasy have marched arm in arm through The Archers' story.

In this book, that recurrent theme, the blending of reality

11

and imagination, has been emphasized by the list of events which heads the account of each year. The list is in two sections: events in the world, and events in Ambridge. The latter happened only in Ambridge of course: but the world events were part of the world of Ambridge too.

1951

THE YEAR OF

The Festival of Britain in spite of continuing austerity and food rationing. C. R. Attlee ceased to be Prime Minister after the General Election in October and Winston Churchill took over again. The Coronation Stone, stolen the previous Christmas, was returned to Westminster Abbey. The Russian delegate to the United Nations appealed for settlement of the Korean War.

IN AMBRIDGE

Dan and Doris Archer's son, Jack, was scratching a living at a small-holding while their other children, Christine and Phil, lived at home. Chris worked at Borchester Dairies and fell in love with her boss who was much older than she, and already married; while Phil, recently out of Farm Institute, disappointed his father by accepting a post as manager on Fairbrother's farm instead of working at Brookfield. Jack and Peggy's third child, Anthony William Daniel, was born on 16 February.

It all began very modestly. Everyone concerned with it knew that this was something experimental, something that had never before been attempted in Britain. There had been daily serial programmes, of course, both on the BBC and Radio Luxembourg. There was the *Dick Barton – Special Agent* type. There had been family serials, too: *The Robinson Family* from London and once-weekly serials from other parts of Britain. *Mrs Dale's Diary* had begun not long before in 1949, but although it was about a doctor's family, its sole aim was to entertain and not to inform the listeners about medicine and the problems of a G.P. (not, that is, until many years later, when it attempted to ape The Archers).

The Archers was different. From the start, the aim was to

13

reflect a completely accurate picture of farming life. It was to give farmers information and even advice that would help them in their daily routines and it was meant to give townsfolk a better idea of the farmers' problems in trying to produce the country's essential food supplies. It was to be information presented as entertainment.

That serious intention, far from being a disadvantage, gave the programme a hidden strength, a rigid framework. By being tied so firmly to the land, and the lives of those who worked on the land, it was never free to slip very far in the direction of the merely trivial or the superficial contrivances of pure 'soap-opera'. It had to succeed in both parts of its twofold aim of informing and entertaining: and if it failed to entertain, it would certainly fail to inform.

Getting that first episode broadcast on 1 January 1951 in the Light Programme was something of a triumph (even if it was to be heard at the rather odd time of 11.45 a.m.). The Light Programme, with its vast audience, demanded high quality entertainment: preaching or teaching were not exactly the order of the day. In a very short time, the listeners would tell us whether the pill was sufficiently well sugared.

Even if the venture only lasted a few weeks, though, it was an exciting undertaking. With luck, it was said, the programme might last three months. The whole team was on its toes.

If the programme failed as entertainment, it would be taken off. If, on the other hand, it didn't succeed in attracting farmers to listen so that they would hear and act upon the advice it offered, again it would not satisfy those who had promoted it as basically an information programme.

For the original idea for The Archers had come from a meeting of farmers who had been invited by the BBC to advise on how factual farming broadcasts could be improved. What emerged from that meeting was that few farmers had serious complaints about the programmes themselves: the difficulty was that farmers in general did not listen to the radio. At this point a farmer from Lincolnshire, Henry Burt, rose to his feet and said: 'What we want is a farming *Dick Barton*.' Everyone laughed, and he sat down.

Dick Barton – Special Agent was a serial adventure thriller, broadcast in fifteen-minute instalments in the BBC Light Programme. Mr Burt, though, was not suggesting that farming broadcasts should be sensationalized. His point was that *Dick Barton* was written in such a way that if a listener heard one

14

episode he was very strongly drawn to listen to another . . . and then the next and the one after that. Each episode ended with Dick in a seemingly impossible situation: hungry lions, a deep ravine, rising flood-waters, a bomb with a lighted fuse – indeed any hazard the writers could imagine, awaited him unless he extricated himself and his companions Snowy and Jock. It was compulsive listening: listeners once hooked tended to become daily devotees.

However, one man, Godfrey Baseley, did not laugh at the suggestion of a 'farming *Dick Barton*'. The idea was certainly unusual, even perhaps absurd . . . and yet! The prospect of a large audience tuning in every evening to hear fifteen minutes about farming problems was a tempting, if fanciful, prospect. The idea simply would not go away. Godfrey Baseley was at the time concerned mainly with producing farming, country and gardening programmes, often taking part in them himself, as chairman or interviewer. Although he had often worked in earlier years as a radio actor, he had little experience in writing or producing radio drama – and a 'farming *Dick Barton*' would need to be moulded in dramatic form. His approach had always been what today is called 'documentary' – using real people: a 'farming *Dick Barton*', would need actors, scriptwriters, radio drama studios. It all seemed too revolutionary to be considered seriously.

The idea persisted, however, and eventually Godfrey Baseley, encouraged by the Controller and the Head of Programmes of Midland Region, began to explore the actual possibilities.

The first problem was the script. To represent a farming family in radio terms meant that a writer with an expert knowledge of radio-writing technique would be needed. Equally important, was the question of authenticity. If the characters' dialogue sounded actor-ish or like stage countryfolk with Mummerset accents, it would be unacceptable to genuine country people. The question developed into a search for either a farmer who could write for radio: or a radio writer who would be prepared to study farming.

When it was learnt that Edward J. Mason – one of the two scriptwriters of *Dick Barton* – was interested, the idea suddenly seemed more viable. Edward J. Mason (Ted) brought with him his fellow scriptwriter from *Dick Barton*, Geoffrey Webb, who luckily was a countryman. Godfrey's expertise on farming matters and the writing skill and experience in serial-writing of Ted and Geoff soon produced draft scripts of what suddenly seemed, after all, to be a workable project.

Throughout this period I was working both in the studio and in a nearby office as a member of BBC Contract staff as a writer, interviewer and producer, and was able to follow the growth of the idea, especially in many conversations with Godfrey and Ted. (Geoff Webb lived some distance away and it was to be some years before closer acquaintance was possible.) Indeed, I was told on various occasions at this time that I was being considered as a possible writer, researcher, and even producer for the show. To each suggestion I reacted positively: but the offer which finally came was to take part as a performer.

Godfrey was determined that the name of the family whose day-to-day life was to be portrayed should begin with an open vowel; and he soon persuaded Ted and Geoff that Archer had the right ring to it. The same principle applied to Ambridge, and that was accepted. The name of the Archers' farm was more difficult though. A name was chosen; but unlike Archer and Ambridge it did not survive – Wimberton Farm.

Midland Region BBC officials were soon convinced that the idea was worth trying and money was made available for five episodes to be broadcast in Whit week 1950.

There were no auditions for that trial run. Eight out of the nine characters who appeared in it were played by experienced radio actors, though I was the only one who had previously appeared in a series of programmes produced by Godfrey Baseley. We were told that we had been chosen because our work at the microphone was known to the writers and producer, but we were to regard the five episodes as a kind of audition. Even if the experiment were successful, and more episodes were asked for, we were not to assume that we should automatically be asked to return to play the same parts. In the event, only two of us failed to please, and later in the year only two auditions were held.

Sitting at the dramatic control panel was BBC Birmingham's most expert senior programme engineer, Tony Shryane, soon to become the programme's producer.

In a daily serial one of the most important elements in attracting the listeners' attention is the beginning of each episode: the opening seconds must be in some way arresting, and yet at the same time set the mood and atmosphere of the programme. It must be counted as one of the happiest accidents that a piece of music called 'Barwick Green' by Arthur

Wood was not widely known in 1950, and that it was discovered by Godfrey Baseley when looking for a signature tune for The Archers. It must now be almost as familiar as the National Anthem and has been heard over the whole world.

It has also been heard in many other programmes besides The Archers – not only in comedy programmes like *The Morecambe and Wise Show* or the unforgettable take-off by Tony Hancock, but in straight plays, as a means of establishing time: the sound of 'Barwick Green' from a radio set signifies 6.45–7 p.m. not only in radio productions, but in the theatre – in *Look Back in Anger* for example. Films, too, have used the signature tune in the same way. It is a hallmark: the sound of 'Barwick Green' has become synonymous with The Archers. Tony Shryane has described it more than once as a tranquillizing shot in the arm, marking the beginning of fifteen minutes' respite from the tensions of real life.

The choice of 'Barwick Green' may be one of the reasons for the surprisingly rapid success of the programme but there were certainly others. For one thing the characters and dialogue had a freshness and naturalness that was new: the atmosphere, the sound effects and the characters' reactions to farming matters were authentic. There was a liberal lacing of humour, and the skill of the writers ensured that the end of each episode left listeners with such teasing and unanswered questions that they felt they had to listen to the next day's episode.

We met to read through the first five trial scripts at 6.30 p.m. on 12 May 1950. The following day we rehearsed all five scripts. And on Sunday 14 May we recorded the five episodes.

Two weeks later, starting on Whit Monday, which was then a public holiday, the first of the five scripts was broadcast. We listened, our families and friends listened – and fifty thousand other Midland Region listeners switched on, too. It seemed to go well: comments were favourable and numerous, criticisms were remarkably few.

Then came a kind of anti-climax. That one week's broadcasts might be the beginning and the end of it: we could only control our impatience while the BBC made up its mind whether the idea was worth pursuing or not. There was nothing we could do but wait. On the day after recording those first five episodes of the trial run, several of us were back in the studio taking part in a serialization of George Eliot's *The Mill on the Floss*. It was, in other words, back to work, while the decision that was to affect our future was slowly reached by the BBC.

One thing was destined not to survive, though, whatever happened: the name Wimberton Farm. By the time the decision was reached to give The Archers a further airing, the immortal Brookfield Farm had been created.

In the months of waiting, after the trial run of the programme the previous May, rumours abounded. The Archers had been rejected out of hand it was said; influential people in the Ministry of Agriculture had appealed to the BBC to save the programme. It was even reported that the Director-General himself, when asked for a ruling, had said: 'No more family programmes unless there's a war!'

There was, in fact, a distinct possibility of war at the time. Those austere years after the Atom Bomb had ended the Second World War were uneasy and uncertain. Having only recently seen the end of another World War, many people still felt on the edge of an abyss. There was an apocalyptic, doomsday feeling.

From its first broadcast on the BBC Light Programme on 1 January 1951, The Archers opened a window on to a more desirable world. Here were people with the same human thoughts, feelings, strengths and weaknesses as their listeners, breathing the same air, battling with the same problems, speaking the same language. Perhaps the sun shone more brightly in Ambridge; and yet, on the other hand, the frost was just as keen, or keener, and the mud as unpleasant as mud elsewhere. From the first, The Archers seemed completely authentic, vivid and real. The explanation, though, is a simple one: from the start the programme relied implicitly on the imagination of its listeners.

Every voice carries with it a different impression for every listener: so care was taken not to conflict with this impression, by giving too many details of the physical appearance of anyone. Grace's beauty was not described; Walter Gabriel's outlandish appearance was created in the listener's mind by his voice. It was the same with Ambridge itself and the individual buildings that made it up. Words are heady stuff: the phrase 'a small country village in a valley' will create a far more vivid picture in the minds of listeners than any painted backdrop.

Early on, the principle was established and drummed into the Cast, that the dialogue was to be not so much heard as overheard: statements were rarely if ever directed at the listener. We tried to build up an audience of eavesdroppers . . . but eavesdroppers who ran no risk of hearing ill of themselves.

Part of the modesty of the programme's beginning was no doubt due to its small budget: yet it was no disadvantage to have so small a cast. A few carefully selected and differentiated characters were introduced and established as real people. In the first episode there were only nine, six of whom were related. The locations were limited as well and all dominated by Brookfield Farm.

Who were these new characters who, within such a very short space of time, were to become household names and national figures?

Basically at first they were one family, with one or two friends. Dan Archer, the patriarch, was a good tenant-farmer, honest, hard-working, struggling. His greatest friend was the lovable but feckless Walter Gabriel, who represented the bad, inefficient farmer. It was a stroke of genius to make the bad farmer who would be the recipient of so much preaching, a comic character. To balance the picture, a wealthy farmer, able to be super-efficient and yet to farm at a loss for tax purposes, was introduced in the shape of George Fairbrother, a plastics manufacturer.

As an essential change of scene, and to provide a commentary or chorus, a village pub with its regulars was included.

And thus the groundwork was complete. Then the elaboration began.

The characters had to be three-dimensional if they were to carry conviction. So Godfrey Baseley, the programme's editor, with Edward J. Mason and Geoffrey Webb, the two script-writers, set a precedent for the creation of later characters by drawing up a complete dossier on each individual, telling their whole lives from their birth.

So Dan Archer was the son of a farmer, John, who had also been a tenant at Brookfield where Dan and his brothers John (known as Ben) and Frank were born.

In his early twenties Dan had married Doris, the daughter of another landworker, William Forrest, a gamekeeper.

They had three children, Jack, Philip and Christine who were aged, roughly, twenty-nine, twenty-three and nineteen. Jack grew up in the late twenties and thirties when times were hard; he had left the village school when he was fourteen so he had had no higher education. Phil and Christine were luckier. When the time came for them to go to school, Dan was doing rather better on the farm and, with the aid of scholarships, they had both won their way to Borchester Grammar School. After working at Brookfield for a year or two, Phil went on to Farm Institute. This difference in education was always a bone of contention between Phil and Jack. But the lines of the characters were drawn with subtlety. Latterday serials seem so often to deal in types or even stereotypes, but the relationship between Dan and Doris's children was as unexpected as life itself. They disagreed, but never came to blows. Jack was by nature lazy, but used his misfortune in being born too soon as an excuse for his lack of achievement. The truth was that both Phil and Chris had rather more in the brainbox than poor likeable Jack. He settled to nothing and was always having brainwaves which were going to make his fortune, but never did.

A family trait of stubbornness was introduced; but the way in which it worked in each of the three children was different in every case and different, too, from their father's stubbornness. Dan was amenable to reason but once his mind was made up, nothing would move him from what he thought was right. Jack, on the other hand, was weak and unpredictable. When he dug his heels in, he appeared obtuse and pigheaded; but it didn't often happen.

Phil exhibited the family characteristic in his early adult years by stubbornly believing that he knew better than most people and by putting his beliefs into practice, sometimes with disastrous results. A know-all, in fact. Christine's streak of obstinacy was softened by inheriting her mother's steadiness of character. She was loyal, trusting and kept her word. It was hardly surprising that she suffered so much in love in her early womanhood.

Jack was the only child of Dan and Doris who was married when the programme started. He had married a girl he'd met in the ATS when he was in the army. They had two children, Jennifer and Lilian, aged six and four respectively, and another child was expected. They all lived at a small-holding, where Jack had settled when he came out of the army, determined to make his fortune by growing tomatoes and chrysanthemums and salad crops. His wife, Peggy, was a Londoner – and this was not an accident. She could represent the townsman's viewpoint until she had assimilated so much of her surroundings she became an honorary countrywoman.

Throughout the serial, some representative of town life has been necessary to draw parallels, to make contrasts and to ask simple questions naturally. No countryman would ask, for example, 'Why do you dip sheep?' or 'What do you use a harrow for?' A townsman would, and did.

One of the early townspeople was Mrs Perkins who came to Ambridge to be with Peggy in February when the baby was due. Mrs Perkins, like the character with which she was paired, Walter Gabriel, was deliberately written slightly larger than life. Ordinariness is a very difficult quality to convey without being dull or uninteresting. Dan and Doris were, and are, ordinary. They are normal, average, good, hard-working people: but it needed the extraordinariness of their old friend Walter Gabriel and his new friend 'Mrs P.' to throw into sharp relief that ordinariness.

From the outset it was decided that stage rural accents were not likely to sound convincing to anyone, as will be shown in a later chapter. But a mere touch of country flavour in the country characters could be enhanced by one or two speakers of 'standard' or 'educated' English. So the Fairbrothers, George and his daughter Grace (he was a widower) were introduced. He functioned, too, as another form of yardstick: material success. Walter floundered with little cash, farming inefficiently. Dan struggled with little cash, farming remarkably efficiently. Fairbrother had no problems financially and needed neither to struggle nor to be efficient – any losses could, at that time, be set against tax.

So, although Dan, Doris, Jack and Walter all had Midland accents, Chris and Phil, anxious to 'get on', had already lost most of their native accent. The phenomenon of children of poor parents having virtually two 'languages', one for use at school and one for use at home, was familiar enough: great play was made with Phil and his pretensions. His conversations at home, especially with Dan were rough and often slovenly: but when trying to impress Grace and, more importantly, her father, Phil's accent went up a grade. It paid off: Phil very soon became Farm Manager for Fairbrother and Grace was his steady girl-friend.

The programme was a month old before another facet of country life was introduced in the shape of Tom Forrest, gamekeeper on the local estate.

All aspects of country life would eventually be reflected, but it is interesting to recall how each one was introduced in sequence. There is a danger in having too many diverse characters in any serial and it was a good idea to make Tom Forrest the bachelor brother of Doris, thus keeping it 'in the family'.

The part, incidentally, was played for a few episodes by George Hart (who now plays Jethro Larkin) before Bob Arnold took over and made the character of Tom Forrest uniquely his own.

One other character appeared in the earliest scripts: Simon Cooper, Dan's farm-worker. In those days the term 'farm-labourer' was still in fairly common use, though in the twenty-five years that The Archers has been running such descriptions have fallen out of favour. The unions especially feel that there is more dignity in being styled a rodent-operator than a rat-catcher, a hosiery operative than a mill-girl; and certainly there are few replies to advertisements for 'a cowman' these days; call the job 'dairy manager' and the replies pour in, even though the wages are the same.

Simon was the epitome of the farm-worker. He was not un-intelligent but sketchily educated; full of country lore and folk-wisdom; knowledgeable about animals and good with them, even though he often spoke to them less than endearingly. What made Simon a character, though, was his mild but cease-less complaining. He appeared to do things grudgingly, especi-ally anything that was in any way different from his usual routine, and he often approached or retreated mumbling and chuntering and whispering dark imprecations under his breath. He was the perfect foil for Dan, just as Dan was the foil for Phil. Simon was the traditionalist, the conservative; Dan was sufficiently aware of changes in the farming world to know that he would go to the wall unless he somehow learned to farm more efficiently; Phil was full of the latest ideas that he had learnt at agricultural college, but lacked Dan's judgement and experience in applying them.

In the background was Simon's sorely tried wife Bess, who, though she may have appeared to henpeck him, really wrapped him round with care, keeping him warm and fed and satisfied in a picturesque but not very convenient cottage and on very little pay.

These then were the characters; and before the first broad-cast of The Archers proper, a programme was transmitted to introduce them to listeners. It was called 'Announcing The Archers' and was heard on Thursday 28 December 1950 from 5.30 p.m. to 5.45 p.m. on the BBC Light Programme.

Added reality was given to this first glimpse of The Archers by the fact that Godfrey Basely, who was well-known to Mid-land listeners for radio visits to real farms to talk to real farmers, was heard visiting Ambridge and Brookfield Farm, and meeting and talking to The Archers and their friends.

We had been thoroughly briefed with facts about the characters we were to play. We felt like secret agents being given a whole new identity. Gwen Berryman, for example, received the following brief:

Mrs Archer

Mrs Archer is aged somewhere round about 55. She is a farmer's wife on a small farm.

Her past history is as follows:

She was a daughter of a Gamekeeper and went to the village school until she was 14, then she went into service at The Manor House, proved herself to be trustworthy and capable and developed through the various grades until she became a personal Lady's Maid to the daughter of the house. She had, by this time, acquired a good knowledge of what you might call 'good manners and behaviour'. She then married Daniel Archer, who was working with his father on a small farm. His father died fairly soon after they were married and Daniel took over the farm. They had a very hard struggle to begin with, through years of depression, but they managed to carry on and Mrs Archer had, during this period, three children – Jack, Phillip [sic] and Christine.

Jack, the eldest, was only able to have an Elementary School education. As times improved, Phillip was able to satisfy something of his mother's ambition for him by passing an examination to the County Grammar School, and from there on to an Agricultural College by the skin of his teeth. Christine, who was younger than the boys, was able to have a better start in life by then, by virtue of more prosperity to the farm. She was quite bright and the play will open with her on the point of leaving school, after passing Higher School Certificate.

You may gather from this that Mrs Archer is ambitious, and I think that what she's trying to do is to copy in some way what was done at the Manor for the children there. She has a certain amount of pride, is a good and thorough housewife, tolerant with her husband who is perhaps a little old-fashioned, but able to understand and appreciate to some degree the ways of youth in a modern world. I don't want the character to have any accent at all, but I want her to be recognized as a country-woman in her manner and speech.

Godfrey Baseley.

19th October 1950   B.B.C. BIRMINGHAM

The rest of the Cast all had singular and equally detailed briefs, but on that December day in 1950 when we first attempted to create the characters on the air for a wider audience we didn't have to keep too closely to a script. Instead, almost like playing charades at a party, we had to assume the parts and were interviewed in the familiar Baseley manner, helped, bullied, cajoled, challenged and encouraged, so that we all played Trilby to his Svengali. The resulting interviews had a freshness and air of improvisation that was new at the time. Since those days the art of improvisation has been re-discovered both in the theatre and especially in television 'dramatized documentaries'. There were few precedents for it on the air in 1950.

That same day, the Birmingham *Evening Despatch* printed a picture of the six of us: Dan and Doris, Jack and Peggy, Phil and Chris. The accompanying story alleged that we had that day made our début by recording 'in secret', and stated: 'Every effort is being made to produce a true picture of life in an agricultural community.'

That newspaper feature is historic: it contained the first photograph of the Cast of The Archers and the first article written about us as we began to be heard by a national, as opposed to a regional, audience.

As if sensing that something of more than passing interest was about to begin, the *Daily Mirror* asked on 30 December 1950: 'What's Mrs Dale going to say about this?'

There were two excellent cartoons, one of Ellis Powell who played Mrs Dale, and one of Harry Oakes, described as 'Farmer Archer'.

The article began with the announcement that the programme was starting at 11.45 a.m. the following Monday morning, when 'Farmer Dan Archer arrives on the Light Programme to introduce his family to Britain's housewives. But it will be no fleeting acquaintance. Farmer Dan is hoping that it will ripen into friendship. The Archers are here to stay.'

Looking back with hindsight, that extraordinary assertion 'The Archers are here to stay' seems like prophecy. The truth is, though, that from the beginning, the press decided to invent a feud between the Archers and the Dales. The writer showed his hand when he went on to report adverse criticism of the Dales and spoke of 'many requests from country folks for a daily serial centred on their own lives'. I suspect more than a touch of journalistic exaggeration in that report.

With remarkable insight, considering that not a single episode had yet been broadcast in the Light Programme, the writer declared that in The Archers there would be 'no suburban small talk or over-the-fence gossip. Cliff-hanging suspense and tricks of that sort will be out', and concluded: 'Eventually, one of these radio families will have to go. So the real test is whether Britain's housewives will stay loyal to the Dales or draw a bow for the Archers.'

The *Daily Mail* quickly caught on and began its long tradition of giving The Archers notable coverage. In its edition for Tuesday 2 January 1951 with a headline over two columns that ran optimistically, 'The Archers begin their daily saga of the land', it printed photographs of Harry Oakes, June Spencer and Norman Painting whom it described as 'Midland actors (as yet) unknown to the outside world'. Both the headline and the article exhibited a confidence that the programme would last longer than three months, which we all found tremendously encouraging. We felt proud and excited at having been selected for even thirteen weeks of steady work. Those few of us who have survived until today can still at times scarcely believe that it has all happened, that what began so quietly should have lasted for a quarter of a century.

Who were they, this group of 'Midland actors (as yet) unknown to the outside world'?

The two main characters were Dan and Doris and by a stroke of luck, or a mixture of luck, flair and judgement, one of them, Dan, was discovered when the programme was given its trial run.

Harry Oakes, like Dan Archer, was born on 15 October 1896; but there the similarity begins and ends. Harry's first profession was designing pottery, though he had wanted to be a portrait painter. He vividly remembered, and described watching as a student, Augustus John at work. Harry also had a fine bass-baritone voice and trained with the same singing-teacher as his friend Marjorie Westbury. He had been broadcasting since 1938, but the potential of his resonant, friendly voice seems never to have been fully realized until he was asked to give a trial performance as Dan Archer. He was right from the start.

The same was not, unfortunately true, of the actress who was originally asked to play Doris. A fine performer though she was, that feeling of inevitability was missing. Dan Archer came to life even in a chuckle from Harry Oakes. He was made for the part and the part was made for him. There is, in the creation of characters in the studio (as in any cast of actors) a mysterious chemistry that binds the group into a team. The programme's trial run on the Midland air had demonstrated this point quite clearly. Two performers, excellent in themselves, did not for some indefinable reason quite 'gell': the chemistry was wrong. And so on 20 October 1950 an actress called Gwen Berryman received the following letter:

'Dear Mrs [*sic*] Berryman,

You may have heard that after Christmas there's a possibility of a daily serial play ("The Archers") coming from The Midland Region, on similar lines to that of "Mrs Dale's Diary".

There still one or two parts not yet cast for this and I wondered whether you would care to come into Birmingham on November 3rd, at 5.10 p.m. to give me an audition for the part of Mrs Archer. I'm enclosing a few details about this character in order that you may be prepared to some extent.

I'm arranging for a special scene to be written for the audition, in which you will play opposite one or two of the characters already cast.

For your information, if you are eventually selected for the part, it would mean recording the five episodes during Saturday, Sunday and Monday morning of each week, and a contract would be issued to cover the thirteen weeks to the end of March.

Perhaps you'd let me know if you are interested in this.'

That letter was to change the whole of Gwen's life. There had been a time when the bright lights of the West End were at her finger-tips; but fate dealt her two cruel blows, which she now dismisses peremptorily with 'I was twice unlucky in love', and she returned to Wolverhampton to live with her parents.

She had been trained for the musical stage. She had studied piano, cello and singing from the age of fourteen. She broadcast first as a singer: in 1927 as Margarita in *Faust* and in 1928 as Susannah in *The Marriage of Figaro*. She went on to the Royal Academy of Music, winning scholarships, gold medals and prizes and appearing in the Academy's yearly opera production at the Scala Theatre. She understudied Mabel Constanduros in *Derby Day* at the Lyric Hammersmith, and played the part when it moved to the Comedy Theatre. She seemed to have arrived. She played in a Gracie Fields film, toured in musical plays and then gave it all up and retreated to her parents' home.

She was not long away from the theatre: she soon joined the local repertory company and for many years was a favourite player, especially in comedy parts. When broadcasting from Midland Region began at full strength again after the war, she found herself drawn back to the microphone, but this time as a straight actress.

She speaks with affection and gratitude of Mabel Constanduros who, in order that her understudy might have the chance of playing the part, made much of a slight indisposition so that Gwen could go on in her place during the run of *Derby Day* in London. Many years later, when Fate was making one of those ironic twists that often occur in the lives of actors, Mabel Constanduros told Gwen how much she, in turn, would like to be in The Archers. She died, though, before it could happen.

Gwen sailed through the audition and landed the part of Doris Archer, which she has made uniquely and lovably her own.

Dan's elder son Jack was a part which presented few problems of casting, for the work of Denis Folwell was well-known in Midland Region. He had served his apprenticeship in provincial repertory theatres, had reached the West End, appeared in films and had experience in management and production. The war, though, intervened and he was commissioned in the Royal Artillery in 1941. After leaving the army in 1945 he joined that other army of actors trying to get back into the theatre. He had regularly broadcast from Birmingham from 1934 until he joined the army and he quickly became much in demand at the microphone. He had a distinctive voice that conveyed a true impression of his own personality: genial, easy-going, likeable.

He was perfectly matched on the air by June Spencer, who played Jack's long-suffering wife, Peggy. Although born and bred in Nottingham, June played the cockney ex-ATS girl with complete conviction. She too had known the hard work of provincial rep, but had concentrated after her marriage on radio work, not only as an actress of wide range and with a whole gamut of regional accents, but on several occasions as the author of amusing programmes as well as writing *Odd Odes* for Cyril Fletcher.

Looking back to the early days of playing Peggy opposite Denis Folwell's Jack, June said: 'Although Denis and I didn't always see eye to eye about things outside the studio, as Jack and Peggy we had a rapport that made our scenes together very satisfying to play. I think this was because his performance was always utterly sincere.' June's own modesty prevented her from stating the undeniable truth that her own performance has always been stamped with the same quality.

The part of Philip, Dan and Doris's second son who was cock-sure, boisterous and ambitious was not, on the surface, one that seemed appropriate to the writer of this book, since I had little in common with a rip-roaring farmer's son. But radio, luckily, is concerned with the capacity of a voice to convey character and my voice projected the required ingredients. It had been heard on the air some three hundred times from both London and Birmingham and so, like those of the other original members of the cast, was not unfamiliar to listeners.

Pamela Mant, who played the Archers' third child, Christine, was equally well-known and was not pleased to see her name twisted into Pamela Iwart in the *Evening Despatch*! Apart from acting experience both for the microphone and in weekly rep., she was a keen horsewoman who enjoyed living in the country, and indeed occupied a gypsy caravan on the riverside meadows that lie under the shadow of Tewkesbury Abbey.

Apart from the family, there were two other characters who formed the original nucleus of performers: Walter Gabriel, played by Robert Mawdesley, and Simon Cooper, played by Eddie Robinson.

Robert Mawdesley's voice was among the most well-known on the Midland air, since, in addition to frequent appearances as an actor, he was also an announcer. His manner was, if anything, more county than country. After studying medicine at Cambridge for a while he had found the lure of the stage too great and had abandoned a medical career for the theatre. Like June Spencer, one of his earliest appearances had been in *A Midsummer-night's Dream*. June had played Mustard-seed at a very early age: Robert had been, when slightly older, an enchanting Puck – a far cry from the rumbustious Walter Gabriel.

Robert had begun to appear in films when the war interrupted his career and he was quickly commissioned in the R.A.F. After the war he joined the BBC as an announcer in the General Overseas Service, working with such colleagues as Bruce Belfrage and Robert Dougall, whom he slightly resembled in vocal manner and voice quality. June Spencer's most vivid memory of the beginnings of The Archers is hearing

Robert produce the gravelly voice of Walter for the first time. It was utterly unlike his normal voice. 'We were all stunned,' says June, 'and then wildly enthusiastic.'

The reactions of listeners were the same.

Eddie Robinson, who played Simon Cooper — Dan's right-hand man — was, as he put it, 'thought to be the oldest member of the Cast, but will only admit to having been born at an early age'. During the First World War he had performed in many old theatres and army stations as a member of a concert-party, and although born in Wednesbury in Staffordshire, built up a reputation between the wars as 'The lad fra' Lancashire'. He was heard frequently on the air in this role from London, Belfast, Manchester and Birmingham, and then gradually found himself in demand by Midland Region as an authentic speaker of Black Country dialect. It is hardly surprising that Simon spoke a dialect of his own: it was remarkably convincing, and yet was difficult to pin down to any precise locality.

So, it will be seen, that although all the members of the original Cast were experienced performers, particularly in radio, none of them was widely known. Post-war conditions had indeed compelled one or two of them to do as many actors were forced to do at the time and take on some other occupation in order to survive. Mischievous critics from time to time have tried to suggest that some members of the cast were little more than amateurs, but the facts are otherwise. All the members of the original team were not only experienced performers, but were also friends and colleagues who had worked together as professionals for some years. This is one more factor in the phenomenal rise to success of the programme.

From very early on there were encouraging signs. The comments of family and friends were more than usually complimentary and the endless stream of letters from strangers began, which still flows in today. From all over the British Isles, from places we had never visited or in many cases even heard of, friendly letters came from unknown people who wrote to us as if we were their closest intimates. One of the first fan letters received was dated 29 January 1951, and ran: 'I feel I must write to you to tell you how much I enjoy listening to the serial play of country life The Archers. I think each person in it is perfect for the part they play in it ...'

This description of the programme as a 'play' was, curiously enough, not typical. It was not accidental, though. The writer continued: 'The play is so instructive. There are lots of things young men and women who intend to learn farming could learn from it, but 11.45 a.m. is rather a difficult time for young people to listen to it. I wonder if one will be able to buy it in book form later on? If so, it would be a book worth keeping.'

Such a letter, with its insistence on the didactic and informative element of the programme, might not encourage the belief that the serial was at the start of a long record-breaking run. What soon emerged, to the surprise of many at Broadcasting House, was that many people actually enjoyed what we in the Cast called 'the bits out of the Ministry pamphlets'. This country, like the USA, has a deep-seated puritan tradition which favours, however silently, the respect for learning. The English temperament in particular is not often given to high-spirited self-indulgence and (so-called permissiveness notwithstanding) leans more towards plain living and high thinking than towards wine, women and song. And so The Archers, this ordinary not-very-affluent country family, quickly caught the interest of a rapidly growing number of listeners, where trendier, more 'glamorous' or 'sensational' characters might have failed.

When Tommy Handley died in 1949 the BBC had begun looking for a successor to one of its most popular programmes, *I.T.M.A. (It's That Man Again)*. Various attempts at comedy scripts were tried out, most of them merely a variation on the *I.T.M.A.* formula. Few people imagined that the programme that was to come nearest to that place once occupied in so many people's affections by *I.T.M.A.* would be filled by something entirely different – an everyday story of countryfolk. It was to be some years before a new kind of comedy programme replaced *I.T.M.A.*: *Take it From Here, The Goon Show, Hancock's Half Hour* and the Kenneth Horne shows, which although they came much later, were much nearer to the *I.T.M.A.* formula. In the meantime, the public took *us* to their hearts.

Within weeks, the reception given to The Archers was very encouraging. Top brass both in London and Birmingham made indications that we were finding favour.

Once the final Cast was assembled, we were told that we had to learn to feel like a family off the air as well as on. There would be no stars in this show; indeed, we would be treated equally in every way, even in the matter of fees.

And so, absurd as it now seems, though clearly well-intentioned, arrangements were made for one large table to be reserved in the BBC canteen so that we ate together on recording days. There were advantages of course: not only the cast, but the editor, producer, technical staff and the two writers got to know each other socially. The disadvantages, though, soon became evident. The rest of the BBC staff and artistes in the restaurant thought we were being stand-offish and giving ourselves airs. Our food was served more slowly than if we had been collecting it ourselves from the serving-counter: choice had to be limited to simplify the service, and lunch had to be at a fixed time, which meant that occasionally those who liked a drink beforehand had to rush. The Cast, incidentally, quickly divided itself into the wets and the dries. Very few, if any, of us were non-drinkers, but half of us kept to the old tradition of never drinking before going on the air, while the other half felt that without a drink they couldn't face the microphone.

The eating experiment was soon abandoned by mutual agreement; but the fact that it was tried, and the intention behind it, does indicate how seriously the whole enterprise was taken from the beginning.

The programme had been running for some seven weeks or so when the good news was broken to us that not only were our contracts to be renewed for three months but *Dick Barton – Special Agent* was being taken off, and we were to take its place at the peak time of 6.45 p.m. It seemed as if all our most extravagant dreams were coming true. During one of those communal canteen lunches, Geoffrey Webb who had both written and produced other serials for commercial radio, had declared that it needed six months to establish a daily serial. We were half-way there! Geoff had also said that if the signs were good at the end of six months, then the length of run was almost unpredictable . . . it might run for two or even three years! How little he knew, or we guessed, how long its life would in fact be!

Towards the middle of March 1951, several of us were sitting at coffee-time in the canteen: Gwen Berryman (Doris), Harry Oakes (Dan), Eddie Robinson (Simon) and myself. Thinking of the future and what difference it would make to all our lives, Harry remarked, almost casually, 'After all, twelve pounds a week isn't to be sneezed at!' He must have been surprised at the effect this simple statement caused, believing, as we all did, that everyone was being paid the same. Eddie and I, it appeared, were getting two pounds a week less, and poor Gwen even less than that!

So, with the hotheadedness of youth, I resigned, or at least made it known that I was not interested in signing a further contract. There was a splendid furore, culminating in a confrontation between myself and the fearsome Godfrey Baseley. The only place for us to talk turned out to be in the largest studio in Broadcasting House, where the Midland Light Orchestra under Rae Jenkins normally performed. It was empty, save for two grand pianos. Godfrey was angry and banged one piano. I retaliated by banging another. I was called an ungrateful stupid young fool: I retorted that rather than work at less than the rate for the job, I'd choose to starve in a garret and write the poems and plays I'd always wanted to write. Eventually, with a resulting increase of respect on both sides, I returned to the studio where I was due to record. 'You've got a job here for ten years if you want it!' Godfrey bellowed after me as he went down the stairs. Now that, I thought, really was fanciful: his famous imagination was carrying him way beyond the bounds of reality.

But he was right.

Two things resulted: the fees were adjusted, so my little skirmish helped not only Gwen and Eddie but also other members of the Cast; and the other was that after some weeks of being in Godfrey's bad books, he buttonholed me one day and said, 'I want to see you!' Wondering what was coming, I followed him into a corner. 'Got a programme I want you to write for me!' I gathered that the past was forgotten. And indeed it was.

Godfrey Baseley in those fire-ball days was not the easiest of people to deal with: in his enormous enthusiasm to get results he trod on many corns and often failed to make people like him. But that was never his objective. All that mattered to him was that The Archers should be a success. For this reason, although Tony Shryane's name appeared on the scripts, it was Godfrey who produced us with Tony's assistance for the first few weeks. And pretty exacting and exhausting they were too. Every line, every inflection, every sound-effect had to be just right – right as he saw it. On more than one occasion Gwen Berryman was reduced to the point of tears and resignation. But the character of Doris Archer as established then, has gone on to make her the most loved member of the whole family.

After less than two months, Godfrey handed over the production completely to Tony. On 30 March 1951, the Head of Midland Region, John Dunkerley, gave a cocktail party for the Cast. Without fully realizing the import of what she was saying, Mrs Dunkerley remarked, with complete truth, that for the first few weeks we all sounded just a trifle tense, but now we had relaxed and settled down splendidly. There were huge grins on all our faces, but no one smiled more broadly than Tony Shryane.

John Dunkerley gave us the feeling that we were part of something new and special. Till then, most of us merely felt that we were employed to do a pleasant job, and were being paid to do it. He suggested that it might become rather more than that. We were curiously elated to be given first a cocktail party and then the official thanks of the BBC. The atmosphere suddenly became portentous for a moment, then Denis Folwell, with that dry manner which he transferred from himself into his performance as Jack Archer said, 'Very nice of you, sir. And thank you for the use of the Hall!' Once more laughter took over.

The following Sunday, 1 April, was spent on a farm in Worcestershire being photographed 'in character, on location'. When those photographs were published they did nothing to dispel the illusion that Ambridge and The Archers didn't exist! There we were for all to see, with cows and milking-machines, pigs, tractors, farmhouse kitchens, poultry and sheep.

New as the programme was, it still managed in its first year to set several precedents. One was the inclusion of topical references which gave the programme the feeling of being immediate and up-to-date. In this way, The Archers were heard discussing the contents of the Chancellor's Budget long before the pundits had reached the microphone. In those days there was no extended coverage minute by minute of the Chancellor's speech. The Light Programme news was not heard until seven o'clock, after The Archers; and on the first occasion when we included a 'topical insert' about the Budget we received a telegram of congratulation from the Head of Light Programme, who declared himself 'astonished at the topicality of last night's programme'. We discovered later that he had heard our episode on his car radio after leaving a meeting at which it had been decided that there would be no comments on the Budget, but merely a plain statement of the facts. This indulgent attitude was not to last throughout the programme's long run: parliamentary voices eventually complained about fictional characters commenting on political facts – but in 1951 those complaints were a long way off.

Another precedent was created in our first year when at the end of November the Ambridge Christmas carol service was recorded in a village church with choir, congregation and vicar on hand to advise. Members of the Cast sat with the village congregation, while the Vicar of Ambridge (Harry Stubbs) and Dan, Doris and Tom Forrest were heard singing solo carols. Recording in this way not only produced a more authentic-sounding programme, it was also very good public relations and played its part in building up public interest and involvement.

Not that there seemed much need to whip up our listeners' interest. Within months the audience grew like a mushroom. By the end of May some of us were beginning to be featured in articles in 'showbiz' magazines. *Radio Review* for 25 May 1951 had put us cheek by jowl with a rising star 'the young bachelor comedian-impressionist, Peter Sellers'! Under the paragraph headed 'It was not a flop', the columnist wrote: 'When the new family serial took over the 6.45 p.m. daily spot from *Dick Barton*, many people thought it would prove a flop. To follow an all-action serial with a story about everyday life and people on a farm seems a little like anti-climax. Well the doubters have been proved wrong . . .' All this in less than five months.

As we reached the end of our first year we realized that we had not turned out to be a damp squib after all. We had gone up like a rocket.

There was one event, though, towards the end of that first year which has never been repeated. We had undoubtedly become a top programme in less than twelve months, and so it was decided to celebrate Ambridge's first Christmas on the air with an Archers' Christmas party. This was to be broadcast live, not recorded, on Boxing Day. This was the only occasion in the whole twenty-five years when a whole episode has been broadcast live.

We assembled at 2.30 on Wednesday 26 December 1951 and began to rehearse. In the best show-biz tradition, there was not the slightest hesitation on anyone's part at curtailing our Christmas, not even from Bob Arnold whose birthday happens to be on Boxing Day! In addition to the dialogue, there were also songs by Dan and Doris and of course Tom Forrest, all accompanied on the piano by Phil. For technical reasons, the piano was at one end of Studio Two, our regular studio at Broad Street Birmingham, while the dialogue was spoken into microphones at the opposite end. This meant that I, as the actor playing Phil, was rather busy! It was a non-stop performance, joining in the dialogue at one end of the studio, helping to persuade Dan and Doris to decide whether it should be

'Down the Vale' or 'The Old Rustic Bridge by the Mill', and then, as Dan said: 'Righto, Phil, ready when you are!' dashing to the piano at the far end of the studio. It was rather hair-raising for us all, and a live episode has never again been attempted.

Oddly enough my memory tells me that for this occasion only, the programme lasted half an hour, but memory must be playing me false, for as I write I have before me the actual contract issued for that occasion, on which the time is stated clearly as 6.45–7 p.m., 26 December 1951.

In preparing this book I have unearthed from my files an extraordinary archive, the collection of more than twenty-five years. Other members of the Cast have been kind enough to do the same, with the result that these words are written with the documents concerned before me. We have all been surprised at the number of times our memories have conflicted with reality.

I have, for example, a memory of the first informal Archers' party. The scene, the Board Room in Broad Street, Birmingham, is lit in recollection by a fading summer evening's light. But the written record of the occasion gives the lie to that. I must have remembered an earlier occasion when, in May 1950, we met to read through the very first Archers scripts. The party, though, did not take place until December. To prove it, I have the list of guests, members of the Cast, the actual bill and the receipt for my contribution. The guests of Harry Oakes, it appears, were Mr and Mrs Baseley; of Miss Berryman, Mr and Mrs Mason; my guests were Mr and Mrs Webb, and the guest of Eddie Robinson was Miss V. Hodgetts, who was to become first our longest-serving 'continuity girl', then 'Assistant to The Archers', and then Mrs Tony Shryane.

Before The Archers was one years old the size of the Cast had grown to around twenty-four, but the main group of originals still carried the bulk of the story.

It was exhilarating and exhausting and for some of us, the strain involved was too great. For the programme itself, continuous publicity and acclaim lay ahead: but for some of the performers, stress, nervous exhaustion and even death waited, much nearer than any of us ever imagined.

1952

THE YEAR WHEN

King George VI died. Identity cards were abolished. Sir Stafford Cripps died. The Lynmouth storm disaster occurred. Tea was de-rationed and de-controlled. A state of emergency was declared in Kenya because of Mau Mau activities. Britain's first atomic weapon, and the US Hydrogen bomb, were exploded.

IN AMBRIDGE

Grace Fairbrother, Phil's girl-friend, returned to Ambridge while Peggy and the children joined Jack in Cornwall. Grace refused Phil's offer of marriage saying 'in five years' time', so Phil turned to pedigree pig-breeding. Jack, Peggy and family returned suddenly from Cornwall. Walter Gabriel was comforted by Mrs Perkins in his distress at being told by the Squire to clean up his farm, and Dan and Doris bought Chris a horse called Midnight. At Easter, George Fairbrother married Mrs Helen Carey in Ambridge Parish Church.

By the time we entered our second year, many things happened for the first time that were soon to become part of our lives for the next twenty-five. We had begun to make personal appearances, for example; we had grown accustomed to receiving fan-mail. We seemed to be constantly posing for photographs; and signing autographs became almost an occupational hazard.

It was then that we first began to experience a sensation that a few of us have enjoyed ever since. It was discernible in letters, in chance encounters with people who knew of our connection with the programme, in trains, planes or restaurants. Most of all it was manifested at fêtes and bazaars, especially those in country villages. The moment we were recognized, a great wave of affection flowed out towards us. It was, and is, one of the great rewards for one's efforts. In those early days, though, we

36

were as uncertain as we have always been, about our immediate future. Yet our audience seemed to love us, and we could not help but speculate: could our modest little programme really be destined for the heights?

So our thoughts turned to the idea of 'taking on', as Wilfred Pickles put it. Most of us had worked with Wilfred in the days when he was a 'five guinea' actor: we had seen him become a national celebrity as the star of *Have a go!* There he was, pink and smiling, in the tiny BBC Club Bar in Broad Street, Birmingham, saying, half-deprecatingly. 'I've took on!' when people tried to congratulate him on his success. Could that, some of us wondered, happen to us? (And was that really what we wanted? at least one of us thought.)

The second year of The Archers, saw changes in the Cast. New characters were invented and the number of performers was greatly increased.

Then came the first case of change of performer. Monica Grey had decided that she no longer wished to continue playing Grace Fairbrother. So the writers decreed that Grace should go abroad where, after some unspecified throat trouble, she should have an operation and so, with a slightly different voice return to Ambridge.

Thus it was that Ysanne Churchman took over the part. Ysanne, daughter of an actor, had never thought of being anything but an actress. Her first professional part, in *Bluebell in Fairyland*, was at the age of twelve and she gave her first broadcast the following year. Trained both as an actress and as a dancer, she had worked in every branch of the acting profession with equal success. Long runs on the London stage and on tour, films, radio, television – all were undertaken with the same enthusiasm and professional skill. Her contribution to the long courtship and short marriage of Phil and Grace, ending in the death of Grace, was of major importance in the programme's sea-change from a possible nine-days' wonder to part of established radio.

Serious illness also struck the programme early. Denis Folwell developed tuberculosis and had to enter a sanatorium. This was a serious blow indeed. He had quickly established himself as a popular character and his distinctive voice meant that re-casting, even if decided upon, would be difficult. Denis needed treatment for at least six months. So it was decided to send Jack into partnership in running a farm in Cornwall with an army friend Barney Lee.

Early in 1952 Peggy and the children joined Jack in Cornwall. It was September before Denis was well enough to leave the sanatorium and take up his work again. So Jack, Peggy and family rather suddenly returned from Cornwall and the script-writers, ever-resourceful, explained that the reason for this was that Jack's partner had become too fond of Peggy.

The beginning of the year brought another innovation that was destined to become part of the programme's accepted format: the weekly Omnibus edition. Our predecessor, *Dick Barton*, was heard in an omnibus edition on Saturday mornings. We had taken his place each Monday to Friday at 6.45 p.m. but now the Omnibus of The Archers was to be heard not at the old *Dick Barton* time, but on Saturday evening from 7.30 p.m. to 8.30 p.m. Then, for the first time, Tom Forrest began that extraordinary series of brief introductions that have gone on almost uninterrupted for twenty-four years – almost uninterrupted, but not quite. There was a time when 'Tom' was 'in prison' and therefore unable to broadcast. But that story will be told in sequence.

There are various means of measuring success in radio. But for those who take part in it, one of the milestones is to appear on the front cover of *Radio Times*. This has happened more than once to The Archers. First in November 1951, with a fire-side view of Dan, Doris and Christine; then in April 1952 with a splendid photograph of Harry Oakes as Dan with a pitchfork-ful of hay on his shoulder. Other occasions were to follow.

The year 1952 also saw the continuation of our now normal practice of using an actual location on which to record the programme in order to increase authenticity. When at Easter 1952 Grace's father, George Fairbrother, married a widowed friend Helen Carey, the ceremony was recorded in a Worcester-shire village church.

Over the years, several places have been used both for photographs and recordings and among them has been the village of Hanbury. In spite of varied claims, there is no single village that is the 'real Ambridge'; but Hanbury has played its part in the Archers' story. With the local vicar to advise and the congregation to swell the singing, the Fairbrothers' wedding was recorded in the church itself, just as the carol service had been recorded the previous November.

Continuing our custom of inserting topical scenes into the programme, the sudden death of King George VI presented a problems. Our listeners had already begun to expect that what

38

happened in the real world would be mentioned in Ambridge, yet how could a suitable reference be made that was not offensive?

The script of the episode originally recorded was looked at, and more problems emerged. As luck would have it, there was one gloomy scene which was attempting to show the 'other' side of Walter Gabriel. We always knew that his hearty manner was a front, a mask which he hid behind. In the episode in question, Walter was found sitting on his 'old granny's' grave, and mourning her death so many years before. Clearly this would not do. The whole episode had to be re-recorded.

Once that material had been removed, and something more appropriate to a mourning nation had been written in its place, it was decided that the Archers would behave exactly as any other family did: they would comment on the news of the King's death as they read it in the newspaper. So this topical insert was in a very low key, with hardly a specific word spoken. Lines like: 'You've seen the paper?' 'Hm.' 'Can't believe it, can you? Like losing a member of the family.'

It was, like our most successful topical inserts, very brief. But it was enough to show that Ambridge, though a kind of Never-never Land at times, was still subject to the same slings and arrows as anywhere else. Some indication of the programme's popularity may be gained from the fact that when the brief black-edged 'mourning' edition of *Radio Times* was published in the emergency following the death of the King among the programmes that continued was The Archers.

On 13 March 1952 the now defunct *Daily Graphic* published the results of a poll organized by their columnist Jonah Barrington. He had asked readers to say whether they preferred the Dales or the Archers, whether they felt that either should be discontinued, and which were their favourite Archer characters.

His readers were so overwelmingly in favour of the Archers that Jonah Barrington could afford to be less than enthusiastic himself: 'A daily serial with the momentum of a steam roller and rather less glamour than a corn-chandler's catalogue is steadily gaining the mass affections of British listeners,' he began. 'Don't ask me why: only a Harley Street psychologist, probably, could faithfully analyse the reason.'

He then went on to speak of the programme's 'background of damp raincoats and wet gumboots, its earthy atmosphere, its daily narratives of small-holders, mangel-wurzels, vets, pigs and leaking roofs', before giving the results of the poll.

The reaction was so great that he felt it showed 'a burning public interest in the programme hitherto unsuspected by me and, I think, many other critics'.

Of the (undisclosed) number of readers who voted, 78.3 per cent preferred the Archers to the Dales; 92.8 were in favour of retaining the Archers indefinitely, while only 7.2 per cent said it should be scrapped, and the most popular characters were Walter Gabriel first, Dan Archer second and Mrs Perkins third.

The piece ends with 'hearty if somewhat earthy' congratulations all round.

For those of us who had unexpectedly found ourselves caught up in this whirlwind success, life had become suddenly breathless. Only two years before, our regional audience had been around 50,000; now it was 8,000,000 a night! We were, as a writer said in *Reveille* in April 1952, 'the second most popular programme on the air'. The name of the most popular was not divulged.

The theme of this article was the true one that the actors concerned with The Archers were all beginning to behave like country people in private life. Robert Mawdesley bemoaned the fact that one farmer wrote to him and offered him a job mucking-out cow sheds, and several listeners asked if they could buy the load of farmyard muck he had referred to in the programme.

Harry Oakes said that he scarcely 'knew one end of a pitchfork from the other until this lark started', and recalled how, going home from the studios on a bus one night, 'a chap tapped me on the shoulder and said, very seriously, that I'd do better if I put my money into Friesians instead of Shorthorns'. Gwen Berryman is revealed as keeping two pigs, and saying: 'I've started keeping these since I became a farmer's wife.' Pamela Mant is reported, correctly, as living in a caravan, and I as 'living in a converted barn in Oxfordshire' (correct) and 'keeps ducks' (not true). John Franklyn, the original Mike Daly, who had been reported in the Christmas 1951 edition of *Smallholder* as a duck expert, is described as having 'bought himself a small-holding'.

'I've never known a group of actors get so caught up in the parts they play,' said Godfrey Baseley, who was then reported as saying that there was a farm in the Birmingham studios – a model one. 'But it's not just a toy . . . each model animal represents so many farm animals on Dan's farm, and by keeping this up to date I've got an accurate check on the stock position from week to week.'

As the programme continued and the number of farms and farmers increased, the model farm idea was abandoned, but it was found necessary to keep an accurate account of each farm's stock because when Dan's flock was referred to in one script as 300 sheep and in another some time later as 100, hundreds of letters poured in from listeners. It had become clear that we had not only to sound authentic: the farming details mentioned in the programme had to be accurate too. So convincing was Dan Archer that farmers all over the British Isles from Cornwall to Scotland were organizing their farming in step with Dan. As Ted Mason is reported as saying at the end of the same article from *Reveille*: 'This farming stuff is a bit tricky. If you're not a farmer it's all too easy to make the same cow calve twice in ten episodes!'

It seemed to those of us who played the central parts in The Archers that it was beginning to matter less and less whether we lived in town or country – we spent less and less time at home and when we did, a great deal of it was occupied in dealing with fan-mail and business correspondence.

Two and a half days were spent in the studio every week, with very few breaks. Every week there were garden fêtes, bazaars, flower shows or other events to open. There were dances, lunches, dinners. There were endless speeches and presentations. There were photo-calls and interviews for the press. And always the signing of endless autographs. In less than two years we had ceased to be private unknown citizens: we had begun to be radio celebrities, constantly and increasingly in demand for public engagements.

For some of us, appearing in public presented difficulties. Not all of us looked the part: not all of us, especially the ladies, specially wanted to. If they were to be guests of honour at lunch, and given pride of place on the platform, presented with the inevitable bouquet, they naturally felt that they should look like Doris or Chris or Peggy wearing their best clothes, not their working ones. All of us, though, found ourselves changing our wardrobes: we chose the sort of clothes that our characters would choose and we suddenly developed a leaning towards tweeds. No opportunity was missed, though, of appearing as much like the character as possible without actually wearing costume.

In August of 1952, for example, Dan, Doris, Phil, Chris, Walter and Mrs P., Tony Shryane and Edward J. Mason all appeared at a flower show and garden party at Wychbold near Droitwich organized by the BBC staff who manned the famous Droitwich transmitter. An episode of the programme was rehearsed and recorded before an interested audience of a thousand people, most of whom, it seemed, then proceeded to queue for autographs.

It so happened that at this time 'Phil' was supposed to be recovering from a tractor accident in which he had hit his head and had subsequently undergone an operation on his eyes. So, when the characters were introduced to the audience one by one, Phil appeared, walking hesitantly, wearing dark glasses and being led by his sister Chris. The moment is preserved for ever on the front page of the *Droitwich Guardian* for 29 August 1952.

That summer was our first experience of having our engagement books full of appointments, mainly to open garden fêtes, Most of us never had a Saturday free and we often spent a good deal of the Friday travelling hundreds of miles to the place where we were to appear, and a good part of the Sunday getting back, ready for rehearsing on Monday morning.

Some of us quickly realized how little it meant to see one's name on a poster or one's photograph in the paper. Occasionally some feature or article would stand out as being unusually accurate, or with particularly good photographs (like, for example the two-page spread in *Everywoman* for October 1952 with the title: 'The most famous farm in England'). But there scarcely seemed time to stop and think about what was happening. There was always another engagement waiting to be fulfilled. It would be misleading to suggest that the pressures upon us were as great as those on present-day pop-stars, but the pressures were there, and they showed no sign of decreasing as each milestone went by.

The first milestone was undoubtedly the week's trial run in the Midlands in 1950. Then came the real beginning on the Light Programme on 1 January 1951. Next was our promotion to 6.45 in the evening after three months, and then came our one hundredth programme. Now we were approaching another milestone: our five hundredth broadcast.

As we look back today, over twenty-five years and more than six thousand five hundred episodes, five hundred seems a small enough number. Yet at the time it seemed yet one more scarcely believable point of achievement. What is undeniable is the extraordinary progress that had been made in establishing a whole new mythology in less than two years.

More than that, not only had a new world been created in the minds of listeners, but behind the microphone too, a new organization had evolved. Writers and editor had to meet and plan the story, which in turn had to be approved by programme officials inside the BBC. Then the scripts, once written and edited had to be typed, duplicated and sent to the actors. A whole filing system of 'continuity' details had to be created and a bank of recorded sound effects had to be built up. All this in under five hundred episodes. It is hardly surprising that those of us in the middle of it all felt we scarcely had time to breathe.

One point may puzzle the thoughtful reader. The five hundredth episode was broadcast on a Wednesday – Wednesday 17 December 1952. It may well be asked why the five hundredth edition did not fall upon a Friday. The programme began on 1 January 1951 and five episodes were used every week. The answer is that when King George VI died, programmes were much curtailed for two days as a mark of respect. It took some years before those two missing episodes were made up, or rather were levelled out by natural wastage – in some years, for example, there was no edition on Boxing Day. At all events, the programme is now on an even keel: each hundredth, each thousandth, episode is transmitted on a Friday.

The five hundredth episode was marked by a small party in Birmingham, again given by the Controller of the Region, John Dunkerley. Kenneth Adam, Controller of the Light Programme, was present. There was a critical appraisal of the programme in *Radio Times*, illustrated with photos of Dan, Doris, Phil and Chris, by John Dewey, a real farmer. He wrote of commercial travellers meeting in a pub to hear the programme in the hope of catching out The Archers. The Archers usually won. He mentioned agricultural officials who told him that 'Some of our technical wallahs listen regularly. What impresses them is that when it touches on weed sprays, or something like that, it's pretty accurate on detail.' He spoke of one farm where all the hands listened when they could. Then he went on:

'Most of the houses in our village turn on the programme, some old dears go in next door for it, and mothers like it because it is "safe" for the children. The girl who helps here in the house stamps her foot with annoyance every night when the programme ends just at the exciting part. She is sighing and dying for Philip to get married. My wife sees budding romance weeks ahead, and her forecast is usually right. I like the practical tips, and would like them more if they were ever on subjects I want advice about! I must say in criticism that the Archers are a gossipy lot. Much of farming is one man on one job, and if he is talking he cannot be working. How that scrounging but lovable old gasbag Walter Gabriel ever makes a living is a mystery. Perhaps he and the Archers, too, have a secret non-radio life when they work like beavers to get some farming done, instead of just chatting pleasantly about it . . . We all wish Dan Archer and his wife and family, and friends and employees, a good long innings, but personally I wouldn't have his job for worlds. Think of the responsibility of the example he sets!'

The responsibility of that example weighed very heavily at times on the production team. How could you explain to a devoted farming listener in the West Country that just because Dan Archer was hay-making it did not follow that he should? Indeed, the chances are he should have made his hay a couple of weeks before Dan! Or how do you tell an equally devoted farmer in the North that he might do well *not* to follow Dan and wait a week or two before trying to get in his hay harvest? Dan Archer, as a character, is something that many great writers have failed to create: a good man who is not a bore.

The five hundredth episode, and its accompanying celebrations over, the programme returned to its normal round. December meant Christine's birthday, on the 21st, shortly followed by a traditional country Christmas. We received an even greater number of Christmas cards, greetings and presents this year than on our first Christmas one year before. But the one I treasure most says:

happy christmas to all the archers and hope peggy is getting well

Dear Philip Archers
I am 9 years old and lived 110 North Station Road Colchester and If grace wont marry you I will. Will you say happy birthday to christine please
And my love
     from Diana

     x x x x x x x

1953

And the end of sweet rationing. Violent gales and high tides brought severe flooding to the East coast, causing extensive damage and loss of life. Amnesty was declared for war-time deserters in Britain. Stalin died and also Queen Mary, aged eighty-five. Winston Churchill was created K.G., and awarded the Nobel Prize for Literature. Edmund Hillary and Sherpa Tensing, under Colonel John Hunt, reached the summit of Mount Everest. The Piltdown skull was found to be a hoax. December was the mildest in Britain for twenty years, and before that for two hundred years.

IN AMBRIDGE

Jack took over as licensee of *The Bull*, Len Thomas replaced Christine who had left the dairy and after working at Brookfield now wanted to work full-time at the riding stables. Dan, Phil and Len helped to rescue Walter's flock after dogs had attacked his sheep. The licence of *The Bull* was transferred to Peggy because of Jack's dilatoriness. Grace announced that she was off to Ireland for a year to study horse management, and Chris and Clive Lawson-Hope, the Squire's nephew, became friends.

Coronation Year, the third year of The Archers, saw a consolidation of the hold which the programme had already made on upwards of eight million daily listeners.

It was a year of Special Coronation Events. There was no ordinary village fête or flower show that year: they all became Special Coronation Fêtes and Flower Shows.

As the year began, the number of television sets licensed was only just above the million mark, while there were eleven million radio sets. The televizing of the Coronation itself gave a

45

great boost to the sales of television sets, but it was to be five years before there were more television licenses than radio ones issued.

It shouldn't be thought that one reason for the success of The Archers is that it began to be broadcast at a time of mounting interest in the radio medium. Although it is true that in 1970 there were as many, or rather as few, licences issued as in 1927, in between these two years there was a steady rise and fall in the number issued. The peak was reached in 1950. In other words, 1951 when The Archers began was the year in which the number of radio licences (11,546,925) began to decline, as television slowly (at first) increased in popularity.

We had the buoyant feeling that our daily audience of eight million was, if anything, increasing, in spite of the possible attraction of television. Our fan-mail continued to grow, and we had more requests to open Special Coronation Garden Fêtes and Shows than we could possibly accept. It was, for many of us, a golden year which carried us on a flood tide of popularity and gave us scarcely a moment to stop and draw breath.

But for some of us it meant change, hard decisions and almost impossible tasks; and sadly, for all of us, our first and devastating bereavement. But death was to stay its hand throughout the summer when every weekend, and sometimes on weekdays too, members of the Cast of The Archers would be greeted by waving crowds lining the streets, or thronging in their thousands on to public parks or playing fields. It was a royal year and for much of it the Archer family was treated like royalty itself.

The year had begun, though, with the resignation of one of the original, and one of the most popular members of the Cast – June Spencer, known and loved by then to millions as Peggy Archer. June and her husband had had to make a difficult choice between the success of their married life and June's continued radio life as Peggy. Hard as it was, no one could blame them for deciding that June should leave the programme and raise a family. We were all sad at her departure although we knew that she might be able to return on occasions after a year or two in order to play one of the increasing number of small parts that were now an accepted ingredient in the programme. None of us could guess at the time that not only would she return in November 1954 to play the part of Rita Flynn, the naughty Irish girl with the heart of gold who tried to lead Philip astray – a part June had created and 'doubled'

46

with Peggy during the first month of the programme – but that she would in time return to play her original part.

An excellent actress and delightful person, Thelma Rogers, had very quietly entered the cast to play small parts, including Elsie Catcher the village schoolmistress, and she was chosen to succeed June.

Inevitably letters arrived saying: 'We don't like the new Peggy!' This was less than heartening to Thelma, who got on well with us all and impressed us with the effort she made to give the best possible performance. But in long-running daily serials, you sometimes have to wait for many years for your rewards. When, in October 1962, Thelma left to continue her stage career, June Spencer returned and once more letters began to arrive, saying: 'We don't like the new Peggy!' What is clear, and luckily the powers that be recognized this from the start, is that listeners to daily serials abhor change of any kind.

As this book shows, all too sadly, some change in cast is inevitable in a run as long as twenty-five years, and eventually our indulgent listeners came to accept the fact. However, there was little evidence to show that we lost any listeners when we had a new Grace or a new Peggy. And during 1953 another change was made which was unrecognized by most of our listeners, even though it was a main character.

Pamela Mant, who had created the part of Christine in 1950 and played it splendidly until October 1953, suddenly left the programme for personal reasons, giving the production team barely a month to find a replacement. Various actresses were tried without success. Then Denis Folwell remembered being asked for an autograph by a girl at a Whitsun Fête in Louth as he sat surrounded by crowds, signing photographs. He had looked up with a start: 'You sound exactly like Chris!' he had said and the girl had laughed delightedly. 'Your laugh even sounds the same.' She was indeed a vocal double, and luckily Denis remembered where she lived and that her name was Lesley Saweard. She was invited to the studio and gave a successful audition for the part. Although her experience was limited – she was nineteen – she quickly brought talent, enthusiasm and hard work to the part, and played it with such success that no one wrote and said: 'We don't like the new Christine!'

But this was not to be until November. Before that, in January the programme was recorded in the BBC's Nottingham studios and for various reasons this visit remained in the minds of the Cast. One of our number, it is true, made the occasion memorable by indulging a shade to freely in the warm hospitality that was offered to us, but the photographs taken by the local press on that occasion reveal more of the spirit of camaraderie than normally spills over into such posed pictures.

We all got on well together and if there were some members of the Cast one liked a little less than others, there was an unusual warmth and toleration about our recording sessions together that made our work a pleasure. The four Brookfield Archers, Dan, Doris, Phil and Chris were often heard at mealtimes, discussing the problems of farming and personal life; and so well did we know each other by this time that our unscripted remarks grew and grew until, on occasions, we were almost improvising. We rarely cut into each other's lines or pauses, knowing each other's timing and phrasing. It was an exhilarating time, and in spite of this freedom of performance 'fluffs' or re-takes were rare, even though we still recorded the whole episode at one session on a single disc.

On the last day of January, violent gales and high tides caused extensive flooding with loss of life along the East Coast (as well as in Holland and Belgium) and one listener wrote suggesting that the Archers should be heard in the programme collecting donations for the Flood Victims' Relief Fund. Now fact and fiction really were becoming mixed: not only did the characters in The Archers give generously, the actors who played the parts did so too, and a very large sum was collected.

In March the deaths of both Stalin and Queen Mary were mentioned topically in the programme. The topical insert on the death of Stalin was particularly memorable, because of the technical difficulties it caused.

Once the news had broken the normal procedure was followed: the script of the episode due to be broadcast that evening was read and a scene selected in which the topical reference could be made. Then new material was written and provision made to cut out an exact amount of the material originally recorded. The new script was then typed, the performers alerted and a new recording made.

On this occasion, though – it was Friday 6 March – the time of rehearsal came, 3.30 p.m., and only Doris and Phil were present. All efforts to raise Dan and Chris had failed: they were both no doubt en route for some public engagement at the weekend. So all the new material was given to Doris and Phil to speak, and this was superimposed on the original disc. In the original scene as recorded, listeners heard Doris cooking breakfast, with Chris at the table already eating. The door opened and Phil and Dan entered, joining Chris and Doris for a scene of general chat mainly about Grace at the riding-stables, and Chris's chances of winning on Midnight at the Little Croxley Point-to-Point.

What was actually broadcast on the day of Stalin's death sounded similar, except that Phil entered alone, chatted with Doris about Stalin's death, while the sound of Chris's knife and fork on plate suggested that she was busy eating. Then the door opened and Dan came in, and the whole family joined in general discussion about the Little Croxley Point-to-Point. It sounded as if the whole scene had been recorded that very day: in fact only half the cast had actually been there!

A major development in the history of The Archers took place in the spring of 1953. The General Overseas Service of the BBC had decided to take the programme, and a means had to be found to bring new listeners up-to-date with all that had happened in the previous two and a half years.

Both Ted Mason and Geoff Webb were extremely ingenious devisers of programmes: both had written thrillers like *Dick Barton*. Geoff had written for commercial radio and Ted had many detective thrillers to his credit. They devised a short series of episodes which formed a clear introduction to all the main characters with their backgrounds and their immediate past actions, so that in a matter of weeks a new audience would be fully in the picture and able to follow the normal episodes thereafter.

And so every week, after recording our usual six episodes we then went on to record a special General Overseas Service edition, which was in the form of a thirty-minute Omnibus. As all this was done within the space of two days it meant very hard work for us all, not least for Tony Shryane the producer who, unlike the performers, never had an episode off. We worked from 9.30 till 6.15 on Monday and from 9.30 till 5 p.m. on Tuesday.

After the overseas programme had been running for a while, a recording was played to us of our own performance as it sounded on the average set in remote parts of the world. The dialogue was at times barely audible under a continuous sizzle and crackle of 'atmospherics'. At fairly regular intervals, the sound faded into distortion and then silence, only to return with a rush into clear speech. We realized that we would have to learn a new technique: the casual throw-away technique which had so quickly won for us the reputation of being 'real', 'natural', 'true to life' had, for the G.O.S. edition only, to be replaced with a slower, clearer, more deliberate delivery.

Far from being tedious, this was a most salutary technical challenge. There were times when we felt that people less fortunate than we, people who found themselves slightly envious of our great good fortune, were hinting that we were becoming smug, complacent, lazy or big-headed. Any serial which is an extended success must expect brickbats of this sort. The whole experience was far too exhilarating, though, for any of us to become smug or complacent, however anxiously our few personal critics waited with baited breath. Nonetheless, the act of applying an entirely different performing technique to the same material each week was stimulating and challenging, and the perfect safeguard against complacency.

As Coronation Day, 2 June 1953, drew nearer we found ourselves fully booked for a series of public events. As early as 9 May, two members of the Cast judged events at a Coronation Year Rally at Harpenden; there was a Coronation Year Carnival at Fazeley in Staffordshire at which members of the Cast crowned the Queen. On August Bank Holiday ten members of the team, including the producer, appeared at a Coronation Year Horse Show and Gymkhana, Horticultural and Dog Show at Wrest Park, Silsoe, Bedfordshire. And individual members of the Cast were called upon for similar functions throughout the summer.

Several of us agreed just a little too readily to 'present the Coronation mugs', not realizing that as every child in the village had to be given one, the process was long, tedious and arm-breaking. It was nice to be asked to fit in a detour to a hospital for long-term patients because something to look forward to 'makes the weeks go quickly and would take a lot of the disappointment away at having to miss the Coronation'. How could anyone refuse such a request? And hectic though our lives were, how pleasant to be told afterwards: '. . . thanks for brightening up our Coronation day.'

A country rector wrote an endearing letter asking Mrs Archer to 'send Phil or Dan or even the Vicar. We would very much like an "Archer" at our Fête. The Vicar could take his fee for his church expenses if he wished . . .' How easy it was to forget that all the Archers, even the Vicar, were actors, who were supplementing their income by taking on such engagements.

Others, equally ingenuous, had no understanding at all of the fullness of our schedules. One letter ran: 'Bye thee way. We have a Corn-nation party here in "St Pauls Street" on thee 6.June.all day and carry on till 3 oclock in thee Morning. Myself and my landlady and lady thats got the Cornation party up for children as well as Grown ups would like to see you.A Birthday Party as well hear.we will have some fun hear in the street.Myself and (Mrs Ellis) said that I was to ask if you would like to come down to Brighton on that evening if you like let me know before thee 6th. June . . .'

In fact, Coronation Day was for most of us a rare day off, our purely predictable comments on the day's events having been included in the night's episode when it was recorded the week before.

Later in June one of the most important national periodicals, *Picture Post*, carried a five-page spread of magnificent photographs by Bert Hardy with text by Brian Dowling. Looking at them now there is one that gives us great sadness, and yet at the time we were completely unaware of how ill one of our best-loved colleagues looked. Carried along on our flood-tide of success we were it seems too preoccupied to notice signs which now are all too clear.

The growing confidence of the production team, together with first-rate national publicity like the articles in *Radio Times* and *Picture Post*, coupled with our continued public appearances all over the country, did nothing to decrease the steadily mounting interest in The Archers. The programme and its characters were now household names; and our fan-mail was prodigious.

All sorts of people, from every social level, wrote to us with equal warmth. There were at this time still remarkably few unkind or unpleasant letters. Many of our listeners, while saying how true and real the programme was, went on to congratulate us on our 'acting skill' and 'the way you play your part'. Many asked if we ever appeared in other programmes.

Letters from children were as frequent and numerous as any others. One little girl wrote:

'Dear Mr and Mrs Archer,
    I thoughoghly enjoy lestening to your programme as it seems to be real and we can imagine just what Ambridge is like.
    We have an Archers Club and have the pictures from

article about the Archers which was in the Picture Post, at the end of each week we make a list of questions about thing we think might come into the following weeks programme then all the members make a lists of their answers and at the end of the following week the one with the most correct answers wins a small prize, we have a member in Torquay Devon who sends her answers by post each week.

Could you let us have a photo of you both for our club-room wall. I enclose stamps to cover the postage.

Our love to Chris.

Eileen

P.S. We're glad that phil and Grace are engaged at last.'

One optimistic couple sent a silver and white invitation card 'requesting the pleasure of Mr Philip and Miss Christine Archer's company at the Coming of Age of their daughter', while a postcard from the P.O.'s Mess, H.M.S. *Flint Castle*, Portland, Dorset addressed to Mr Philip Archer, Ambridge Farm, c/o BBC Birmingham, Warwick, bore the message: 'Regret that we overlooked your Birthday, Please accept our apologies, and our Belated wishes for your Birthday. From Ken, Alex, Harry, Aubrey, Charles, Philip.'

During the late summer of 1953 several letters were received from a devoted listener whose handwriting bore witness to the fact that she was crippled with arthritis, but she could still knit. In spite of our protestations, beautifully knitted socks eventually arrived at the Birmingham studios – something in return for all the pleasure the programme gave to a grateful listener.

We were often touched by letters and subsequent gifts of that sort, and on more than one occasion suspected that some of the gifts were more than the senders could easily afford.

Mothers often wrote on behalf of severely handicapped children and it was not difficult to read anguish and fortitude between some of the lines. Heartbreaking letters, revealing agonizing personal problems were not infrequent – some of them being very hard to answer.

Other listeners wrote with unconscious humour: 'I am making a collection of radio stars' one alarming letter began, while a young listener from Norwich wrote, disarmingly, for a photograph, 'as I am a great fan of yours. I have seen many photographs of you, but They all seem to be different.'

A listener wrote from an address in Great Portland Street,

London, asking for 'an assigned photograph'; while from Dordrecht in Holland came a letter asking for help with certain English words, after expressing interest in the programme.

Occasionally – very occasionally in those sunny days – there was adverse comment. We all received unpleasant letters at various times, not all as amusing as one addressed 'To "Phil" the "Posh" Archer' and sent, surprisingly enough, from London S.W.1. It began, without address of sender or any preliminaries:

> 'Just burned down 3 more Haystacks, in protest against your "La di da" affected "*voice*", telling me not to – and when I can save up I'm going to buy your "*sister*" a picture of a *horse*, – so she'll know one when she sees one. "*Moonshine*" & his "snorts" is obviously "a Boy" & "props". More broken glass and chasing dogs tomorrow – until you talk like an Englishman & some "sense".'

During the summer of 1953, a London impresario tried unsuccessfully to negotiate with the BBC for a stage play based on The Archers, to be written by Edward J. Mason and Geoffrey Webb, and to be mounted using the original radio cast. So the play was produced with other players and caused a certain amount of confusion. Avid listeners went along to their local theatres in response to posters urging them to 'see your old friends Dan and Doris and Walter' and of course found themselves confronted with different interpretations from those they knew so well over the air.

Another event took place during this unforgettable Coronation Year – an event which had already cast its shadow before, but, as I have already said, we were all too occupied to notice it. Among the photographs published in *Picture Post* was one of Robert Mawdesley, the original Walter Gabriel, which to the eyes of hindsight shows a very sick man bravely hiding what was soon to be discovered as an inoperable complaint. For some months Robert had exaggerated the role he enjoyed playing in the studio of a crabby misanthrope.

Those of us who knew him well realized that this was a kind of act: we knew quite well that if we said, 'Good morning, Bob', he would reply, 'Morning!' But if we began by saying, 'Morning, Bob!' he would say with a correcting manner, 'Good morning!' He had the warmest of natures and a quiet humour, though he often amusingly pointed out that he felt he was no longer the darling of the gods. After broadcasting with him in

London, I suggested travelling home with him. 'Love it, old boy!' he said. 'But I warn you, I'm a jinx.'

As we waited at Paddington Station, he suddenly announced that the rain was coming through the roof. I was perfectly dry but he was right. In the one spot where he was standing, the rain was dripping through on to his head!

'See what I mean?' he said. 'And you see. When the train comes in, it'll stop with either a guard's van or a first class compartment opposite where I'm standing!'

He was right – or nearly so. It was a closed restaurant car in fact.

'See what I mean?' he queried. 'I told you, I'm a jinx.'

Gradually, one or two of us began to wonder whether this half-comic, half-serious crustiness wasn't a cover for feelings too awful to be expressed. He began to have difficulty with reading his scripts, and on one particularly frustrating occasion spoke of double-vision.

On one occasion, he and I travelled together from his home in the Cotswolds to appear at a function and, as he no longer had a car of his own, I suggested that he might like to drive. He eagerly agreed but within minutes of his doing so, we both realized that it was a mistake. His sight was clearly playing tricks and after several miles of weaving about from side to side of narrow country roads, he feigned some excuse, pulled up and I took over again.

Yet throughout this time when, as we now know, he was refusing to face up to the bitter truth, his performance as Walter had the same richness, the same humanity and the same quirkiness that had endeared the character to so many people. Then, suddenly, he was no longer there. We heard that he had taken to his bed in a state of complete mental and physical collapse.

By the end of June we heard from his wife that 'Robert is a *very* ill man, far more dangerously so than even I could have imagined.'

The feelings of the whole team were changed by this news: from feelings of light-hearted absorption in an exhilarating project, to a mixture of sympathy for a sick colleague and an anxiety for the programme. Walter Gabriel was a key character and probably the most popular: Robert's performance was unique.

Clinging to the hope that complete rest and careful nursing might restore him to perfect health, the production team decided that a temporary understudy would have to be found; someone who could, by attempting some sort of impersonation, at least keep the character ticking over until Robert was well again.

By far the most acceptable performance came from another old colleague, Chris Gittins, and to him fell the almost impossible task of playing Walter.

The story was given to the press early in July and immediately Robert's illness became dominant in listeners' letters. A postscript to a fan-letter dated 18 July 1953 said: 'I'm very sorry to read about Walter being ill. I hope he soon recovers. "The Archers" would not be the same without him.' And another, on 5 August, said: '. . . if you should see Mr Mawdesley "Walter" in the near future while he is in hospital please convey my good wishes to him and tell him I hope he gets well again soon.' Barely a letter reached us that did not express sadness, concern and anxiety.

When we met the public at our never-ending round of fêtes, fairs and shows, the enquiries that always greeted us reflected an enormous anxiety that seemed to fill the whole nation.

Knowing as we now did what resentment there was from the public who disliked changes of any sort, especially of former, we were concerned both at Robert's illness and Chris's difficulties in playing the part. We had to assure the crowds who flocked to see and hear us that although seriously ill, Robert was in hospital receiving the best possible treatment, and in the meantime we hoped that listeners would not frown upon the 'new' Walter, who had the unenviable task of trying to imitate the inimitable. We dared not say more of what was in our hearts.

It was an occupational hazard for someone playing the lusty young romantic lead to be the object of interest of certain types of female listener. This was certainly my experience. During the summer I had begun to receive letters of growing passion from one young woman in particular. By September I think she had overcome her infatuation, and had also taken the hint from the somewhat off-putting tone of my brief replies to her earlier missives.

Early in October I was not pleased to recognise among my morning mail another letter from the same young woman. Its contents, however, were not on her usual lines. Her letter was dated 1 October 1953 and read: '. . . This evening I was listening to "The Archers" and I was surprised when the programme ended three minutes before the time, and then I heard Mr Mawdesley's death announced. Words cannot explain the shock I got. Well I pray that God will grant him happiness in the next world and I will always think of him when I hear Walter Gabriel . . .'

I think Robert would have liked that.

_1954_

THE YEAR THAT

All food rationing ended in Britain after fourteen years. Oxford won the 100th Boat Race and Roger Bannister was the first man to run a mile in under four minutes. Anthony Eden was knighted, and Sir Winston Churchill celebrated his eightieth birthday. He was presented by both Houses of Parliament with a portrait of himself by Graham Sutherland.

IN AMBRIDGE

Dan Archer ceased being a tenant-farmer and bought Brookfield when the Lawson-Hope estate was sold up. Carol Grey bought the small-holding and an ex-university lecturer who had won the pools, John Tregorran, arrived by gypsy caravan and settled in Ambridge. Chris decided not to marry Clive Lawson-Hope, but Grace agreed to marry Phil.

As another year began, we found ourselves looking forward to another milestone. It was to be in November: our one thousandth episode. There seemed little doubt in any of our minds now that the programme would last that long and that our contracts would be renewed. But what then? Television was gaining in popularity by leaps and bounds: we all had sets and watched them in what small leisure time we had.

Even in what we now recognize as those early days we began to entertain a thought which, once introduced, has been our dark companion throughout the years and is still an unwelcome member of the team. It is the thought: Will 'they' take The Archers off when it is at the height of its popularity?

We felt it as we approached each new milestone, even when we began to count in thousands of episodes and not hundreds. We felt it when we began to count in years: five, ten, twenty,

twenty-one twenty-five. We felt it for the first time as we approached our one thousandth episode.

It was not irrational. The whole phenomenon of our incredibly swift rise from modest obscurity to being a household word seemed, in our few moments of reflection, dreamlike and unreal. Creating a fantasy world of Ambridge and the Archers seemed in itself a fantastic experience for us all. We felt then, as many of us feel now, that one day we might wake up and find it all a fast-moving extended dream.

We were now called upon to appear at rather bigger functions drawing thousands of people, rather than the smaller groups at village fêtes. Some of us preferred then as we do now the small village occasions, although today if an 'official opener' is invited at all – and it is a declining formality – a star from one of the regular television serials is more likely to be chosen. We don't complain: we have had our wonderful day. Whereas before we had to decline as many as we accepted, now it is a pleasure to be asked, and to know that we are still of interest and still able to draw the crowds after so long.

Back in 1954, however, we were regarded as probably the greatest attraction possible for a country event. We even found ourselves called upon to attend the great agricultural shows. We had made 'topical inserts' into the programme from the more important national events like the Royal Show and the Smithfield Show. When we appeared at the Poultry Show in December 1953 for example, large photographs appeared of Dan, Doris, Phil and the new Chris with such captions as 'The Archers' day at Show', 'Radio Archers go to Poultry Show' or 'Radio Farmers Come to Town'.

There was still a tendency to treat us as country bumpkins and although it looked as if we were beginning to be accepted, there was still no strong feeling that we really had 'arrived'.

Events during the next year or two, however, were to alter that.

The changes in the Cast seemed to be accepted, after an initial period of mild resentment on the part of our listeners. Lesley Saweard's taking over as Chris caused very little comment, and soon the sincerity and integrity of Thelma Rogers's performance as Peggy won back for that character her high place in listeners' affections.

Chris Gittins had a rather rougher time as Walter Gabriel. The physical effort alone of producing some approximation of Robert Mawdesley's gravelly voice was very taxing. Chris explained that in order to sound 'Walter-ish' he lived on a diet of rusty razor-blades and throat pastilles. The extraordinary thing was that Robert Mawdesley had been able to produce that voice without the least effort or strain. When asked how, he replied, 'I don't know. I just think it and out it comes. My infant grandson can do it!' And indeed, although the strain of being one of the original Archers was as great for Robert as for the rest of us, the effort of producing that voice was minimal.

On more than one occasion Robert played both parts in a duologue: when Mr Robertson the Vet chided Walter for his lack of hygiene for example, the listeners heard two quite separate personalities: a gruff-voiced countrified Walter and urbane, well-informed lighter-voiced Robertson. No one could have guessed that they came from the same actor. It was as if Robert could throw some unseen switch and in a fraction of a second assume the whole *persona* of Walter Gabriel.

When he died, it was the greatest compliment that an episode was shortened so that the editor could pay an obituary tribute to an actor we all felt was irreplaceable, both on and off the air.

Chris Gittins was faced with several problems: apart from the physical production of the voice, he was told to aim at re-creating the character, slowly bringing to it his own interpretation, so that eventually he could give his own performance and not an impersonation. We had no doubt that he could do it: he had been a familiar radio voice since 1935 and had specialized in radio when conditions in the theatre made it very difficult for a young actor to make a living.

Once it was clear that the inevitable change of performer was not materially altering the popularity of the programme as a whole, Chris relaxed and began the uphill task of creating his own version of Walter. Within a year or so he found himself saying that although he had tried faithfully to follow the character created by Robert Mawdesley, his own impression of Walter was based on an old local poacher who was Chris's mentor in country-lore as a child in his native Worcestershire.

While it was unthinkable that Walter Gabriel and his series of comic encounters with Mrs P. should become other than major ingredients in the Archers' formula, it was decided to take the spotlight off Walter for a while to give Chris a chance to work his way into the part. After all, he had stepped into a major role with all its concomitant public appearances photographs, interviews and lack of personal privacy. The rest of us had experienced a (slightly) slower indoctrination into a very wearing and hectic way of life.

So Ambridge saw the introduction of two new characters who were to become firm favourites: Carol Grey, who was to marry Grenville before eventually becoming the wife of the other character who entered the programme in 1954, John Tregorran.

By this time, the writing and editorial team of Baseley, Mason and Webb were past-masters at the extraordinarily skilled task of marshalling the development of the story. They had first discovered and then mastered a technique for blending solid farming material with human drama. They would trail a coat, and the moment it caught the general public interest it would reveal an agricultural purpose.

Over a period of years they used the apparently insatiable curiosity of the public in Philip's love life to extend what appeared to be a love story into what was in fact a monumental information project on the problems of pig-breeding! It was managed like this:

In the very first episode Phil and Grace had been heard in a close embrace after the New Year's Eve party. It was to be four years before they were eventually to marry. It was, not accidentally, a stormy and eventful courtship with several estrangements in which it looked as if each were about to marry someone else.

Grace was the daughter of a rich plastics manufacturer who farmed for fun and didn't mind if he made a loss: Phil became manager of Fairbrother's expanding farm.

Fairbrother was friendly with a widow, Helen Carey, whose son, Alan, had not fully recovered from his wartime experiences. Alan, also wealthy, arrived and cut Phil out with Grace. When, however, he proposed marriage, Grace declined his offer and went abroad with her father, who had lost face in the village by proposing to start mining ironstone in Ambridge.

Phil, realizing that financially he could scarcely seem an attractive prospect as a husband for Grace, consoled himself with a succession of girl-friends from Jane Maxwell to Marjorie Butler.

In 1952 the marriage of her father put notions of marriage into Grace's head once again and Phil, having had plenty of time to think while recovering from his tractor accident in hospital and wondering how he could ever provide Grace with the life-style to which she was accustomed, asked her to marry him in five years. By this time he hoped to be better off financially. Grace not surprisingly, refused; but this made Phil even more determined to make some money. And how was he to do this? By setting up a pedigree pig-breeding scheme.

If the 'story so far' is analysed it will be seen at once that for over a year the listeners had been conditioned to want Grace, above all else, to marry Phil. When it had been made clear beyond doubt that neither would be happy with anyone else, the stumbling-block was revealed as being a simple financial one. Money must be raised and the method was farming. Suddenly millions of listeners found themselves desperately wanting a pig enterprise to succeed.

Then authenticity had to be considered: even if the pig-scheme were successful, Phil wasn't going to make a fortune overnight. The couple were very much in love, but as the permissiveness of the sixties was still some years away, they were allowed serious petting but nothing more. As Barbara Cartland has said: 'As far as the bedroom door but no further!'

With the love-scenes becoming more and more torrid, something had to be done. And so, in 1953, Grace with a sort of desperate hopelessness, suddenly decided that she would go to Ireland to study horse-management. The atmosphere of her departure was not improved when Phil, helping Len Thomas the shepherd to catch a train home to Wales, where his wife had been killed in a car-crash, arrived too late to say goodbye to Grace. During her absence, Phil consoled himself with Anne Trentham.

In September 1954, after a stormy home-coming, Grace agreed to marry Phil, money or not. Even then, the wedding was not immediate: public anticipation had to be fed and built up, so Easter Monday the following year was chosen. Even then, minor tiffs, misunderstandings and varying moods kept the interest alive.

There is no doubt that this section of the long saga of The Archers provided the greatest public involvement in the programme. The largest number of letters ever received was sent, urging Phil on or advising him to send Grace packing.

Here, from a large number of those letters which still survive is a selection, without commentary. They date from early 1953 up until the wedding in 1955 and tell their own story.

From Peterborough, 8 January 1953:
'Take my advice and drop that nasty piece of work Grace Fairbrother *at once* . . . she's just dying to be married. Let that Clive Lawson-Hope have her . . . he'll have none of her rotten bursts of temper . . . Take off those blinkers, choose a wife who'll be a helpmeet, an even-tempered and industrious person with similar ideas to yourself . . . "Get weaving" and Good Luck to you. I'll be listening. Believe me to be A Wellwisher.'

From an Aberdonian:
'Grace never mind fit Phillip says.
Pull yer goonie over yer taes.'

From 'two lonely little patients' in a hospital near Swansea, 8 April 1953:
'We feel we must write to you after listening to last night's broadcast. We thought your technique was terrific and we do hope that Grace will respond to the right treatment. If not, *we* shall be very pleased to co-operate. Having been in bed for 8 months we look forward to moments such as these . . .'

From 'Ye olde worlde Academy, Bristol':
'Miss V want too No wen You R going to smak Grace's btm – if you dont reely want that there Wring send it hon to hus has we ave ere two or free Spin-stirs wot will be glad to where it as they will ave no hother chance.
    We feels as ow they oughter to took hoff the shelf and dusted.
I am Yours
Miss Fanny Flannelpants alias Miss Droopydrawers.'

From Four Admirers (aged 23–25) Merthyr Tydfil:
'We listen every night at 6.45 patiently waiting for your entrance. We are really dying to hear you in a "Love Scene" with either, Anne Trenton or Grace, a *full five minute* scene; please try to do something about it.'

From Walsall, Staffs. 9 April 1953:
'I am pleased you have made it up with Grace again perhaps when you have sold all your little pigs you will have enough money to get married.'

From Catherington, Hants. 1 May 1953:
'I do wish you would hurry up and get engaged to Grace –
then I should have no need for any consternation concerning
"Clive" – whenever I hear the tune "Boric Green" I am a
very fond lover of all animals – except pigs!'

From 'A listener – one who is fed up' Leicester:
'Instead of the Archers been a pleasure to listen to it's
getting nothing but a nuisance. let it be farm life not so
much of the courting businnes if Grace fairbrother wants to
go away for a year why be mardy about it she is right when
she says get on with your pigs . . . good luck to Grace keep
as you are. stick to your guns.'

From Old Coulsdon, Surrey:
'I am glad to hear you are going with Grace again and that
your pigs so far have not gone swine fever. Hope you have
a nice Coronation Day.'

From Co. Limerick. 12 May 1953:
'Well what I want you to tell me is what is your work each
day are you a farmer or just one in the programme. Tell me
do you love Grace or not.'

From Broadgate, Coventry:
'Well we all hope your pigs are progressing and that they
will do well & get a good price for them. For it takes a lot
of money to get married on. However you have got two years
unless Grace's scheme should fall flat. We think here in
Coventry you have made a good choice. For by the manner
of Grace's voice she will be if not now a very beautiful lady
. . . So God Bless all.
yours ever so much
Peeping Tom.'

From 'Well wisher'. 11 April 1953:
'This is just a word of warning – if you marry Grace Farebrother you will regret it to the last day of your life. She is
utterly selfish, bad tempered and altogether detestable – she
was a perfect little fiend to her father when he married again
& when his baby was coming, & most unsympathetic when
your eyes were bad & she was only fit to marry Clive Lawson-
Hope, where she would meet her match! *You* wait for some-

63

one else, & if you can't wait, you'd do much better to marry
Margery (who helps with the pigs) or even kind little Mary
Jones, who at least has a heart, & is kind to her old father.
Everyone I know if of my opinion, so take heed & "don't"...'

From the Royston District Calendar Girls, Herts:
'Dear Phil we think it's time you wed,
And so our few pennies we have shed
to help you buy the engagement ring
And make the wedding bells ring,
We think you are so very slow,
Go on Phil and have a go.
When next you meet, Grace your'e girl
Kiss her, and make her all awhirl
Sweep her right off her feet
And give us, Calendar girls a treat.'

From Witney, Oxon. 27 September 1953:
'You're Breaking our hearts Phillip Archer,
You really are causing us pain.
By letting Grace buzz off to Ireland.
You're slipping Phil Archer thats plain.
We always thought you were a nice guy,
So just to please us Phillip dear,
Go on take the plunge and get married,
Instead of wasting a year.
We are all very fond of you "Archers".
We never miss listening to you.
But by heavens if you don't get married.
There's no telling what we might do.
There is plenty of ways we could end this.
But the one we think is most true
Is just to say Thank You Sincerely
From all of us here to all You.'

A 'bunch of Archerites' sent this from Derby:
'If you would please give your Archer fans
Follow her – courage take in both your hands,
The Story makes you do the decent thing.
Then do it now – and with you take the RING.
Put on her finger, third, its proper place
Kiss it, look up, and see a smiling Grace,
and when she sighs, and says, "It's lovely Phil"

We listeners too, will all enjoy the thrill.
For every nice girl, whate'er her age or state
A token likes – to show she has a mate.
You've helped others theirs troubles to pull through,
Tis high time now they do the same for you.
So haste to Ireland, do not long delay,
And prove again that Love will find a way.
Forgive the doggerel and thanks for happy listening.'

From Bonchurch, I. of W.:
'What an idiot you are! You didn't have to stop for all the odd moments – seeing Len off on the train etc. For Heavens sake be a *man* and get engaged . . . You really do infuriate us all, though we can't help liking you – but don't let "keeping the programme going" stop you from behaving as a *real man* would.

Good luck in your mission but don't let every opportunity go!

One of your many well-wishers & friends.'

From an eleven-year-old, Carterton, Oxon.:
'This is what will happen to you if you do not watch your step.

Love is sweet
But oh how bitter,
to love a girl
And never get her,
Now Grace lives over the sea,
What a good swimmer you ought to be.

We listen to you every night, your love affair is getting very monotonous please do something about it.'

From Salisbury, Wiltshire. 2 November 1953:
'Congratulations on your engagement to Grace, but PLEASE don't get tired of waiting for Grace to come back, and get rid of the ring and have the piggeries "modernised and air-conditioned throughout" instead.'

From Carlisle. 5 February 1954:
'I am most surprised to learn that a man so astute in business as yourself should decide to marry on Good Friday.

Unless you wish to lose much of your profit on the pig

sales, you must ask Grace to advance the date a few days & reclaim a year's marriage allowance.'

From Northwood, Middlesex. 14 February 1954:
'Well Philip hurry up and marry Grace, & as a suggestion could you compile a Book on "The Life of The Archers" it would be grand & I know a number of folks who would welcome a Book in their home to be able to read the Story from its onset.'

From Tamworth, Staffordshire. 4 February 1954:
'Will you get married to Grace or Ann please let me no in the letter who you will marriey . . .'

From two eleven-year-olds, Loughborough, Leicestershire:
'My friend and I are writing to ask if you are one of the people in The Archers would like to come *to tea* at the above address, do you really kiss Grace. Will you please let us know the date you can come we will write back and tell you if its O.K.'

From Manchester. 12 September 1954:
'I must say it is a very interesting show. The only trouble is we do wish you would hurry up and marry Grace. You see in our own minds we have got it all planned out very nice, but I don't suppose it will end that way. Still we don't want it to end for a long time yet.'

From Carterton, Oxon. 4 September 1954:
'Please find enclosed two verses we think John Tregorran might add to his "What can the Matter be?" repertoire.
Yours sincerely,
Anne Taylor aged 13.
P.S. Sorry the writing is not very good but I have been out of training for the past 8 weeks.
It's about all your girl friends
that we are complaining,
We've listened for four years
they seem never ending.
It looks to us that
another is pending
It's nothing to laugh at at all.

We've listened thro' Rita, Jane,
Maxwell and Mary
Grace Fairbrother, Anne Trentham
It's getting quite dreary
So we are all switching over to
Mrs Dales Diary
IT'S NOTHING TO LAUGH AT AT ALL.'

From Knaphill, Woking, Surrey. 28 September 1954:
'I not with some relief that you and Miss Fairbrother have at last "named the day", but I suggest that you give some thought to your position under P.A.Y.E. before making arrangements for Easter 1955.

As a single man, I have no doubt that you are paying a sizeable amount in Income Tax under P.A.Y.E. so, if the happy day is fixed before April 5th, 1955, you should be entitled to a useful refund – it might even be enough to pay for the "top hat and tails". Yours truly.'

From Bray, Co. Wicklow. 8 September 1954:
'Well done Phil, at last you have got engaged to Grace, my goodness you have taken a long time. I have been waiting for it for months. Congratulations to you and Grace.'

From Richmond, Surrey. 11 December 1954:
'Just a note to wish you all a happy Xmas and New Year – it's a bit early I know, but you will be inundated later!! I am still glad you haven't married Grace yet.'

And so it went on, a never-ending flood from every corner of the British Isles. Not only letters were sent – Valentine cards, rings, family planning articles, colourful engagement cards, and every possible sort of reference to pigs from comic seaside post-cards, cartoons and technical articles from farming journals to plastic pigs that would walk down inclined surfaces. *The Leader* on 5 March published under the heading 'Welcome – Jack, Peggy, Phillip and Christine' a photograph – of four lambs!

Among this collection of letters from listeners – an extra-ordinary series of social documents in a way – there is one of a different order. I was pursuing my career as a writer, in what little time was left from being 'Philip Archer', and about this time a series of plays of mine on the lives of the saints was being broadcast. The leading part in one of these was most sensitively and movingly played by an actor who has since become a star in a rather different field – Kenneth Connor, one of the most consistently funny stars of the *Carry-on* series. In reply to my note of thanks for his performance as St Philip Neri he wrote a splendid letter back, which contains this paragraph:

'It must not smack too much of mutual admiration, but we listen to the "Archers" as voraciously as anyone & some of the love scenes between Grace and Phil I think are amongst the most alive & absorbing moments in radio. I mean that.'

If to quote those lines seems immodest, let me add immodesty to immodesty by saying that one of the things that sustained many of us through what was in fact a most nerve-wracking time, was receiving comments of that sort from distinguished members of the acting profession, whose judgement we valued. Notables as varied as Dame Marie Rambert and Sir Ralph Richardson have been known to make favourable comments upon our work.

One more message from a listener must be mentioned. It was a postcard and arrived on 2 February 1954. It read 'When you see Jimmy Edwards at the Radio Awards tell him he's been holding out on you. After he'd taken his girl round his pigs he proposed to her. She knew there was more in pigs than bacon, but he let you let your girl slope off to Ireland, the mean thing.'

The Radio Awards mentioned were of course the *Daily Mail* National Radio Awards founded in memory of Tommy Handley. We had reached another, and unexpected, milestone. We were joint winners with the immensely popular *Take it from Here* for the most entertaining radio programme. Oddly enough, most of us were completely bowled over at winning this award: we had been so caught up in the unrelenting demands of our schedule that we never gave a thought to such things. As the news sank in we were all enormously elated.

The awards – silver microphones – were presented at the end of an hour-long live broadcast from the Scala Theatre on 20 January 1954. Sidney Lipton, who conducted the orchestra, was kind and helpful in the extreme and declared himself a fan. And Gilbert Harding, winner of an award for the most popular personality, turned out to be by no means an irascible ogre.

I cherish the memory of a fleeting moment when I found myself next to him in the wings, as he waited to go on. He looked furtively around, realized that no one but myself could see what he was doing, whipped a tiny moustache comb from his food-stained bottle-green waistcoat pocket and tittivated his moustache. Then, raising an eyebrow at me, asked in a whisper, 'Is that all right?' I nodded and, as Franklin Engelmann announced his name and the orchestra played, he made his entrance.

Some award-winners, possibly through nerves, fell into the obvious trap of treating us like provincial bumpkins. Not Gilbert Harding, nor Sidney Lipton, and certainly not Richard Dimbleby. The broadcast over, we found ourselves at the reception afterwards rubbing shoulders with all the great names of the radio world, and receiving the congratulations of BBC officials from the Director-General down.

But Richard Dimbleby, apple-cheeked and plump, dazzled us all by his brilliance in knowing all our real names, as well as those of our characters and of recent events in the programme. He had that great gift of giving you the impression that of all the people there you were the one he was most anxious to talk to. 'Yes, Norman,' he said, 'I was just talking to Harry about that – Harry Oakes!' The names tripped from his tongue as if he'd known us all his life.

Gwen Berryman and I moved from group to group and at one point became aware that Harry Oakes was trying to call us over. We went and found Harry talking to the Director-General and his wife, Sir Ian and Lady Jacob. With his most expansive manner Harry presented us, adding, 'This is Sir Jacob and Lady Isaacs!' Our confusion was covered by yet more embarrassment. Gwen gazed at Lady Jacob, who gazed back: both were wearing almost identical dresses! There was nothing to do but laugh: within minutes we felt like old friends.

The following day, Monday, was for once free and no recordings were made; but by Tuesday we were back at the microphone, the bright lights and the dizzy heights behind us. Yet some of the stardust lingered: our work had a new confidence, a new assurance. With a vast and still increasing audience and a National Radio Awards Silver Microphone presented to us, we had perhaps achieved something out of the usual run of things.

The summer was fast approaching when we needed all our strength for the effort of travelling around the country opening fêtes. There were two main reasons for this: in the first place it had started by being good publicity for the programme and was regarded as good public relations. And secondly, it was one way of supplementing our income, which was still very much lower than many people imagined. It was to be some years before our basic weekly salary rose to twenty pounds.

Nonetheless, the future seemed bright and beckoning and our engagement books were as full as ever, when suddenly a bombshell exploded. We were firmly requested by the BBC to attend no more fêtes of a political nature.

Now it so happened that we had received very few invitations to speak at garden parties arranged by the Labour Party, whereas almost from the start we had been extensively booked by Conservative associations. We often pointed out that our appearance at a given function bore no political significance and that we were merely there to meet the many friends we knew from letters we had in that part of the country.

It was at the end of April that the Labour M.P. for North Norfolk, Edwin Gooch, complained to the Board of Governors of the BBC that two members of the Cast of The Archers had been booked to appear at Felbrigg Hall, Cromer, on 31 July 1954. The *Daily Express* reported him as saying that the Archers were used to attract crowds who would provide money to fight him at the next election.

Our reaction to this was that our services were available to open fêtes organized by *any* political party; but the BBC thought otherwise.

On 28 April, we were officially informed that the BBC would be grateful if we would not seek or accept any further engagements at political fêtes, and if possible to withdraw from bookings already made. This was far from easy.

Mr Gooch's slogan, 'The Archers are helping the Tories' was very effective in embarrassing the BBC. The various local Conservative associations on the other hand, sensing no doubt that the publicity would ensure even greater numbers at the fêtes we were booked to open, were very reluctant to release us from a binding contract.

A compromise was attempted: we could appear so long as we did not use our 'Archer' names. So Harry Oakes and Gwen Berryman could and did open the Conservative Fête at Felbrigg Hall, but the names of Dan and Doris Archer did not appear in the announcements.

Gwen Berryman has a poster advertising a fête at Thoresby on Whit-Monday, 7 June, with personal appearances of FAMOUS RADIO STARS, with their real names in small type, with ARCHERY DEMONSTRATION as one of the attractions, and a bold silhouette of an Archer in the centre of the poster. Among the many events listed, apart from the 'archery demonstration' was a speech by the Minister of Transport and Civil Aviation, Rt. Hon. A. T. Lennox-Boyd, M.P.

Uneasily through the summer, we continued to open fêtes, even political ones. At the end of May, for example, four members of the Cast opened the Monmouthshire Conservative Fête at The Priory, Caerleon, at which the Minister of Food, Major Gwilym Lloyd George and his wife were present.

This particular event is remembered, however, not for the political awkwardness of the occasion but because of an incident that happened to Chris Gittins, who was just beginning to experience the joys and miseries of this sort of public appearance. Gwen Berryman, followed by Leslie Bowmar and Joy Davies (George and Helen Fairbrother) had mounted a hay wagon and were seated. Two seats were left and as Chris climbed up, he asked one of the organizers where he should sit. The organizer indicated a chair, but at that moment his attention was distracted. Attempting to draw the chair nearer for Chris, the organizer in fact pulled it sharply from under him, and poor Chris did a backward somersault into the crowd. He got the biggest laugh of the afternoon. But it was more than a month before the pain left that part of his spine he had hit on the edge of the hay wagon in his fall.

We had all been called shortly before this to a very uncomfortable interview with the Controller of Midland Region, John Dunkerley, a man of sterling integrity and fairmindedness, whom we knew to be our friend. But he was powerless in the face of the BBC's decision to avoid undue embarrassment at all costs. We were again asked not to associate our Archer connections in any way with political events, to withdraw if possible from commitments previously entered into, and in the case of any engagements from which release was impracticable, to give the BBC the relevant details.

This was of course done, but to appear in public and pretend we had no connection with a programme called 'The Archers' was clearly impossible. The 'spectacular Fête' at Willey Park, Brosely, for the Ludlow Division Conservative Club, together with the Rt. Hon. Harold Macmillan, then Minister of Housing and Local Government, was one that we remember without much delight. The programme bore our own names under the heading 'The Archers'. Beneath were four spaces for signature marked 'Dan Archer', 'Doris Archer', 'Chris Archer', 'Phil Archer'. We all felt embarrassed and uncomfortable, and not only because we had been asked to sit on a hay wagon, on straw bales that slowly became colder and damper in the Shropshire drizzle.

Reluctantly we agreed that it would be far better not to accept any engagements for political organizations. Some of us, though, could not help agreeing with parts of an editorial in the *Sketch* for 6 May 1954:

'A branch of the Norfolk Conservative party decided to hold a fête this summer at Felbrigg, and they invited along the BBC's Archer family.

'The local Socialist M.P., Mr Edwin Gooch, lodged a protest. Hundreds of his constituents, he complained, would object to Archers appearing at a political gathering.

'Nobody would blame Mr Gooch for trying this on: the BBC is fair game for politicians. And you would expect the BBC to reply, in the same spirit, treating his protest for what it is – a joke.

'But what do they do? They fall on their knees, say they're very sorry, and promise to behave better in future.

'In a letter to Mr Gooch, Sir Alexander Cadogan, chairman of the governors, admits that "there is a danger that such actions might appear to associate the programme itself with party politics".

'And he announces that the cast have been instructed not to accept engagements of this kind in future.

'Well, really! How spineless can you get! It makes us wish we could come up behind the BBC, while they are bowing and scraping, and give them a good, swift kick in the seat of their corporation pants.'

Whatever the rights and wrongs of the case, no political fête has been opened by an Archer, as such, since that cloudy summer of 1954.

But the year seemed destined to end on a happier, upward note. We did indeed survive to see our one thousandth episode and the celebrations of that event were extremely enjoyable. But after them further controversy lay in store.

Once again, Dan and Doris were seen on the front page of *Radio Times*, while on page four there was an article by Tony Shryane on 'Putting Ambridge on the air'.

'I come fresh each Sunday to the mechanics of production, eager to supply a backcloth of reality to the scripts,' he wrote. 'For four days I am in the studio rehearsing and recording five daily episodes for listeners in Great Britain – a week in ad-

Doris (Gwen Berryman) and the original Dan (Harry Oakes), 1957

The creators of The Archers – Geoffrey Webb (writer), Tony Shryane (producer), Ted Mason (writer) and Godfrey Baseley (editor) – learn the facts about farm life at first hand with Dr W. Blount

This photograph of Harry Oakes as Dan Archer and Eddie Robinson as Simon Cooper did nothing to dispel the illusion that the Archers were real

Philip (Norman Painting), Simon Cooper (Eddie Robinson), Mr Fairbrother (Leslie Bowmar) and Dan (Harry Oakes) supervise a flock of sheep

Jack Archer (Denis Folwell) and Dan Archer (Harry Oakes) watch a needle-match of dominoes between Simon Cooper (Eddie Robinson) and Walter Gabriel (Robert Mawdesley). Tom Forrest (Bob Arnold) pegs

The Archer family signs autographs at Wrest Park fête

Walter, played by Robert Mawdesley, with Mrs Perkins (Pauline
Seville). Their friendship gave the villagers of Ambridge cause for
endless discussion about a possible marriage

Walter, played by
Chris Gittins

A family gathering.
Doris and Dan Archer
(Gwen Berryman and
Harry Oakes) entertain
Peggy and Jack Archer
(Thelma Rogers and
Denis Folwell), Jill and
Philip Archer (Patricia
Greene and Norman
Painting) and Christine
and Paul Johnson
(Lesley Saweard and
Leslie Dunn). The two
younger members are
Jennifer and Lilian
Archer (Freda Hooper
and Margaret Lane)

Harry Oakes

Edgar Harrison

vance. Then there is the half-hour programme for overseas listeners, and an edited version in omnibus form for Saturday nights.

'My job is made easier by the fact that the cast are absolutely sincere in their portrayal of the Ambridge characters ... That, together with their devotion to the programme as a whole, results in a team-work that has played no small part in making *The Archers* a success.

'The same spirit is to be found among the "back-room boys" – studio managers and engineers – on whom the success of any programme so largely depends. Then there is the editor, Godfrey Baseley, who first dreamed up this fabulous family and who remains a tower of strength; the scriptwriters, Edward J. Mason and Geoffrey Webb. All three go to great lengths to ensure the authenticity of the programme.

'An old Persian saying has it that a man may count his wealth by the number of his friends. If that is still true today, the Archers are multi-millionaires, for never has any ordinary British family had so many loyal friends, both at home and overseas.'

The thousandth episode was, at least in theory, a perfectly normal one, but Ted Mason who wrote it contrived to include as many of the cast as possible – seventeen members in all. Mike Daly, an Irish vagabond, had bought a rare book in a junkshop for five shillings and had found that it was worth much more and so had given a party to celebrate. The first scene was one of the classic Brookfield farm breakfast-scenes with Dan, Doris, Phil and Chris, with interruptions by Simon, and the third and last scene was the party itself which ended with John Tregorran proposing marriage to Carol Grey.

We gathered at five o'clock on 22 November 1954 and over tea met the press informally. Then we moved into a room with dozens of chairs set out for guests, and after some astonishing tributes had been paid to the programme by the Director-General, Sir Ian Jacob, and by our good friend Sir James Turner, now Lord Netherthorpe, who still knows some of us better by our 'Archer' names than our real ones, we solemnly listened to the actual transmission of the episode.

The surprise of the evening came when Richard Maddock, who often recorded the introductions to the daily episodes, wheeled in a table on which were arrayed engraved silver cigarette boxes which Sir Ian presented to the regular members of the Cast. There was one engraved with the initials R.M. – it was received by Gwen Mawdesley, Robert's widow, to stirring affectionate applause.

Among the official guests in the front row watching all these proceedings was Mr Edwin Gooch, M.P., president of the National Union of Agricultural Workers.

From 7 to 8.30 there were what the official invitation described as 'refreshments'. It was in fact a Champagne party: the day of our thousandth episode, which also happened to be Gwen Berryman's birthday, St Cecilia's day, was celebrated with genuine enthusiasm, and dutifully reported in the Press.

Less than a week later, the programme was in the headlines again. 'The Archers banned from the TV screen' said the *Daily Mirror*. 'Archers can be seen but not heard' said the *Daily Express*. '*What's my line?* row over the Archers' said the *Daily Mail*.

The headlines referred to the fact that the previous day most of the regular Cast had been invited to the Shepherd's Bush Empire at 3.30 p.m. to rehearse for an appearance as the guests on that evening's live television transmission of *What's My Line?*

But something had gone wrong with the staff work. We were ushered into a dressing-room and kept there under a kind of amiable close surveillance. Finally H. Rooney Pelletier, Head of Light Programme, arrived and explained to us that there had been a mistake. We should *not* have been invited to London, arrangements for us to record our week's programmes in London should *not* have been made; he gave us an unconditional apology for the inconvenience caused and pledged his personal word that a short film would be made for television, in which we could be seen 'in character and on location'. It was not BBC policy for us as actors to appear as ourselves.

This really was becoming mind-boggling: we could not appear in public at political fêtes as 'Archers': we could not appear on television as ourselves.

We laughed it off, as always. Seats were found for us in the circle of the theatre and from there we watched the show go on, at which we were to have been the star attraction.

We all drew out breath when Eamonn Andrews asked the team to put on their 'black-outs' as it was 'time to meet tonight's guest celebrity'. On walked a smart and smiling figure. We in the audience were shown the usual placard which duplicated the caption which viewers at home were seeing on the screens. The name was difficult to read, as it was scrawled in black ink, whereas all the others had been printed in heavy, easily-readable type. Then we realized who it was. It was Cyril Stapleton, the dance-band leader, who had at minutes' notice been almost hauled out of his bath to appear. The audience applauded. The girl with the placards put the one bearing his name face down on the pile of ones already shown . . . Then there was a mild gasp. Printed in heavy type on the reverse side, easily readable from the back of the theatre were the words THE ARCHERS. And they were crossed out!

Some time later, BBC policy was changed: the promised film in which we should have all appeared in character on location was never made, but Gwen and Harry did appear as 'The Archers' on *What's my line?*

One way and another, 1954 had been a year to remember. As it ended we looked to the future with rather less eager anticipation than we had the previous New Year's Eve; none of us quite knew why.

In some ways we were right: in others we were perhaps over-anxious. Yet, in many ways, 1955 turned out to be easily the most eventful year so far.

1955

THE YEAR WHEN

Anthony Eden took over from Winston Churchill and Hugh Gaitskell succeeded Earl Attlee. Albert Einstein died. The bank rate was increased from 3% to 3½%. Germany attained full sovereignty and the Western European Union came into being. The general election was won by the Conservatives with a majority of 59. On 22 September the Independent Television Service began and shared headlines the next day with the death of a mythical girl in a radio serial.

IN AMBRIDGE

Grace married Philip on 11 April and died on 22 September trying to rescue a horse. The Manor House became a nursing-home and Jack became Carol Grey's foreman at the market garden.

This memorable year began well. After a National Radio Award and over a thousand episodes to its credit, the morale of the whole team had rarely been higher. Difficulties caused by changes in the Cast had been overcome and the listening audience, large as it already was, appeared still to be growing.

The momentum of the story-line had never been greater. Human drama and agricultural information were inextricably blended in the Phil–Grace situation and the listeners were still encouraged to feel that the wedding planned for Easter might still not take place. A second line of defence for future development was the Carol–John situation.

John Tregorran's proposal, made in the closing seconds of the one thousandth episode, was, in fact, declined, but not irrecoverably, by Carol. With a kind of light-hearted inevitability the Archer saga rolled on, urged forward by the tidal wave of interest and enthusiasm of millions of completely involved listeners.

The year's round had scarcely begun when news came that we had again won a National Radio Award. This gave the lie to the impression given in certain professional quarters that our first silver microphone had been won by a fluke, and that we really weren't quite up to the highest standards. On the first occasion, Ted Mason's very funny script had been reduced to a fraction of its original length, so that in the hour-long broadcast, most of the time was devoted to the other award-winners and The Archers didn't appear until the closing moments of the programme when they had a few lines each. This can still be heard from the rare private recording I have of the occasion.

There was no such shabby treatment this time. Not only had we won, but we had won outright, sharing the award with no other programme: we were proclaimed the most entertaining radio show.

Anxious to avoid the embarrassment of the previous occasion when she and the Director-General's wife wore identical black dresses, Gwen bought a magnificent full-length white dress. It wasn't perhaps the perfect choice – as Gwen herself agreed when Arthur Askey remarked to her that she looked as if she was ready for her coffin! – but at least no-one else was wearing anything remotely like it!

With two silver microphones now on display at Broadcasting House, Birmingham, we settled once more to our unrelenting task of recording episodes. In a successful serial, the public demand for a bright new episode every day sometimes gives those involved the feeling that they are feeding some insatiable monster, some Moloch who devours two hundred and sixty episodes every year.

The milestone we were now approaching was not an 'external' one of numbers of episodes or years, but an internal one: the marriage of Philip and Grace. This had been heralded for so long, had been so built up, that it had to be a notable occasion.

We were inundated with listeners' letters both for and against and many people sent cartoons, advertisements – anything and everything with the remotest connection with weddings or marriage, amusing, informative and occasionally tasteless.

The Income Tax avoidance question rumbled on until well after the wedding, with the most detailed advice from accountants and tax specialists. One letter, with photograph, even purported to come from a Large White Pig, saying: 'Dear Uncle Phillip, I was sorry to hear this evening that your piggies value had gone down. Why not buy me, for luck. Then naughty Auntie Grace could marry another boy . . .'

We were asked to send a telegram – which we did – to a young couple who on the day that Grace became Mrs Philip Archer, became Mr and Mrs B. Everard. We were asked for wedding-day pictures and we were even advised that Ben White the Ambridge baker was cheating us, as a rich fruit wedding-cake should be made three months ahead. One listener sent us a sad cutting of a small ad. offering an unwanted 3-tier wedding-cake going cheap.

Some were outraged at the thought of altering a wedding date for tax purposes: 'Much as I dislike Grace Fairbrother I would not stand by and see her bought as a chattel in a market for £90 . . . as a lover you make an efficient farm manager . . .' But several people, including London accountants who enclosed their business card, pointed out that Phil would save not £90 but the tax on £90 (and, as one pointed out, if Phil's salary wasn't high enough to be liable for tax at that rate, he should have married the girl for her money years ago!)

In a typically informal manner, one listener wrote, offering an alternative plan:

'In our home you & your family (& others) have become our friends – your programme is so realistic that you really have become *actual* friends of *ours*, we talk over all you say, just as one does in actual life. Now dear old Gran has taken such a liking to Ann Trentham & insists that we write & ask you to have her, & *break off* your engagement with Grace, whom, by the way, we all think is a spoiled brat & she says tell Master Phil not to stand any nonsense from Mr Fairbrother. Why not start a farm with that John Tregorran, he has £12,00 [*sic*], she says, & doesn't know what to do with it – so there's an idea Philip, & she says don't let Tregorran leave he is the life & soul of the party.

Bless you all, & thanks for bringing so much happiness into the lives of many lonely people, who look upon you all as their true friends . . .'

One lady wrote from a very 'good address' in Kent on die-stamped writing-paper (we drew our listeners from an increasingly wide social range by this time). She had strong personal reasons against changing the wedding date:

> 'Please, please let nothing stop your wedding to Grace at Easter, as my husband who is in Central America on business for three months (where I keep him informed of the doings of Ambridge) is dashing home to listen to your wedding ...'

The wedding did, of course, take place; and, following Archer precedent, it was recorded in the village church at Hanbury, where previous carol concerts and George and Helen Fairbrother's wedding recordings had been made. On former occasions the Vicar and his smallish country congregation were present. This time it was different. The news had been 'leaked' and coach-parties arrived from all over the Midlands. 'Archer's mock wedding fills village church' headlined one newspaper; 'Philip Archer "weds" Grace in church: mile of cars – 500 congregation.'

It was, in fact, very nearly a disaster. The groom stopped to ask the way, having got lost in the nearby country lanes, and was told: 'No, I will not tell you the way to Hanbury Church!' The reason, it eventually transpired, was that several local churches had had the lead stripped from their roofs, and this local worthy saw no point in publicizing their whereabouts.

Chris Gittins remembers how he arrived to find that he could get no nearer than a mile to the church when he was stopped by the local police who were out in force.

'But I've got to get there,' he said, 'I'm Walter Gabriel!'

'They're all trying to make us believe that!' was the intractable reply.

There was nothing for it.

'All right,' said Chris, 'you listen!' And there and then, with cars arriving, crowds passing on foot and hooters sounding, he gave an impromptu performance. It must have been the most convincing one of his life: the police allowed him through.

Leslie Bowmar (Fairbrother) and his life-long friend Denis Folwell (Jack) were less fortunate. They had to walk that difficult crowded uphill mile to the church – and Denis was only recently back in harness after a second spell in a T.B. hospital (described in the programme as a short visit as a voluntary patient to a mental home).

So there we were, waiting at the church, not for bride or

bridegroom but for the best man and the bride's father, who was to give her away.

The old gallery in the church hadn't been used for many years, but it was full to capacity, giving the Rector one of the many anxious moments he had that night, as he was afraid that it might give way under the thronging crowd.

Inside the nave and chancel it was pandemonium: we were jostled and hustled and I was horrified to see two press cameramen take a short-cut by climbing over the altar to reach a better viewpoint.

Then the Rector hushed the crowds and called for the owners of certain cars which were blocking the entrance to the churchyard. 'Will they please move them,' he said, 'so that the BBC recording car can get to the church, otherwise there will be no recording.'

Eventually Tony Shryane and the recording engineers arrived, microphones were rigged, and the script of the ceremony carefully rehearsed. The noise was indescribable and no one heard what we were saying.

Then, at last, we were ready. The Rector climbed into the pulpit, called for order, reminded the sightseers that they were in the house of God and led them in a short prayer, followed by the Lord's Prayer. This helped those of us with acting parts to play to get more into the mood of a marriage service and less of a feeling of being at a circus. As the congregation – the largest for years, possibly ever – all joined in the Lord's Prayer, I wondered how long it had been since those old walls had echoed to so many voices joined together in the family prayer that is common to so many Christians of so many different sects.

The 'Vicar of Ambridge' had been coached by the Rector of Hanbury, The Rev. Leonard Birch. The brief whispered exchange between Dan and Phil while waiting for Grace was not heard by the assembled congregation. But when the organist played the 'Bridal Chorus', the twitterings and whisperings of the excited congregation were utterly authentic. In an episode of just under fifteen minutes it is only possible to include selections from the marriage ceremony, but the essential vows were heard. Even in so short an extract, the scriptwriters managed to include one of those small touches of authenticity which have so often struck chords in the hearts of listeners. How many of us at weddings have heard the second name of the bride and groom for the first time? So it was on this occasion:

'Philip Walter' began the Vicar . . . and again the ohs and

ahs of the congregation, as they realized afresh that Philip's godfather was none other than their and Dan and Doris's old friend, Walter Gabriel.

Soon it was over, the crowds demanded autographs from us, while the Rector proffered his collecting box to them. After brief refreshments in the Rectory it was all over. Or so we thought.

There were to be repercussions. A writer in the *Church Times* attacked the whole incident, but not everyone agreed. One newspaper writer, under the heading 'That "wedding"', commented:

'What a fuss there is about that "wedding" of Philip Archer and Grace Fairbrother in the BBC's rural serial "The Archers". When the Rector of Hanbury allowed the "ceremony" to be recorded in his church to provide authentic atmosphere he said he expected criticism.

'Now he has got it – from the *Church Times* which hopes directions will be given to ensure there is no repetition of the incident.

'To be sure, the BBC – experts with sound effects – might well have manufactured an equally convincing atmosphere in a studio. But it is difficult to see what harm could be done by using this Worcester church.

'In "The Archers" the church plays a vital part in the village life. This programme is heard by millions every night, and some even find it difficult to believe that the village of Ambridge is fictitious.

'One would have thought that anything which helped stress the significance of the Church would be welcome to its supporters and spokesmen.'

The Rector's collection was later swelled by a Midland Bank Gift Cheque for ten shillings, drawn in favour of Mr and Mrs Philip Archer and signed enigmatically: 'A. L. L. ENGLAND'. Whether this was a *jeu d'esprit* on the part of a listener sending the good wishes of All England to the newly-weds, in whose courtship the question of money had played no small part, or whether indeed we had a well-wisher who really was called England and had those three initials, we did not know. We sent the cheque to the Rector for his church funds and asked, even if it were honoured, for it to be returned. It was honoured and I have it still.

Enough time has now passed for the contents of parts of the letter I received from the Rev. Mr Birch on 14 April 1955, to be

divulged without hurt or offence. After asking Ysanne Churchman and me to endorse the gift cheque on the back using our
real names, and commenting on a good radio feature programme by Colin Wills about The Archers and how the programme was put on the air, Mr Birch continued:

'There has been an astonishing reaction to the wedding
recording here – literally hundreds of visitors over Easter. I
got a mild rocket from the Bishop, by the way, but I think he
was secretly rather amused. I have been invited to preach
in the Cathedral on Rogation Sunday when the Farmers
Union and Young Farmers Clubs attend. I am terribly
tempted to observe that "it is nice to see the Dan Archers,
Tom Forrests, Walter Gabriels, Phil Archers etc of the Worcestershire countryside in this Cathedral this afternoon". But
I am not sure I shall get away with it.

I hope you are having a pleasant honeymoon.'

A honeymoon of sorts was being enjoyed by all of us. These
were the happiest days of their lives for Phil and Grace; but for
the whole of the Cast these years of the mid-fifties marked the
crest of the wave.

Listeners sent us things beginning with 'C' – cards, cartoons,
contraceptives and cakes.

One Dorset newspaper reported that a seventy-four-year-old
listener from Upwey had written to say that she would always
remember the Archer wedding, as 11 April was her birthday.
The report continues:

'On Easter Monday a telegram came from Norman Painting
saying: "Many happy returns; cake following."

'The cake duly arrived this week with a card attached, "Ben
White's Best". It was one of the many wedding cakes which the
BBC actor has received from fans all over the country.'

Following in the footsteps of Dan and Doris, Phil and Grace
were invited to open the proceedings of the Shanklin Carnival
on the Isle of Wight in July. We had been told what a rapturous
reception was waiting for us, but nothing had quite prepared
us for what actually happened.

We were taken in a place of honour in a long line of decorated floats through the streets of the town where people stood
four or five deep waving flags. It was a royal progress indeed,
with posters everywhere, declaring 'Shanklin welcomes The
Archers'. People thronged roofs and balconies, handkerchiefs

were waved, a band played. We entered the County Ground, where we were to declare the proceedings open, to a roar of welcome from thousands of waving enthusiasts.

Gwen Berryman had told us how she and Harry the year before had been moved to tears by the warmth of the welcome. Ysanne and I felt the same. We were given a glimpse into the lives of the Royals, and quickly learned some of their problems: with cameras on every hand, your nose must not be scratched no matter how it may itch, your face is becoming numbed and painful and your smile terribly fixed, but you cannot relax for a moment. With cheering crowds below, above and all around you are vulnerable and exposed, but wrapped in a supporting embrace of warmth and welcome.

We both remembered previous occasions when the crowds were great. At Ripley Show, for example, when we were escorted by the police as we rode in country fashion in a buggy with a trotter. Ysanne sat beside the driver and I perched on the back axle, astonished at the cheers of the crowds and the fingers that were wagged (Phil was having one of his occasional affairs at the time). When the driver of that buggy died, his relatives sent me a silver egg-cup which he had won at trotting, in memory of him.

On another occasion, Ysanne and I appeared at a flower show in a Nottinghamshire mental home and we were both fascinated and appalled to hear a visitor say to her friend: 'There they are, look. You can't believe it's really them. I wouldn't dare speak to them!'

The older members of the Cast often look back to those years with great affection. The memories are very varied. Gwen often recalls an elegant dinner in a stately home where the lighting by candlelight was so discreet that nobody could see what they were eating. When a dish of fried chicken with banana was offered by the butler, Gwen had nothing but banana, Harry little more than sweetcorn fritter and his real wife, Dorothy, managed to get chicken but went on to the fruitless attempt of cutting the contents of a finger-bowl with a knife and fork.

On another occasion which was also formal, the butler was seen moving from guest to guest with something covered by a napkin. 'Excuse me, sir (or madam),' he whispered. 'But is this, by any chance, yours?' Each member looked with some anxiety, and most shook their heads, until it was Denis Folwell's turn. His eyes brightened at the sight and he eagerly retrieved the object he must have lost during the main course – it was a single false tooth on a gold plate.

The whole 'family' were being entertained to lunch on one occasion before a personal appearance and, as the meal was served, our host proudly told us that the Queen and the Duke of Edinburgh had eaten there only a day or two before. The words were scarcely spoken when someone lifted a forkful of cabbage to his lips revealing the corpse of a large black beetle lying in state on the remaining cabbage. In response to a quiet signal, a suave waiter sidled up.

'Yes sir?'

Silently, the body was indicated.

Undiplomatically, but involuntarily, the waiter gave a gasp that was so dramatic that all eyes round the table clicked on to the offending plate. Recovering quickly, the waiter whisked the plate away, profusely apologizing and offering the choice of the whole cuisine in restitution. Appetites suddenly waned, and one could almost hear the staff sighing with relief that the incident hadn't occurred on the royal occasion only such a short while before.

Having handed the part of Peggy over to Thelma Rogers, June Spencer was once opening a fête as Miss Rita Flynn, the sometimes too friendly barmaid. Suddenly her little son David who had somehow evaded June's husband, burst through the crowds heading straight for her just as she was doing her 'Miss Flynn' act, and crying, 'Mummy, Mummy, look what I've found on the junk stall!'

In the very early days, Leslie Bowmar (Fairbrother) was opening a fête at which, after a lengthy introduction, he was triumphantly introduced as 'Mr Bertie Bowman'. With his charming diffident smile, Leslie stepped modestly forward on to a part of the wooden platform which promptly gave way, and he disappeared up to the waist on to the ground beneath.

Chris Gittins recalls a fête on a Somerset vicarage lawn one wet day when, as Walter Gabriel, he was introduced by a very tall vicar. Advancing to the microphone stand, acknowledging the applause, Chris could see at once that the microphone was far too high, and so grasped the mike stand in order to lower it. No one had told him that the sound system had been made by a local amateur. The stand was alive and a mighty shock promptly threw Chris across the vicarage lawn! In retrospect the incident seems amusing, but at the time, especially as the lawn was wet, it could have been disastrous.

So great was the number of invitations to appear at public functions, that we often found ourselves doing more than one in a single day, opening a bazaar in the afternoon and appearing at a charity dance in the evening in a different county miles away.

But inside the story itself, that summer of 1955 brought Phil and Grace 'the days that are not long, the days of wine and roses'.

Grace had changed her mind about having no family for five years. Married life softened her character: her moods of irritability, her tantrums, her jealousy all disappeared. It seemed a perfect match, an idyllic marriage.

Then the month of September approached.

It had become The Archers' policy to start a particularly enticing story at the end of the summer, to win back that margin of listeners who had temporarily fallen out of the habit of listening at 6.45 because of rival claims of outdoor sports, gardening or annual holidays – these were the days before transistor radios, remember. There were so-called 'portable' sets, but most radios were a fixed piece of house furniture – as much a focal point in millions of homes as television is now.

As the fifties progressed, television became more of a rival to radio. There were now only twice as many radios as television sets, and within two years the numbers of each would be more or less equal.

So a particularly strong September story was needed this year – one that would not only bring the listeners surging back but one which would gain as much publicity as possible. Various storylines were discussed, among them the announcement that after all Philip and Grace were to become parents. It was agreed that Grace would tell Phil the good news fairly early in the autumn or late summer, but this was scarcely a big enough story.

Then the extraordinary idea of the first real Archer death was mooted. Both Geoff Webb and Godfrey Baseley later claimed responsibility and others have also alleged fathering the thought. Knowing Ted, I feel sure that at first he would be against the idea. But again, knowing him, I feel sure that he would see the extraordinary dramatic value of the plan.

The more it was considered, the more the idea commended itself. There was no doubt that it would create a mild sensation: (the precise reaction when it happened was far greater than most people thought). If Phil or Grace died it would solve the well-known problem of serial-writing: lovers are of greater interest to listeners than newly-weds. But, and of far greater importance, it would strike a death-blow at the criticism that The Archers was really only a soap-opera after all, because it was so cosy.

There was a self-defeating quality in thrillers like *Dick Barton*, who had always escaped from no matter what impossible situation he had found himself in; or cosy-comfort-escapist programmes like *Mrs Dale's Diary*, where everything always turned out All Right no matter how worried Mary was about Jim. But if one of the Archers should die, a very important popular character, no one could ever again accuse the programme of not being 'really true to life'. There could be no 'Oh, it'll be all right tomorrow!' reactions to the evening's cliff-hanger: the formula could only be strengthened. Furthermore a death in the family would affect not only the Archers but the whole village.

The bold step was decided upon: Grace would die. Then came the question, when? Letters from listeners made it quite clear that many of them reacted unfavourably against an unhappy unresolved story, no matter what suspense it generated, that lasted over a whole weekend. Eventually the fatal date was chosen – Thursday, 22 September 1955.

Now it so happens that this was also the date on which the first regular commercial television programmes started. Coincidence or deliberate choice, it is probably no longer possible to be certain. I lean towards the view, knowing how such dates are decided at Archers' writers' meetings, that it was almost certainly pure coincidence. After all, what advantage could there be to a radio programme, that would have gone off the air before the commercial television programmes began, to choose that particular day? No one in the BBC, I am certain, had the least inkling that the public reaction would be quite as extreme as it was.

Whatever the reason, the plan was laid, the date was fixed. The next problem was the element of surprise. Although at this date scripts were still written not more than a week ahead (sometimes no more than a few hours ahead!) a week was quite long enough for the story to leak out, and the impact of the actual broadcast removed.

It was therefore decided to record the programme in London for that particular week and to prepare each episode daily. The whole operation even had a 'cover story': it was to be an 'experiment in topicality'. Each day's episode was to be written in the morning, liberally peppered with items from that day's newspapers, and recorded in the afternoon.

It worked like a dream. The ominous Thursday arrived. We had all wondered whether the rumours we had heard about a sensational story in the programme for that week were true.

I had, each day that week, been spending sessions in Harley Street discovering that I had an ulcer, and on Thursday, 22 September arrived at the studio with only minutes to spare, in pain and in a taxi. Ysanne met me outside the studio door, clutching a script: 'It's true,' she said with a tight transparent smile. 'They're killing me. Today!'

I collected my script and saw the whole of the production team lined up like the supreme soviet. There was the tense feeling of an important occasion. We were told that after the script was recorded, representatives of the press would come to the studio to interview us. Suddenly we all felt that this was to be an historic occasion.

The contents of the episode are well-known. The Fairbrothers were abroad and Phil had given a party at Grey Gables. Grace went back to the car in search of a lost ear-ring, saw smoke rising from the stables where a favourite horse Midnight was locked up for the night. Trying to rescue Midnight, a beam from the burning building severely injured her and she died in Phil's arms in the ambulance that arrived to take her to hospital. The last line gave us some trouble. As written, it was Phil telling his father and sister Chris what had happened:

'She . . . she died in my arms . . . on the way to hospital.'

We rehearsed and rehearsed it. We all knew we were tense: besides the producer, Tony Shryane, there were two writers and an editor in the control cubicle, all with ideas of how to say it. Now, although the actors had been given freedom to improvise in certain types of domestic scenes, it had been laid down early on that the tag-lines of a script were inviolable. So we worked on and on: try as I did, I could not make the line work. Several suggestions were made and tried.

Then, diffidently, I asked if all the weight could not be put into the last word. What did I mean? I suggested my version. There was a silence. All right. Try it. I did. The first complete line I had ever written for The Archers (later I was to write millions):

'In my arms . . . on the way to hospital . . . she's dead!'

(DOOR OPENS AND CLOSES IN BACKGROUND)

CHRIS: 3. That somebody just come in? Not Mum, surely.

Too early for her to be back.

DAN: 4. Might be your uncle Tom or Phil p'raps —

INNER DOOR OPENS

CHRIS: 5. Its Phil.

SLOW FOOTSTEPS APPROACH

DAN: 6. Didn't expect you back quite so soon. Chris and I

were ..... (SUDDEN REALISATION) Phil ... Phil lad ..

Approval What's gone wrong.

PHIL: 7. (DAZED, HELPLESS, UNABLE-TO-BELIEVE IT HIMSELF)

~~She~~ ~~drooped~~ In my arms ... on the way to hospital...
She's dead!

Remarks: Non sig. tune —

The page of script showing the vital change.

There was a long pause. Then, after a murmured consultation Godfrey Baseley said: 'Yes. That's it. We'll buy that!'

So it was.

Tony Shryane is a perfectionist: we had rehearsed ourselves almost dizzy. Now we began to record. The first take was perfectly adequate. Tony felt it could be better. We did it again. Soon it was complete. Before we could collect our wits, a hoard of raincoated journalists swarmed in, shepherded by the Assistant Head of Light Programme. They listened in stolid silence to the official statements of what was about to happen, poker-faced and unemotional.

88

The first to speak asked bluntly: 'What about your switchboard?'

No one understood the question. It was repeated and explained. 'Surely hundreds of listeners will ring up and complain?'

The official reply was: 'Oh no, we don't think so. We have certainly made no special arrangements.'

The BBC telephone switchboard was in fact jammed for hours.

The sensation caused by the death of Grace was far greater than anyone had imagined it would be. It was treated like a national disaster, and reported in the international press and in foreign newspapers. It is to be doubted whether any radio programme before or since has had such wide coverage in the British press, or was dealt with in such complete seriousness. Newspapers as far away as Malaya, carried the story on their front pages: 'It's a sad day as BBC kills off Grace . . . British housewives wept to day for the fictitious heroine of their soap opera . . . A family in Dover pulled down the blinds in their home as a sign of mourning.'

At home it was headlines and front-page photographs in all the major newspapers, London and provincial.

The *Daily Mirror* reported that someone travelling by car from Ashford to Dover saw people in villages standing at their doors openly weeping for Grace Archer. One family in Romney Marsh were collecting flowers to make into wreaths and crosses to send to the funeral. One man said: 'The emotional level of the end was disgraceful. My Mother – who is not over-sensitive – was quite upset.'

Ysanne Churchman, whose smiling face beams out under gloomy headlines was reported as saying: 'I am very sorry so many people are miserable about the death of Grace Archer. It was no wish of mine. I have enjoyed taking the part.'

The following Saturday saw no abatement of interest. The *Manchester Guardian* reported an interview in the television programme *Highlight* with Ted Mason and Geoff Webb, who are reported as 'remaining inscrutable throughout'. They spoke of the programme lasting for five more years, and insisted that the step of killing Grace had not been taken lightly. The paper reported a BBC request that no more flowers should be sent!

As ever, the newspapers vied with each other for a new angle. One reported that Ysanne Churchman was a 'lively ghost' as she appeared as a guest star on a television programme called *It's Magic* on Friday night. Others reported on the number of distressed people who made phone calls to the BBC, some anxious to be reassured that it was only the character that had died and not the actress. Many reported that the decision to 'kill' the character had been made in March, before the 'wedding of Phil and Grace'. Ysanne Churchman revealed that she knew the character was to leave the programme, but only recently learned for certain that she was to die.

The *Daily Mirror* printed a Londoner's comment: 'I thought I was in for a lively party when I was invited next door for the first night of ITV. Instead, it was like a house of mourning – because Grace Archer had been "killed off" in that radio serial at 7 p.m. How can people get into such a state over a harmless fairy tale? How do they get so worked up over a bit of synthetic sob-stuff?'

The Omnibus edition of the programme on Saturday night drew one of its largest audiences ever, and discussion of the incident went on in the Sunday press. Terence Feely in the *Sunday Graphic*, under two-inch high heavy black headlines 'Britain's Sob Sisters' began: 'May I respectfully suggest to the women of Britain that the death of poor Grace Archer is something less than a national disaster,' and, in exhorting the women of Britain to 'be their age' makes the point: '. . . this emotional binge was a true, full-blown phenomenon in its own right.'

The *Manchester Guardian* printed a pretty parody of Wordsworth:

Grace Archer
(*Dulce et decorum est pro BBC mori*)

She dwelt unseen, amid the Light,
Among the Archer clan,
And breathed her last the very night
The ITV began.

A maiden in a fantasy
All hidden from the eye –
A spoken word: the BBC
Decided she must die.

She was well-loved, and millions know
That Grace has ceased to be.
Now she is in her grave, but oh,
She's scooped the ITV.

M.C.

One of the performers who had played one of the previous minor characters to die in The Archers (there had been three to date) wrote to the *Birmingham Post* complaining that when his character fell down the stairs and broke his ungodly neck not a word of regret was expressed!

So much interest was still being aroused, that the BBC called a Press Conference in Birmingham, four days after the original broadcast. The previous days' series of statements and interviews had clearly not satisfied the press's demand for copy.

At the press conference, Denis Morris, Head of Midland Regional Programmes, explained that the decision to 'kill' Grace had been jointly taken many months before in order to reduce the number of characters, to exploit the new situation created by the death of a major character, and because Ysanne Churchman was 'an accomplished artist' and the BBC wanted her to come back into the main stream of broadcasting.

So once more the incident was given space in Tuesday's national press: the *Daily Mirror*, *Daily Herald*, *News Chronicle*, *Daily Sketch*, *Daily Mail*, the *Birmingham Post*, etc., etc. The 'six guilty men' who 'killed' Grace are listed by name: Denis Morris, Head of Midland Regional Programmes; Rooney Pelletier, Controller of the Light Programme; Tony Shryane, producer; Geoffrey Webb and Edward J. Mason, scriptwriters; and Godfrey Baseley, founder and editor.

By this time, the humorists had had time to get to work: 'Will the BBC kindly supply Mrs Dale with a blazing stable?' wrote one; and one of a group of workmen digging up the road outside Broadcasting House, Birmingham, heard a car backfire and commented: 'Blimey! That's another one of the Archers gorn!'

There was bathos, too, as well as pathos. 'At first I couldn't believe my ears,' wrote a Kettering woman. 'Grace Archer dead? I said to my husband, "She mustn't be!" Then I felt quite cold and had to put my woolly on!'

The story continued. The *Birmingham Mail* reported that the Journal of the Salvation Army, *The War Cry*, had an article headed: 'Inquest on Grace Archer', and gave a full report.

The papers kept the story alive by starting various hares, mainly a kind of 'indictment' of the 'guilty men' who murdered Grace'. So we read such headlines and comments as: 'Alas, poor Grace!', 'Death of Grace Archer "inevitable"', 'The Archers may live happily ever after', 'A master stroke of BBC showmanship', 'He's glad they killed Grace Archer' – the latter being a successful attempt to inspire correspondence by publishing controversial views.

The *News Chronicle*, commented on Wednesday, 28 September that Denis Morris had been 'obliged to make a statement at the news conference . . . under close questioning from Press watchdogs'. At least a large part of the Press appeared to be treating the matter as of serious national concern, and this paper went on: 'Surely it would have been more in keeping with the best traditions if Sir Ian Jacob, as Director-General of the BBC, had come forward and said: "The responsibility is mine. I alone must take the blame."'

Even the 'radio doctor' was brought in: 'Come to that, why has the Postmaster General remained silent? If Mr Macmillan is prepared to receive all the kicks for the Burgess and Maclean scandal, why shouldn't Dr Hill take the rap for what the BBC did to poor Grace?

'It is astonishing that no M.P. has yet announced his intention to put down a question about this dreadful affair. Lt. Col. Marcus Lipton must be slipping.'

A week later, the *Daily Worker* entered the arena with 'Steam radio still packs a punch', and 'Archers – what next?'

Then, having squeezed the story dry, the *News Chronicle* turned to pontification. Under the heading 'That stunt', an editorial commented: 'Grace Archer has died. Women are alleged to have wept in the streets: the BBC has blushingly turned away offers of cash for wreaths. If all this hubbub is an odd reflection on Light Programme listeners, the scriptwriters don't come too well out of it, either. This was a silly, cheap, unworthy way of getting BBC publicity on the night ITV opened. The men who run "The Archers" have clearly turned their mission to mirror "life" into a mania. They should get back to the notion that their first job is to entertain.'

This somewhat pompous comment narrowed the meaning of the word 'entertain'. Many would have argued that the incident marked a very high point in the year's radio entertainment.

After a week the Press dropped the story. But in its issue for 7 October, *Radio Times* printed a selection of letters representative of the main views expressed by its correspondents. One clergyman wrote: 'The death of Grace Archer knocked me flat and I burst out crying out loud', and another welcomed the fact that this 'splendid programme' had now shown that it could embrace genuine tragedy. One writer said the incident was as out of place as it 'would have been in Jane Austen's

Emma', while applauding the whole production, especially the silence instead of signature tune at the end, and failing to see why so many should object to the incident.

The day after the death of Grace we had one more episode to record in our week of 'experimental topicality'. It had been a gruelling time. As I left the studio a letter was put into my hand. In a daze I opened it. It was from Godfrey, Ted and Geoff, dated from Broadcasting House, London, 23 September 1955, and ran: 'We would like you to know how much we appreciate your superb performance in "The Archers" last night. We realize just how much was at stake and also how much depended for its success on you. It was an occasion we shall remember for a very long time – mainly because of the part you played in making the emotional experience really live. Yours very gratefully.'

I took in the mere gist of this extraordinary letter. The sight of those three signatures below the words 'Yours very gratefully' was almost too much for me. My head swam. Emotion chased reason and fantasy confronted fact. At that moment several colleagues, who never before had seemed to take me seriously as an actor, arrived and I found my hand being shaken, my shoulder patted. I was too stunned to speak. Declining offers of drinks and celebration I dashed over to Euston in a cab and caught a train to the country.

The ordeal was far from over. A torrent of listeners' letters began to arrive, divided sharply into two sorts: those who treated Grace's death as a personal bereavement, and those – the majority – who, surprisingly enough, wrote congratulations on the way the episode had been put over.

Cards and letters poured in from all over the British Isles: from St Neots, Easington, Saffron Walden, Hereford, Kendal, Epsom, Cheltenham, Galashiels, Tisbury, Accrington, Leeds, Worthing, London, Inverness, Dorchester, Rochester, Leominster, Reading, Redditch, Pontefract, Norwich, Swansea – no corner seemed unconcerned.

One old lady from Co. Durham was so upset she lost count of the days:

'I am one of the Old Listen on the Radio I was just enjoy it on Wednesday night I heard you shoing for Grace to come Back it has given me a terable shok. And I have not sleep since Wednesday night will you tell me the true if she his realy Dead I want send Flower But I will Pray for every night.

Please Answer this to And Old Pension.
I Enjoy thee Archer & more so than Anythink Else on the Radio.'

One listener could not bear to remember the love scenes, so recently heard (or overheard).

'Whoever they find to take the place of Grace, never speak to her in that kind tone of voice you used to speak to her it would be horrible to hear you speak to some one else like that unless of course they had given you time to have a child that was like her.
a follower of the archers but not the archers any more.'

Some found expression in verse:

'A cruel death, it would not be denied,
That cut the bonds of love so lately tied.
I did not think the call would come so soon,
I found it night ere I thought it noon.
Then come to my grave, my loved ones come,
Wherere it may chance to be.
And if any daisies should peep from my grave
Be sure they are kisses from me.'

Others mixed condolence with business:
'Every night my family and I listen to "The Archers". When Grace was supposed to have died I felt awfully sorry for you. I would be very pleased if you would send me a photograph and autograph. Yours affectionately.'

Indeed, many letters received were the sort that would normally be sent to the bereaved after a friend's death:
'I am very sorry to hear of your wife's death. I admired her courage. I wish to convey to you my deepest sympathy.'

'I wish to send you my sincere sympathy at your loss.'

'May I on behalf of my husband and my two neighbours say how sorry we are to hear of the death of your dear wife and with such tragic suddenness too. Will you please accept our dear sympathy and may God comfort you in your sorrow.'

Others seemed able to eat their cake and have it:

'I can't tell you the awfull feeling I had when I heard that Grace was dead. It was like as if it had been someone I had known and liked very much had died. I have never before written to anyone like this before, but I felt just as if I wanted to comfort you, you sounded so heartbroken it was hard to believe it was just a play. Never before have I been so carried away by a play on the wireless, and I am longing for tomorrow night to here the next instalment.'

'Please accept my sincere sympathy in your loss. You made everyone in this village shed a tear. So please next time don't make it sound so real.'

'We shall miss her dreadfully although we didn't know her personally, and have grown to love you all. Please convey our deepest sympathy to Mr and Mrs Fairbrother, & Mr & Mrs Archer in their great loss . . . It is a wonderful programme – so very true to life that is hard to believe sometimes it is only a play.'

There were some listeners, though, who not only consoled themselves by saying that it was 'only a play', but that, in true soap-opera style, it would all turn out to be a mistake, and like the heroines in a fairy story, Grace would revive:

'On the night of the fire, I wasn't upset, because I felt, like others, Grace would come to. Afterwards, I cried every night until Wednesday, & when even last Saturday evening tears came again, when you said "You had everything at Coombe Farm, but your wife. It was all acted so perfectly, that was why, we felt it was real life, & so very touching.'

The same listener tried to justify the incident by putting two and two together, with the usual inaccurate result:

'We have heard rumours Ysanne Churchman is going to Commercial Television. Of course one can't blame her if she is getting more money. [This was not, of course, the reason.] Sorry to say we are not interested in Television.'

One long letter, lamenting the whole sad episode, ended: 'P.S. We daren't tell Gran!'

It has been often said that most listeners believe The Archers to be true. As I have tried to show elsewhere in this book, this has never been the case. A small proportion of listeners appear to be unable to accept the fact that it is 'only a play', and there has been a steady stream of applications for jobs at Brookfield, holidays on the farm, and offers to buy various articles that characters in Ambridge were trying to sell.

But from the very beginning, listeners have spoken of 'the acting', 'the way you play your parts', 'you all make it seem so real'; and, as has been pointed out, although numerous photographs have been published of the Cast 'in costume, in character and on location', very few, a very small minority, have ever really been taken in.

By far the greatest number of letters written after any sensational incident speak specifically of the acting. And when those few of us who have remained in the programme for twenty-five years analyse the reasons why we stayed with it, high among the reasons comes the fact that it is always satisfying for a performer to feel that his efforts are convincing.

On the one thousandth episode, as has been said, we each received an engraved silver box, but what touched us more was to receive a letter from Tony Shryane thanking us for our sustained hard work: 'Working as you do, week after week, you could quite easily feel that all your efforts were taken for granted. Let me assure you that this is not so. Your loyalty to the programme during the last four years has been greatly appreciated.'

Over the years, individual actors have been given chances to show a greater range of emotion than in the normal everyday-life scenes; but even in such unusual opportunities like the death of Grace, the fact that the Archers was a team show meant that the effort was spread over the whole Cast. No one performer could have created the effect which caused such comment, single-handed. This was always a show without stars.

Everyone shared the pleasure of receiving letters which were complimentary about our acting. And indeed for many years, we passed letters round when we met each week – apart from letters that were couched in such superlatives that modesty forbade.

The steady stream of praise for the 'death of Grace' episodes gratified us all. What actors could not fail to glow at reading such words as: 'Congratulations to all the Archers on Thursday and Friday's performance . . . you must all be very proud of your achievement . . . superb acting . . . I don't think I have ever heard such beautiful sincerity over the wireless before . . . I'm positive that there has been nothing on the radio for twenty years to compare with the stark realism & pathos . . . sincere and masterly portrayal . . . very authentic and true to life, it brought a lump to my throat and I consider myself pretty blasé . . . sensitive treatment of this has made it a most moving experience.'

In case those brief extracts give a false impression, let me stress that they are the merest fraction of the comments received, and the more fulsomely flattering ones have *not* been included!

Letters were received from every social level, from people in all walks of life – even members of the BBC administrative staff.

Not that the incident pleased everybody, or affected everyone in the same way. Some were flippant: 'We thought you were very good when Grace kicked the bucket,' wrote a group of regular listeners. Others were regretful: 'I was sorry to hear they have killed Grace off. I think they have spoiled the "Archers" now . . .' Others quickly tired of the sorrowing widower: 'I think our friend Phil is taking his loss too far and is becoming an ungratful [*sic*] and uncivilised prig.'

Almost our favourite letter came from Swansea:
'For the sake of our sanity, please, oh please, give the sorrowing widower a break. Grace should have died last March, when she wouldn't marry you, to have tax rebate, it was quite clear then, she wasn't long for this world, but I must say this, you did slip up badly, when the stable caught fire, you should have sent Mrs Dale in after her and lock the door on the both of them, men have had a George medal for less, my hair was black before grace started talking but since it has gone quite white. Yours in sorrow.'

In spite of muted threats from some listeners about being so disappointed in the programme because of the death of Grace that they would no longer listen, the audience was, if anything, increased. Not everyone it seemed agreed with the listener who sent a telegram to Ted Mason congratulating him on the death of Grace and urging him on to kill off the rest of the Archers!

Some of us, though, did wonder if we had not, perhaps, reached a high point that could never be surpassed. With the

1956

THE YEAR OF

The Suez crisis. Terrorist activity in Cyprus was increasing. The bank rate was increased from 4½% to 5½%, the highest since 1932. Archbishop Makarios was deported to the Seychelles. The Queen laid the foundation stone of the new Coventry Cathedral. The first atomic power station in Britain began working at Calder Hall. 1 February was the coldest day since 1895, and May was the sunniest month at Kew since 1922, and the driest since 1896. British Railways abolished Third Class travel. Col. Nasser was elected President of Egypt. The transatlantic telephone cable was inaugurated. Israeli forces invaded Egypt.

IN AMBRIDGE

Dan Archer felt he was losing the results of a lifetime's work when an outbreak of foot-and-mouth disease necessitated the slaughter of all his stock. Simon, Dan's farmhand, retired and was replaced by Ned Larkin. Chris, spurning the advances of Nelson Gabriel, married Paul Johnson.

There is in show-business a well-known injunction, 'Follow that!' It refers to the task of having to follow a particularly brilliant piece of bravura performing, or a particularly strong and telling scene.

At least half our critics were poised, as the year after the death of Grace began, with those words on their lips. And not only our listeners, but some of us performers, wondered how the future could seem anything but an anticlimax.

We were forgetting, as so often happens, the expertise of the writing and production team.

The abnormality of the dramatic scenes over Grace's death was emphasized by a deliberate return to ordinary low-key daily behaviour. In the episode following the death of Grace Dan Archer firmly set the mood with 'life goes on'.

What was needed, clearly, was a complete diversion and this was achieved in two ways: by another sensational happening and by the introduction of a whole new set of characters.

But what sensational happening? Clearly not another death – at least, not a human one. Various ideas were floated, rejected, and noted for further use. In good serial writing, several birds are often hit with one stone and the chosen story accomplished this.

At Brookfield, Dan was milking dairy shorthorns, in common with many other farmers of his type. Anxious to bring him more in line with other more progressive farmers, Godfrey Baseley wanted to change Dan's breed of cattle. The Shorthorn Society were not very taken with this idea and at one time there was even the possibility of legal action being taken to restrain Dan from pursuing a course which hundreds of farmers would no doubt instantly follow.

So a direct change was impossible. Dan would somehow have to alter his pattern of farming, switch from milk to beef for some years before returning to milk-production with the desired breed of cattle.

The reason for this change came in a very dramatic way although it was one that was, and still is, by no means unknown to farmers: an outbreak of foot-and-mouth disease.

The whole story from the first suspicions that the Brookfield herd might be infected, to the terrible day of slaughter when the repeated sound of the humane killer punctuated Dan's waking hours was treated fully and effectively. Old-age pensioners sent postal orders and small boys arrived at Broadcasting House with their money-boxes to help poor Dan to recover from his financial loss. Letters of sympathy arrived and although the impact could not be compared with that of the death of Grace, the interest aroused by the story showed that our audience was still following our progress with undiminished attention.

And indeed, that small hopeful minority who gave the impression that they believed in the actual existence of Ambridge and the Archers still continued to write.

Quite early on, letters like this had arrived:

'I your addition of "The Archers" tonight, you spent out 63s on nylons for your sister & Miss Fairbrother. if you can afford that much for a sister and friend. how about me. I've never had a really decent pair of nylons because they are so expensive, and I even the girls who can afford them.'

We were invited to weddings, harvest festivals, coming-of-age parties; and requests for autographs continued to pour in with, occasionally, a rather dubious use of English: 'Will you please send me a photograph of yourself as I save radio stars' ... 'Have you got any film-stars if so How much are they?' ... 'If you will send me your photograph to complete the "Archer" family and to add to my collection of radio stars.'

One bemused little girl, clearly uncertain where the border lay between fact and fiction, wrote: 'I'm sending this care of the BBC as I have no idea where else to send it.'

We are often told that 'my friend and I are very keen on the "Archers" and often act them' or 'My little girl loves your programme and insists on being called Philip. She does not answer to any other name.' This phenomenon was, and is, by no means uncommon.

One girl worried her parents who felt she was in danger of becoming an arrant snob. 'She will not let us listen to the Archers,' her mother explained, 'because she says they are common. But she doesn't mind the Dales because they are professional class!'

Characters only had to mention articles for sale and in would come the enquiries: 'I am interested in buying the pony which you said you had for sale' ... 'In case Peggy is not interested in buying your Welsh Dresser I am prepared to offer you 50/- for it. C.O.D. How do you feel about it.'

The most casual mention of labour problems produced applications for jobs:

'I have gathered that you require a Secretary ... I believe I could help you keep the papers and letters concerning the running of the Fairbrother Estate in perfect order ... My speeds are approximately 100 w.a.m. shorthand and 50 w.a.m. typewriting. I hope you will give my application your favourable consideration ... P.S. I'm very good with Large Whites and Herefords adore me.'

Two 'very experienced punch-card operators' wrote from Somerset on 20 January 1956:

're your remarks made in tonight's broadcast about office efficiency . . . we can operate the following: Hand punch, hand verifier, Automatic key punch, Sorter, Interpolator, 5 and 8-unit tabulator plus summary punch, 3 unit Tabulator, Reproducer, Interpter, Multiplier Punch . . . P.S. Dad says we are quite capable of mucking out ! ! ! '

Some requests, though reasonable, did seem a trifle odd:

'Would you please send us a boy's & a girl's name suitable for a pig? We want a choice as we are not sure what sex the pig will be. This village comes to a standstill at 6.45.'

Writing to inform us of the amount of money raised at a church fête for the restoration fund, one man ended his letter:

'I am enclosing a small snap of our beautiful church, which I thought you might like to see, as you have so kindly helped in its restoration.'

It is perhaps not surprising that some members of the Cast gradually took on more and more of the attributes of the characters they played, especially after a series of personal appearances. Some of us found appearing at village fêtes and other occasions, where the public had direct access to us, extremely exhausting: we felt we were being asked to impersonate the character completely. It felt like trying to play the leading part in a charade, with no preparation, having to improvise the sort of reaction that the character would have to any situation, rather than responding as oneself.

Bill Kings, who gave a delicious performance as a vinegary old humbug, Ben White the village baker, who was 'agin' most things, sent his friends a most amusing Christmas card. It bore a photograph of himself in full make-up behind a baker's counter and the wording echoed Ben's general misanthropy. The front of the card merely said 'Greetings' in large type and 'don't believe in 'em' in small.

Inside, the wording ran: 'I think it's a waste of time and money, but I expect the Archers are doing it, so . . . Happy Christmas and Prosperous 1954 from Ben White, Ambridge (Cash) Bakery, First Quality Bread, Cakes etc. Families waited on daily.'

When later Bill Kings was in hospital for Christmas, the

whole Cast recorded a Christmas card in verse written by Ted Mason. It was broadcast over the hospital radio system and, as Bill confessed afterwards, 'I wept like a child.' His death robbed the Cast of a distinguished performer who brought great wit to the creation of a character who might otherwise have seemed unreal or unpleasant. The busybody type of 'irritant' character is an essential part of the Ambridge recipe.

Certain details were carried over from the actor to the character, especially in the very early days. Harry Oakes, for example, was born on 15 October 1896, so that became Dan's birthday. Chris was given Pamela Mant's birthday of 21 December 1931 and from the beginning, St George's Day was not only my birthday but also Phil's. Phil then, was born on 23 April 1928; but for some reason, Doris Archer's birthday, and year of birth, were muddled. Gwen Berryman's birthday is 22 November: Doris celebrates 15 July.

When I acquired a Corgi, it was decided that Walter should give Philip a Corgi, too, with the same name, Timus – short for Septimus. He travelled around with me, and often made personal appearances himself. He was photographed and written about, and he recorded his complete repertoire of barks, whines and snuffles. When a listener wrote suggesting that Timus was clearly an actor doing animal imitations – not very well – he wrote a dignified letter to the Editor of *Radio Times*, who printed it.

I have said that it had been decided to give the programme one sensational story – the foot-and-mouth epidemic, which has been described – and one major diversion.

The diversion was to be the introduction of a whole new family: the Hoods.

As one of the published reasons for the death of Grace had been the need to keep the number of characters in check, there was considerable anxiety among members of the original Cast when it was heard that a whole new family was moving to Ambridge. No one need have worried: the experiment was short-lived once it had served its purpose as a diversion. The Hoods today are barely remembered in Ambridge, apart possibly from Joan Hood who married Nigel Burton; and Doughy Hood who makes occasional visits (when the actor who plays the part, Arnold Ridley, is not busy being Private Godfrey in the television show *Dad's Army*).

If I remember the advent of the Hood family more clearly than most members of the Cast, it is because, as on so many occasions, I was employed as a kind of sounding-board during the auditions.

Whenever new characters are introduced into The Archers, scenes are specially written so that the actor applying for the part can see clearly what is envisaged. The scenes are usually duologues and it so happens that on many occasions the other person in the scene has been 'Philip Archer'. This gives the intending performer a chance to play opposite an established Archer and thus get the feel of the thing.

I have been employed for many such auditions: first with Harry Oakes, when Gwen Berryman gave her successful audition. Several actresses had attempted the part while I listened unseen with the editor and writers. Then we heard the studio door open, whispered greetings between Harry and Gwen, and then peals of laughter. A good start, we all thought. The peals of laughter have gone on ever since.

My presence on that particular occasion was to read opposite the candidates for 'Grace', an exercise that was repeated a year later when Monica Grey left the cast and was replaced by Ysanne Churchman. In 1953 I read the other part for the auditions for both Chris and Mike Daly, as Pamela Mant and John Franklyn who originally created those characters left the programme at the same time. Later I was both to write the audition piece and read in the opposite part for several major characters. But that is to leap ahead.

As in real life, the events of every single year in the life of Ambridge are not necessarily memorable in themselves. 1956 was, quite appropriately (but how courageously!) a quiet year.

The story-line dealt with the rebuilding of the stables after Chris had been left a sufficient sum of money to do so. For a time the relationship between Chris and Paul Johnson waned, and it was the end of the year before Chris had declined an offer from Nelson Gabriel and had married Paul instead.

February saw Dan's life's work in ruins, when the outbreak of foot-and-mouth disease caused his herd to be destroyed. The Hood family arrived in April and were used largely as a device to explain both past history and present problems to listeners who had not been with us from the beginning.

Pru Harris was an Ambridge woman who became barmaid at The Bull. When her mother died, it was revealed that Tom Forrest had been made an executor of her will and thus Tom and Pru began to become closer friends.

It was all pleasant homely human stuff: even the foot-and-mouth disaster was dealt with in human terms. A less expert team might have been tempted to 'follow that' death of Grace incident with bigger and more sensational events. Rightly, they held their hand; but there were more sensations to come.

Yet, in spite of everything, 1956 was to be a memorable year. For in it, the death of one favourite character caused the appearance of another. Following the death of Eddie Robinson, one of the original cast, the part of Simon Cooper, Dan's right-hand man died with him. An entirely new farm-worker was introduced, who quickly became one of the best-loved characters ever to appear in the programme. His name was Ned Larkin.

1957

THE YEAR WHEN

Anthony Eden resigned and was succeeded as Prime Minister by Harold Macmillan. Sibelius, Toscanini and Dorothy L. Sayers died. The Pope, Dr Schweitzer and Mr Nehru appealed for the banning of nuclear tests and weapons. Petrol rationing was ended after six months. The first Premium Bond prizes were drawn. The first earth satellite was launched by Russia. The world's largest radio telescope at Jodrell Bank went into operation. Russia launched a second satellite with a dog on board. The Queen's Christmas broadcast was televised for the first time.

IN AMBRIDGE

Ned Larkin's no-good brother, Bob, arrived and made advances to Pru Harris which annoyed her long-time admirer Tom Forrest. Tom was arrested after a poacher – Bob Larkin – had been shot, but was acquitted at the Assizes. Dan's brother Frank died in New Zealand and his widow Laura came to Ambridge. At the village fête, Phil met Jill and they married in November. Len Thomas left Brookfield to become Fairbrother's shepherd, and Jimmy Grange came as apprentice to Dan.

After the excitements of 1955, with its sensational events and its wide treatment in the press, 1956 and in part 1957 seemed to take the programme on to a plateau. It was a high plateau, it is true, maintaining, and indeed increasing for a period, its audience which at times exceeded ten million nightly.

But somehow there was still a feeling that we were perhaps a nine days' wonder. Many people made great play of the fact that they never listened to us; some chose to laugh at us or patronize us. Many listened to us in secret, but rarely owned up to it. We had not yet reached the status that was awaiting us, still some years ahead, of being a National Institution.

After that tremendous orgy of press coverage in 1955, the treatment of the programme by journalists was, with a few exceptions, muted. It was as if we were still not totally accepted, as if we had not yet 'arrived'.

Fan-mail continued to pour in. We all made as many personal appearances as before, though not now, of course, at any event organized by a political party.

These opportunities of meeting the public gave us enormous encouragement. We soon learnt to smell a badly organized event from miles off! Often the initial invitation was enough to make one hope one was already booked for the day in question; but always, within minutes of meeting the organizers, one would know whether it was going to be a success or otherwise.

Not that the well-arranged events gave us any more memories than those not so well thought out. Events held in confined spaces, like vicarage gardens or small village greens, often seemed to be more bustlingly successful than those spread out on playing fields; but we always carried away from them that wonderfully sustaining feeling of being literally loved by so many people. Of all the rewards that is certainly the greatest.

Not that everything went smoothly. Dan and Doris were once introduced by a man who had been Mayor for so long that he was accustomed to declare things open himself. So by the time they stood up to open the fête, it had already been declared officially open. On another occasion, this time a lunch during a carnival week, someone anxious to smoke, suggested to the chairman that the time had come to toast the Queen. Without hesitation he jumped to his feet and proposed the toast — but to the local Carnival Queen!

At personal appearances, we were always asked questions about future developments of the story, according to what particular crisis in Ambridge or Archer life was being dealt with at the time. We used to give parliamentary answers, or else say: 'You listen and find out!'

Some questions are perennial, though. 'How long will they keep it on?' or the variant, 'I hope they'll never take The Archers off' have been heard from the beginning.

Another comment, always made as if it is the day's most penetrating observation, comes after one has been sitting signing autographs for some time: 'You'll have writer's cramp!' is announced with a beaming smile. After twenty-five years, we still haven't thought of a suitable rejoinder to that one.

A question that was increasingly asked from 1957 onwards, as television became more widely seen was: 'When are we going to see you on the telly?' Although always asked with a friendly smile, the question always seemed slightly doomladen: the voice of the people was telling us that they were transferring their affections from sound radio to television.

Originally we had been told that the programme would naturally graduate from sound to vision. As our life grew longer, though, the enormous technical problems that would arise in translating the programme into television terms became all too clear. Those of us who played farming characters would have to learn how to handle machines and animals, and whole sections of the 'out of doors' part of the programme would have to be filmed on location, a costly and very time-consuming business.

Some of the newspapers did float the idea from time to time. 'Archers on TV' ran one headline over a story in which the editor said the idea of televising The Archers was being considered, but 'we have not yet reached the planning stage'.

Denis Morris, Head of Midland Regional Programmes, explained that one problem was that TV dialogue is usually much slower than in sound broadcasts, 110 words a minute as opposed to 150. He added: 'We listened "blind" to recordings of *What's my line?* to see if additional commentary to cover pauses would convey an adequate sound picture. The idea had to be abandoned.'

Such an idea is unthinkable today, but it is interesting to look back and see that even by the mid-fifties, television had by no means found its identity.

Tony Shryane often stresses the influence which the casual, almost improvised, dialogue of The Archers had on later TV successes like *Z Cars* and *Softly, Softly*. It is certainly easy to forget how very revolutionary the basic dialogue technique of The Archers was at the time. It is clear from listeners' letters that a team of writers, actors and technicians working together really did convince some listeners that we were not fictional characters in a play, but real people – though, as the letters following the death of Grace have already been quoted to prove, some listeners wanted it both ways.

Not all of us really look the part, in spite of wearing clothes that are in keeping with the parts we play when appearing in public. But this has never seemed to discourage our audience. After all, how many farmers really look like farmers?

We were, and always have been, essentially a radio programme, using words and sound-effects to provide fuel for the imagination of listeners. Whenever we did appear, either in photographs or in person, we attempted to look as convincing as possible; and authenticity was also obtained by occasionally introducing into the programme real-life personalities. The Ambridge Fête was opened by Gilbert Harding on one occasion: in this year, 1957, by Humphrey Lyttleton.

Various well-known figures from the agricultural world have appeared from time to time, among them Sir Richard Trehane of the Milk Marketing Board for example.

Famous horsemen and women too. Recently Ann Moore made a successful series of appearances, and in 1957 fantasy and fiction were closely mixed when Chris's horse Red Link was ridden by Alan Oliver. There was of course a real Red Link and Alan Oliver rode it at Badminton on 24 April 1957. At the Richmond Show in June, Red Link came third and on 14 September Red Link qualified for the Foxhunter Competition by coming second at Dagenham, again ridden by Alan Oliver. On 8 October, Red Link came second in another Foxhunter Competition, and in December Chris sold Red Link to Alan Oliver (who had of course been the real owner the whole time, but who had collaborated closely with the editor and scriptwriters throughout).

The advantage of a tie-up of that sort was that many people attending Badminton, Richmond and Dagenham and the rest of the places where Red Link was entered, would know from listening to The Archers that this particular horse 'belonged' to Christine, and they could follow his progress in 'real life'. The results were broadcast in the programme of course, and so it was not easy to disentangle truth from fiction.

It was equally difficult when Dan went to the sheep sales on the Welsh Border. By prior arrangement with the auctioneer whose voice was recorded throughout an actual sale, the words 'Sold to Dan Archer', or usually just 'Archer', were said as the hammer fell on the sort of sheep Dan would really buy — the real purchaser always played ball and never seemed to mind Dan's name being used instead of his own.

The major story of the year 1957, though, was Tom Forrest's accidental killing of a poacher and his subsequent arrest and remand in custody on a charge of murder. I have already indicated that the editor and writers, having resisted all temptations to follow Grace's death with an even more sensational one, had allowed life in Ambridge to return to a lower key for well over a year.

Their calculations were correct, and their preparation thorough. The poacher who was accidentally killed, Bob Larkin who was Ned's no-good brother, had already fallen foul of Tom, because of his interest in Pru Harris, so the cards of circumstantial evidence were heavily stacked against him.

Shocked as listeners were to learn that Tom was in custody, several lawyers among our listeners viewed the matter with professional coolness and consulted their books. Then they wrote in to say that on the evidence offered no court would convict. And so, the charge was changed to manslaughter.

The full dramatic effect of a much-liked popular character like Tom being kept in prison was too good to miss. But once again, the ways of the law were more complicated than the scriptwriters had realized.

Bob Arnold, who plays Tom Forrest, remembers Geoffrey Webb saying: 'We're in trouble with you. We've got you remanded in custody and now we find the courts are in recess. You'll have to stay there for weeks, unless we can get round it.'

The trial did not in fact happen until July and Tom Forrest was away from Ambridge for some weeks. His introductions to the Omnibus edition could not take place, so Jack Archer brought listeners up to date with the news.

In real life Bob was doing a great deal of charity work at the time, appearing in variety concerts and quizzes and similar events. The imaginative organizer of one such affair announced that by special arrangement Tom had been allowed out of prison to be with them, whereupon Tom appeared from the wings accompanied by a policeman, who remained in view during his entire performance!

During this same time, Bob and his wife Dorothy went shopping in the country town where they lived and he was about to enter the bank when he was spotted by an old lady, who he knew was an avid fan.

'Hey, what are you doing here?' she asked, in broad Cotswold dialect, 'I though you were in prison. How did you get out?'

Tom was always a quick thinker. Without a flutter or a vestige of a smile, he replied soberly: 'That prison's terribly cold.

They've run out of fuel for the heating. So the Governor said to me, "Tom, take half an hour off and trot round the town to get warm," so here I am!'

'There now,' said the old lady, believing every word. 'That was kind of him, wasn't it?'

And happy and completely convinced she went merrily on her way.

However, the writing team at this time was not content with a story-development which provided mere temporary excitement: any especially sensational incident was justified by the deliberate probing into the effects that such a happening would have in real life. So we heard of the distress that confinement had upon a man who was always used to walking the open country, virtually his own master, and without a strict timetable. The mental effect was also illustrated: even if he were released, would Pru now want to marry a 'jail-bird'. Someone on remand (as Godfrey Baseley, Ted Mason and I learnt some ten years later when we spent a day in prison learning all the details for Nelson Gabriel's remand in custody after the Ambridge mail-van robbery) has a much freer life than a sentenced prisoner, but even so the experience was shown to have a deep effect on Tom.

Not content with exploring these human reactions to the situation, the writers then went on to provide one of the most memorable episodes of the programme when, on his unconditional release, Tom returned home to Ambridge in triumph. It was, of course, the sun shining in his face, not the spontaneous warmth of the village's welcome home, that brought tears to his eyes!

Although this incident received nothing like the enormous coverage in the press that the death of Grace did, it had a profound effect upon the status of the programme. People felt they could trust The Archers: another sensational death, even more gruelling than the first might well have had the opposite effect. Instead, the audience could only agree that what had happened to Tom could easily have happened to them and they looked upon us as warmly as ever. This opportunity of identifying their own lives with those of the inhabitants of Ambridge was a vital factor in the programme's continued success.

The balance of light and dark was carefully kept, too. The grimness of an imprisonment of an innocent man was balanced by the joy of his release. The sadness of the mourning Phil was dispelled the moment he met Jill Patterson. The second anniversary of Grace's death safely passed, Phil and Jill were quietly married on 16 November 1957. In Ambridge, as in the real world, everyone was anxious to turn their backs on the shadows of the past and look for whatever brightness could be found in the future.

And for those of us who were now dedicated to little else but bringing Ambridge and its people to daily life, that future was to hold more for us, both of darkness and light, than any serial-writer would dare to contrive.

1958

THE YEAR WHEN

Krushchev became Prime Minister of the USSR and, following a referendum, De Gaulle became President of France. Pope Pius XII and Ralph Vaughan Williams died. The Queen's Opening of Parliament was televised. Gatwick Airport was opened. The first barons and baronesses under the Life Peerages Act were named, Cardinal Roncalli, Patriarch of Venice, was elected Pope John XXIII. The Campaign for Nuclear Disarmament, CND, was launched under Bertrand Russell and the Clean Air Bill came into force.

IN AMBRIDGE

Birth, marriage and death. Lettie Lawson-Hope died and left Glebe Cottage to Doris for her lifetime. Jill had twins in August and bachelor Tom Forrest married Pru in September. Dan had problems: potato blight and a barn full of oats burnt down. Doris began a long campaign to persuade Dan to retire and for them to move into Glebe Cottage. It was to take her twelve years.

While it is perfectly true that among the records we Archers claim is the fact that throughout the whole twenty-five years of our life, there has never been a serious disagreement between members of the Cast, it would be unreal to suggest that times have always been sunny.

From time to time, tensions have built up, often for no easily discernible reason. Looking back, these occasions seem to have been when several minor irritations had combined to produce the temporary feeling of unease.

Although it might be thought that after seven years, the basic members of the Cast ought to have made the necessary adjustments to living a new kind of life, I am far from certain that this is so. After all, we lived from month to month: in spite of our success, we always felt that 'they' might take the programme off when it was at its peak, rather than allow such a phenomenally successful show to dwindle into extended mediocrity. In the event, of course, neither happened: but we never at any time felt that we could see more than six months or so ahead. So with our popularity we ate the bitter sauce of uncertainty and that inevitably produced tensions not far below the surface.

Grace, one of the most popular characters had been 'sacrificed' in order to produce the most valuable publicity the programme had ever had. We would not have been human if we had not at times wondered whether another victim might be needed. The writers of those two satires on serials, *The Killing of Sister George* and the unforgettable Tony Hancock take-off, touched a central nerve when they portrayed the anxiety of central characters in serials, and their almost paranoid fear of 'being written out'.

The most innocent remark given by a scriptwriter to a character can suddenly be read as an indication that the character might be leaving for the Antipodes, or developing an incurable disease. Some new ruling on BBC policy, some change in recording times or procedure, some unexpected criticism or some development of the general story-line – all these can, on occasions, unsettle a cast. For a great deal of the time, we worked happily together. The hours sometimes seemed long, especially in the summer; but it was always fun, even though we worked hard and used up a great deal of nervous energy. Only after one had been ill – after, say, a brief attack of flu – did one realize, when returning to work before fully recovered, just how much nervous energy was discharged in the recording of even a short scene.

All these factors could, on occasions, suddenly give rise to shortness of temper, or a feeling of tension in the studio. The usual times for these infrequent interludes were when we were in need of a break or, curiously enough, just before we celebrated one of our slowly mounting number of milestones.

1958 saw yet another of these milestones: our two thousandth episode. To mark the occasion it was decided to publish one edition of Ambridge's local weekly paper, the *Borchester Echo*. A fuller account of this remarkable publication appears in later pages of this book; but it is mentioned chronologically here because the work involved in its production did produce extra work for the Cast.

The first *Borchester Echo* was a complete mixture of fact and fiction: articles on Walter Gabriel's old Granny, rubbed shoulders with accounts of the BBC's technical staff, with photographs of studios and recording apparatus; a portrait of Valerie Hodgetts our 'continuity girl' jostles with a digest of Ambridge events from 1951 to 1958.

There were three tributes: from the Rt. Hon. John Hare, M.P., Minister of Agriculture, from Sir James Turner, President of the National Farmers' Union and from Alderman E. G. Gooch, C.B.E., M.P., J.P., President of the National Union of Agricultural Workers (whose name we had learned for the first time in a less celebratory atmosphere four years before).

In the place where the leading article would be in a real newspaper, there was an article by H. J. Dunkerley, Controller, BBC Midland Region on 'The Archers' Achievement'.

He wrote: 'Now that it has survived 2,000 episodes and is still listened to regularly by millions, we can permit ourselves a sense of pride in contemplating its history. It began as a proposition thrown out by a Lincolnshire farmer at an agricultural meeting over which I presided in 1948; it simmered and developed in Godfrey Baseley's mind for eighteen months; and in Whit-week 1950, the end-product – "The Archers" – was tentatively tried out on a morning audience in the Midlands.' He then sketched its history to 1958, when he continued: 'Not even the advent of 6–7 p.m. television could shake the loyalty of "The Archers" ' audience. Some transferred their allegiance from the nightly episodes to the Sunday Omnibus edition; but most remained faithful.'

The rest of this first single edition of the *Borchester Echo* was devoted to such articles as 'Writing the Archers story', 'Three people who lead double lives' and 'My job is to keep "The Archers" true to life'. Throughout there are photographs: a double-page centre spread called 'Sunday at Brookfield Farm' for example, and 'What of the future?' And it was the taking of these photographs that added to the general tension in the studio. It is a far from simple matter to arrange photograph calls for some twelve to twenty people, and to provide them with suitable clothes or accessories, correct implements, animals or machines against authentic backgrounds. These photocalls had become something of a bone of contention, as on occasion inadequate notice was given and we suddenly found ourselves in bad odour for mildly complaining at having to give up a whole Sunday – which might have well been the only free day in a couple of weeks or so.

The photographs invariably were taken and we all ended up smiling, if at times a little icily.

But at last the *Borchester Echo* was in the press and Kenneth Bird, whose idea it was, could feel a sense of achievement.

The Cast, though, through a mixture of irritation, frustration and tiredness were going through one of their niggly periods. One recording day, not long before we celebrated the two thousandth episode, Harry Oakes – who as Dan, the head of the family, was usually our spokesman – looked in on Tony Shryane who was sitting at the producer's controls ready to begin the morning's rehearsal and recording and said: 'Could we have a word with you at lunch-time? Won't take a minute.'

Tony recognized the formula and suspected that trouble was brewing. All through the morning he racked his brain to think what possible cause the Cast could have for feeling uneasy; he succeeded in imagining several reasons, all of which he hoped were too fanciful. The morning's work over, Tony screwed up his courage, cleaned his teeth (a life-long ritual this – he always cleans his teeth before lunch) and, straightening his tie, entered the tiny space we laughingly called the Green Room. There we all sat, quiet and poker-faced.

'Well? What is it this time?' Tony asked, with some edge.

'Oh, it's just that to mark our two thousandth episode together, we'd like you to accept this wrist-watch, Tony!'

Tony tells the story against himself: in fact, it is recounted here because he was good enough to recall it for me. The watch, which he has still, was engraved with his name and a brief note of the occasion. But as on countless occasions, that small incident broke the tension, and by the time the celebrations were over, we were all back in our usual mood.

The idea of publishing a souvenir edition like the *Borchester Echo* had also occurred to the *Daily Sketch* who commemorated our two thousandth episode with the first of several pull-out pages from the newspaper called the *Borchester Sketch*. Again more photographs, articles, the same mixture of fact and fantasy; but, more surprisingly, advertisements such as: 'At *The Bull* Jack Archer's regulars agree SmIThs CrISps improve the taste of every drink' and 'Harry Oakes of The Archers recommends "The Dan Archer Collections"' (of bulbs and flowering plants).

Already the feeling that this everyday story of countryfolk was being extended into a family saga was being exploited. Under the thick black heading: 'Remember?', a reporter wrote about 'All the people who made their mark in Ambridge and then left' and 'What they are doing now'.

There were pieces about Dorothy Oakes, Dan's real wife; John Tregorran's engagement – to someone other than Carol; a marriage-guidance column centred on the marriages of Dan and Doris's three children, answering the question 'Does Doris worry over them too much?'; and recipes from Gwen Berryman's recently published *Doris Archer's Farm Cookery Book*.

But perhaps it was the 'news item' on the front page of the *Borchester Echo* that set Fleet Street wondering whether perhaps we were not of more continuing interest than the odd sensational story had led them to believe. Under the headline: 'Round the world with Mr A', Leslie Watkins reported that from Christmas 'the Ambridge story will be broadcast nightly in Canada, Australia and New Zealand ... It should prove a great shot-in-the-arm for the Boost Britain Campaign.' This meant that as well as the special Omnibus edition being available to listeners in the General Overseas Service of the BBC, we would now be heard in Canada and 'down under' as a *daily* serial, just as in what was then still called 'the Mother Country' or 'back home'. It was an immediate success, and our fan-mail told us that for British people living in those distant countries the programme was a vivid and vital link with home.

Radio Times not only gave over the whole of its front page to a photograph of Gwen and Harry standing in a rural setting reading the special edition of the *Borchester Echo* with its headline: 'The Archers celebrate 2,000 broadcasts', but readers were directed to page three where Kenneth Bird's lively article spoke of the programme's 'unique place in the history of broadcasting'.

Far from declining, the programme seemed to be consolidating its position. Some began to declare that if we had been going to fade away we should have done so already. Those most closely concerned with the programme began to talk of the next milestone: our tenth anniversary.

They did more than talk: they made a conscious effort to stand back from the programme and try as honestly as possible to make a critical appraisal of it. One more reason for the programme's long survival! Laurels were never rested on: resort was never made, in major developments, to 'the mixture as before'.

Nor indeed did those who guided our destinies fall into the trap of trying to out-Herod Herod, to indulge in sensationalism for its own sake. Here the programme's basic formula was a great life-saver: no matter what flights of imagination the writers indulged in, The Archers was tied inextricably to the soil. Country life was not full of weekly disasters: the rate of birth, death, imprisonment, inability to have children, failure at work or in emotional life, had to be no greater in Ambridge than elsewhere. The balance of characters had to be maintained: not too many rich; not too many poor, nor quirky, nor lazy, nor inefficient, nor over-efficient. Characters who had served their original purpose and now seemed to have no more to give were eased out, new characters introduced, and the established characters were given a detailed inspection.

So some of us received a two-page closely typed letter beginning: '. . . almost at once we are going to change the character you play . . . I want to get a much bigger note of confidence in the way you are playing the part . . . I think you will find that the two authors will write your material quite differently, and I hope in a manner which will help you to achieve this new characterization . . . we are planning to make very drastic alterations in the whole pattern of the programme . . .'

This brief extract from a very long letter, the confidentiality of whose contents has now long passed, is quoted to give proof positive to those latterday critics who choose to believe that they alone have invented change or 'up-dating'. Clearly, if the programme had been the tired, flabby, unprofessionally-created, insipid and fossilized affair that some writers in some newspapers were anxious for their own reasons to prove it to be, it would never have survived to its tenth, let alone its twenty-fifth anniversary.

Inevitably there have been developments that didn't pay off: stories and new characters that seemed excellent in prospect were flat in realization. But the obsessive dedication of the editor, writers, Cast and producer have ensured that the programme has done more than merely survive. It has won not only that unique place in the history of broadcasting that Kenneth Bird referred to in his *Radio Times* article, but it has also won a place in the social history of this country and in the affections of very many people, both here and abroad.

Personal appearances, brief television appearances, articles, advertisements, a souvenir booklet of photos and biographies, 'novelizations' (*The Archers of Ambridge* and *The Archers Intervene*) and a stage play – it seemed as if the characters of Ambridge had infiltrated into every field, except possibly feature film and gramophone records.

There had indeed been brief film appearances, of a documentary nature, but our first appearance on a gramophone record took place towards the end of 1958. It was a 45 rpm disc, and was recorded by arrangement with the BBC in our usual studio in Birmingham. We were all glad that we were able to perform in familiar surroundings, especially Harry, Gwen, Bob and myself (Dan, Doris, Tom and Phil) as we were required to sing or play the piano. Basil Jones (John Tregorran) also contributed a tenor line. Both Harry and Tom were uneasy about the singing, in spite of having sung for years, and got me in a corner, anxiously persuading me to arrange the musical items in a comfortable key. So I dutifully transposed 'When we are married', and a Mendelssohn duet which was finally not used. I had great fun in making a special arrangement of 'When Jones's ale was new' for Bob to sing to my piano accompaniment.

One side of the record was a party at Brookfield, in which all the current characters were introduced and some were asked to do their party piece.

The other side of the record was Dan and Doris remembering highlights of the previous years: the birth of Tony Archer (then always called Anthony-William-Daniel – all in one breath), and the climax of one of the most successful episodes ever broadcast in the series, Walter Gabriel's distress at the results of sheep-worrying by a stray dog.

To launch the record, Pye Records arranged a publicity stunt which was duly reported in the national press. We arrived at the Dorchester Hotel in 'Walter Gabriel's bus', which was suitably labelled as such, and looked remarkably smart and fresh after our journey from Ambridge. (The journey in fact was a short one: we had been recording the programme in London not far away.)

Tanfield's Diary for 21 November 1958 gives an interesting hint to the way we were beginning to be regarded by the National Press.

We had of course to be yokels. So the line had to be 'the country comes to town . . . aaaarh!' The young journalists who collected material for the column were charming and disarming. They put us at our ease and were immediately surprised to find that we weren't yokels at all.

So, inevitably, the journalistic twist then became an attempt to show us as a group of townee socialites.

'I found them in the bright lights of the Dorchester drinking Champagne and eating scampi' says the columnist, who launched immediately into a report of Gwen Berryman sighing into her glass of bubbly and saying what a strain it was being an Archer. Gwen, in fact, adores good food but is very abstemious when it comes to drinking. But here was an irresistible picture: cosy country Doris drinking Champagne. And then, to add a kind of verisimilitude, the writer raises an Aunt Sally (our old favourite one about being 'real people') only to knock it down. 'I'm single in real life you know', Gwen is reported as saying, 'but when I went to judge a contest in an old people's home one of the inmates complained: "How can you possibly say you're single when I know you have three children and three grandchildren?"'

By this time, of course, we were becoming used to the ways of the press; but even Harry Oakes and I were mystified by apparently pointless changes in the truth. We had begun our chat with one of the journalists by remarking that it wasn't in character for either of us to be drinking what we were in fact drinking. Harry was drinking gin, but normally drank beer; I was drinking a small whisky when normally I drank one glass of red wine. The report made some play on the fact that 'Dan Archer was toying with a whisky while his son Philip favoured gin.' Were the copywriters beginning to re-create us in their own chosen image?

Although it was now more than three years since the famous 'death of Grace', the fact that the coffin-handles and nameplate saying 'Grace Archer 22 Sept 1955' which had been sent to me were now in the possession of Ysanne Churchman and 'go down awfully well at cocktail parties' was given full coverage. Once again, a silent contrast was being drawn between the image of the Archer character, and the way the actor playing the part speaks in real life.

'In a cosy corner,' the diary continued, 'I spotted Beverley Nichols chatting with Carol Grey the hard-bitten market gardener of Ambridge.'

Now truth and fiction really were being mixed. Beverley Nichols is given his real name: the rest of us were referred to only by our character names.

' "I'm here because I'm an Archer fan," said Beverley. "I like them because they're real people. Earth under their finger-nails instead of varnish on them." '

And the column ends:

'Carol looked guiltily at her finger-nails . . . spiky and shock-ing-pink.

' "But I'm quite earthy too," she said hastily. "I ordered a couple of rhododendrons at the Chelsea Flower Show and they've just been delivered . . ." '

We were getting used to this 'double-life' thing by now; but we had made a commercial recording and we were thought sufficiently newsworthy to be dealt with in one of the day's most popular gossip-columns under a three-inch headline: 'Dan hits Town with the Archers'.

We seemed, at last, to be arriving in what is called The Big Time.

Or were we?

1959

THE YEAR IN WHICH

British scientists isolated the basic molecule of penicillin. The first Oecumenical Council since 1870 was convened by Pope John. Britain recognized the new Cuban government of Fidel Castro, and the Dalai Lama fled to India. The Mermaid Theatre was opened in London. One of the longest droughts ever recorded ended, and the Conservatives won the general election with a majority of 100. The first section of the M1 was opened. Archbishop Makarios was elected first President of Cyprus.

IN AMBRIDGE

Oliver Charles Grenville took over the estate when George and Helen Fairbrother went to live abroad. He also bought Arkwright Hall but no one knew this until John Tregorran and Ned found a small fortune in gold sovereigns there while ghost-hunting. The village was again threatened, this time by a by-pass. Laura Archer came to the aid of Jack and Peggy by putting up most of the money to enable them to buy *The Bull*.

The number of regular listeners to The Archers now often exceeded ten million: sound radio was still holding its own against the slow advance of television.

One extraordinary manifestation of this was the publication in January 1959 of another four-page special 'for 10,000,000 Archer fans' of the *Borchester Sketch*. The news from Ambridge was treated like 'real' news in such headlines as 'I track down the MAN OF MYSTERY', 'New boss is tough – but no monster', which dealt with the arrival of Oliver Charles Grenville to take over Fairbrother's estate.

It went on to feature an alleged interview with Dan Archer under the headline 'My greatest Gamble', and reported Dan's anxiety at taking on an overdraft of nearly £3,000 to modernize

Brookfield farm. Another item was headed 'Bachelor-again-Tom reflects,' which explained that Tom Forrest, who married late in life, was now without his wife Pru for some months as she has entered a sanitorium. (The truth behind this event incidentally is that the actress, Mary Dalley, had been given a once in a lifetime's chance to visit relatives in New Zealand, and so had to be 'written-out' for some months . . . a fact not publicized at the time.)

But in the middle of all this alleged 'news' from Ambridge there suddenly were genuine news items, like 'Blind to get news of Archers' (reporting the Braille edition of the *Borchester Echo*), 'Leo Genn makes a début', not to mention the real times of radio and TV programmes and a column of film reviews.

The *Borchester Sketch* also had women's interests in mind: 'You can cook like Doris', 'Don't forget the wine', 'Why can't Chris have a baby?', 'The life Mary misses' and a letter from a real-life fan who with some pride announces: 'I have a budgie who always sings and whistles The Archers' signature tune at 6.45.'

The whole four pages were illustrated with photographs of the cast, captioned only with character names: Jimmy Grange and Joan Hood, Dan and Doris and so forth.

Today, looking back, the note of greatest reality is struck by a vast advertisement for Meggezone throat pastilles. After all, in spite of the make-believe of photo-calls and press reports, we in The Archers earned our living by using our voices. I often wonder whether the inclusion of that solitary ad. was accident or subtlety.

Later in 1959 the news of Chris Gittins's illness was widely reported from local papers to the *Sunday Times* and *Reynolds News*.

Chris had been booked to appear at Camborne in Cornwall. Bob Arnold had been the first member of the Cast to go to this part of the world where a very enthusiastic caravan-site owner organized a steam engine rally. Bob had never seen such crowds, nor such demonstrations of affection from an audience in his life before. I followed on 12 July 1958 and, in spite of torrential rain, was equally impressed by the vast numbers of fans and the long queues for autographs.

Chris Gittins went with high hopes to appear at the same function on 18 July 1959, but was taken ill with a minor heart attack and admitted to a hospital in Truro.

He was put in a private ward. There would have been precious little rest for him if he'd been admitted to a general ward, and rest was what he needed. It wasn't, however, as simple as that. The news soon spread through the hospital that 'Walter Gabriel' was there. In the early hours of one morning, a drowsy Chris woke from a drugged sleep to find himself the object of close scrutiny by two old ladies from a ward on the floor below. They had seized their only opportunity, and had stolen up to see what he really looked like at dead of night. This story often comes to mind when the arguments for and against private medicine are discussed. I know Chris felt then, as we all were feeling increasingly, that the number of places in the world where we could find peace was relentlessly diminishing.

A small item in the *Sunday Times* for 6 September 1959 under the heading 'Archer wedding', reported the marriage of Mary Dalley. *The Observer* of the same date reported 'hundreds of admirers of the BBC "Archers" serial and several members of the Cast attended the wedding.

One trivial incident stays with me of that occasion. We were all announced as we arrived for the wedding reception, and naturally gave our real names. Bob Arnold was, of course, an important guest and he not only brought his real-life wife, but also his daughter. Several of us were amused to hear them announced in a stentorian tone as : Mr, Mrs and *Miss* Bob Arnold!

Truth and fiction merged again in September 1959 when at a function held to inaugurate an appeal for one million pounds for the Royal Agricultural Benevolent Institution, members of the cast of The Archers did a demonstration of how an episode is recorded. The *Manchester Guardian* had as its heading: '£1m Farm Pensions Fund Appeal: "Archers" join in'; while *The Times* put us into the headline: ' "Archers" assist £1m Farm Charity Appeal!'

This appeal was launched by Lord Netherthorpe, President of the National Farmers' Union who had always been both a friend of the programme and known as a very friendly person to many members of the Cast. It will be remembered that as Sir James Turner he stirred us with his words at the celebration of the one thousandth episode.

The *Daily Telegraph* announced in October that 'Dan Archer' was ill, and the *Daily Sketch* reported over three columns: 'Radio Farmer Dan Archer is in Hospital'. But now, alas, there was no mixture of fact and fantasy, no matter how the headlines phrased it. The sad fact was that our friend and colleague Harry Oakes had been admitted to hospital, suffering from nervous strain and exhaustion. The *Daily Sketch* went on to say that the BBC had said that it was 'pure coincidence' that in the serial Dan Archer had been rushed to hospital with a broken leg.

Having been present on more than one occasion when the editor and writers have to decide how to cover the enforced absence of one of the actors, I know how difficult it is to deal with the problem.

The reason for the sudden departure has to be plausible; if it is known in advance how long the artiste is likely to be away, the problem is fairly simple. But no-one knew how ill Harry was at this time, just as in later years we had a similar situation with his successor, and on several occasions with Doris. All one is told is that they are ill and in hospital. They may be there for a week or two, or possibly for months. And so some ailment or condition is chosen which can either be cured fairly quickly or which can be extended indefinitely.

When we visited Harry in hospital he was as cheerful as always: his wicked smile and his inextinguishable sense of fun were as evident as ever. What some of us saw, but not alas Harry himself, was that this was a warning: the pace of being Dan Archer was too exhausting. And yet, the moment he was released from hospital, Harry threw himself into his double-life with as much zest as ever. He was allowed out of hospital to make a single appearance for Christmas. Dan's arrival at Brookfield on Christmas Eve was intended to be a wonderful surprise for Doris. We know that when that warm chuckle and the resonant tones of the one and only Dan were heard saying: 'Merry Christmas everybody!' there was scarcely a dry eye for miles around. It was a sentimental stroke that was also a stroke of genius. Listening to the episode at home during a family Christmas party, the children suddenly hushed, the conversation stopped. I felt a lump in my own throat, even though I knew what was happening. My mother's eyes filled with tears and in a choked voice she said to me, 'Is it really him?'

I told her he had been allowed out of hospital specially.

'Aah!' was the reply.

Dickens couldn't have done it better. Dan Archer, a thoroughly likeable man, a good and ordinary man, a friend as close as one's closest friend, was out of danger, out of hospital, and home for Christmas. Now everything would be all right!

Sentimental, cosy-comfort listening? Undoubtedly. But never cheap, never maudlin: a true opium of the people. After all, as one writer wrote to the *Sunday Times* many years later, when the press was having one of its recurring bouts of 'Why-not-kill-the-Archers?'-itis: 'There is no proven evidence that listening to The Archers is injurious to health.'

Agreed. It might even be that the opposite is true. Tony Shryane often refers to the signature tune as the injection of a drug. Perhaps he's right. The Archers may well be a habit-forming drug, but it certainly isn't harmful.

1960

THE YEAR WHEN

A royal wedding was controversial: Princess Margaret married Antony Armstrong-Jones. Mr Macmillan delivered his 'wind of change' speech to the South African Parliament. The last British Railways steam locomotive was named. Africa also saw the Sharpeville shooting, and the opening by the Queen Mother of the Kariba Dam. Boris Pasternak and Aneurin Bevan died. Cyprus became independent. The Archbishop of Canterbury visited Pope John. John F. Kennedy became President of the United States. The farthing ceased to be legal tender.

IN AMBRIDGE

Arkwright Hall was given to the village by Grenville, as a kind of 'community centre'. The new decade made Dan and other local farmers examine their farming methods and consider the future. The local branch chairman of the N.F.U., Fred Barratt, made himself unpopular by saying that too many local farmers weren't as efficient as they thought they were. Dan began seriously contemplating the idea of a farmers' co-operative.

During the first ten years of the run of The Archers there must have been, I sometimes think, officials in the BBC who felt that it was some sort of monster that had arrived from outer space, and just would not go away. After all, it had started quietly in one of the regions and was given no special treatment or publicity in its early years.

But it would not go away. The half a million listeners who heard that regional trial run in May 1950 had grown to more than ten million by 1960, and the programme certainly seemed to have established itself as part of the accepted pattern of broadcasting.

At this time there was renewed talk of changing the various

services. Home, Light and Third, into separate continuous speech and music channels. In March 1960 the *Daily Telegraph* radio and television critic said that the idea which he had promoted for a 'constant hot music' channel was being opposed inside the BBC by some people who felt that 'the Corporation has big audiences for such spoken-word programmes as The Archers and is most reluctant to make any change that would upset them.' He goes on to say that while realizing that it is impossible to please everybody, it ought not to be beyond the wit of the BBC to put all the light music tidily and conveniently on one channel, and thus obviate needless switching back and forth.

That word 'tidily' is a dangerous one. There is more mischief caused by people with tidy minds, especially in positions of power, than by those who apparently bumble along. The *Telegraph* critic did not give his authorities for the confident statements he made about BBC reluctance to change our channel: but there might well have been something in what he said. By the 1960s it was becoming clear that The Archers had not only arrived, but would not go away.

By this time, too, people were beginning to assume that if The Archers could be so successful in passing on farming information and in interpreting the countryman to the townsman, then it might also be made to serve their own pet cause, whatever that might be. So we were inundated with requests for special mentions of anything from road safety to breast-feeding.

The editorial policy had become clearly defined by now. It was to *reflect* the contemporary scene as it was. In other words Dan Archer could be shown doing any of the things which most farmers were doing on their land. Out-of-date methods were represented, of course, but greater care had to be taken with very new ideas. They were presented as novelties, as experiments which were not typical: hence the many scenes in which Philip and his employer, first Fairbrother who was not very knowledgeable, and then Grenville who was extremely so, put forward *avant garde* ideas which usually scared Dan by their strangeness.

But the supporters of other matters not specifically agricultural attempted to get their point of view over in The Archers.

The *Guardian* reported that the League Against Cruel Sports had decided on two courses: one to write to the Home Secretary complaining about hare-coursing (which was predictable enough); the other, though, was to protest to the Director-General of the BBC about the inclusion of a fox-hunt in The Archers' programme one Monday.

Clearly The Archers was now regarded as a force in the land; what now at this distance seems fascinating is the weight that was being put, by lobbies anxious for maximum publicity, on the persuasive powers of The Archers.

Those of us who play the main parts have continually found ourselves of interest to the press. I have to admit that I am not a regular reader of the daily newspapers – a fact which caused great distress to Gwen Berryman in April of this year 1960. Hurrying to get a taxi after arriving at Paddington, she fell down a flight of stairs and broke her wrist. Shocked and in pain she was moved to a hospital where she tried to get in touch with me. It so happened that I had moved to a flat quite near by, but for some reason her attempts to reach me by phone were unsuccessful. The result was that she had a traumatic stay in hospital which in fact marked the beginning of a decline in her health, and especially in the condition of her hands in which she now has arthritis.

If only I had read the newspapers! 'Doris Archer, the kindly farmer's wife in the BBC radio series The Archers was in hospital last night with a broken wrist. Actress Gwen Berryman, aged 52, fell down a flight of steps at Paddington Station, London, yesterday.'

It was 13 April. Gwen has remained superstitious about that day ever since. Not only was the accident itself bad luck: the fact that I was unable to rescue her and help her to recover in friendly and comfortable surroundings close at hand was even worse.

Gwen has several memories of that stay in hospital. She made her first entrance into her ward on a trolley which made rather a noise as it went along. This did not endear her to the other patients:

'Oh, you would make a row,' cried one with some vehemence, 'just when we're trying to listen to The Archers.'

Gwen realized it was just after 6.45 p.m.

Some days later, a repentant fellow-patient came to Gwen's bedside and with tears in her eyes apologized. 'I don't know what I said,' she admitted, 'but I know I was very rude. I'm so sorry. I'd no idea you were Mrs Archer!'

Gwen's accident did not help the situation in the studio,

where anxieties about Harry Oakes's health were increasing. Those of us who had been with the programme from the beginning had one perpetual dread: that we should be 'written out'. The idea of ceasing to be the characters we played seemed akin to murder. The cynic will say that we were afraid of losing a steady job and that, no doubt, played a part in our thinking. But the younger members in particular realized that they could not expect to spend the rest of their lives playing their one Archer role. Yet we all felt the same. Attempts were made to persuade Harry to take a complete rest abroad — and it was intimated to him that financial help would be forthcoming. But he was adamant. While he had life and breath, he would play Dan Archer. He *was* Dan Archer, just as the rest of us felt (for at least part of the time) that we were the characters we played: some members indeed grew more and more like their Archer characters until they became submerged in them for seven days a week.

But for poor Harry, the nightmare happened. We could all imagine his feelings when his health made it impossible for him to go on. We hoped that he would not read the press reports, especially those like the one in the *Daily Sketch* for 1 June which spoke of 'Dan Archer the second'.

Our concern for him grew when we read on: 'Understudies are to take over from the stars of The Archers, the marathon radio serial. The BBC revealed last night that following special auditions, Monte Crick will replace Harry Oakes as Dan Archer for a week from June 17.'

The important part of that report was 'for a week'; but it must have seemed like a death-knell to Harry . . . 'Dan the second' . . . 'take over' . . . 'replaced by'. We all shared some of the apprehension. Perhaps no single event brought home to us how much we had become absorbed in, and dedicated to, and fused with, these fictional characters that we gave life to every week.

By now we all knew Monte Crick. He had for some time been playing small parts in the programme and we had all noticed a vocal similarity between him and Harry. Some of us, like millions of radio listeners, also knew him in a different role: as accompanist to Ronald Frankau and composer of many tuneful songs. We were to get to know him very much better in succeeding years, but that will be recounted in its place.

The programme continued its daily progress. By now nearly three thousand episodes had been broadcast and its popularity was undimmed. In June 1960 the Rhodesian radio service started broadcasting. The Archers (we were slowly building up a world-wide audience through the BBC General Overseas Service and Transcription Service) and at once the Rhodesians found they had a problem. Our signature tune, 'Barwick Green', had been used for fourteen years out there to introduce a weekly programme of agricultural advice by the Rhodesian Government's Natural Resources Board, for farmers and ranchers in remote parts of Central Africa. Clearly it was unthinkable to have the same tune for both programmes. The Archers won. Our programmes continued to be begun and ended by 'Barwick Green'. The other series was introduced by a new tune called 'On the Veld'.

Today the word 'permissive' is all too familiar: when The Archers began there was little general use of four-letter words, full-frontal nudity was rare, and kitchen sink drama had not yet dominated the theatrical scene. As the years went by, however, a curious thing happened. The flood of letters from listeners, and their reactions when we met them in the flesh, all emphasized one aspect of the programme: its wholesomeness. Conventions changed, speech and conduct became freer, words like 'abortion', 'homosexual' and 'drugs' became freely used in normal conversation; but the least divergence from the old-established 'Archer' convention brought storms of protest. Slowly the writers and editor were pushed further and further away from their brief to reflect life exactly as it was. Strange as it may seem, it was a case of not being trendy if we were to hold on to our listeners.

In practice, this was not nearly the strait-jacket it might seem to have been. We soon found that there was no subject under the sun that could not be discussed in the programme — even the current obsessions with abortion, homosexuality and drug-addiction. But — and it perhaps should be in capital letters — BUT such subjects could only be discussed and dealt with from a conservative point of view.

The tone of the letters already quoted earlier in this book will bear this out and so will press reports like, for example, the headline in black type in the *Daily Express* for 18 November 1960: 'THE ARCHERS: A DIVORCE'.

This is how the four-column article began: 'Is a terrible scandal brewing in the "Archers" family? Five million women throughout Britain — and almost as many men — face the shattering possibility that the BBC's "everyday story of country folk" is soon going to be involved with – a DIVORCE!'

Let me say at once, lest the passage of time should mislead, that this was not a send-up. The tone was serious, not ironic, and even the last lines were not to be taken with tongue in cheek, no matter how they may strike a reader today: 'Death ... murder ... now divorce? What are the Archers coming to?'

The article dealt with yet another example of the plot-lines being tangled by the illness of one of the performers – in this case Lesley Saweard who played Dan's daughter Christine, married to Paul Johnson. Lesley had to go into hospital and so a story was contrived where Paul and his brother-in-law, Phil, should go to Paris for a holiday and there Paul would meet an old flame, Marianne Peters. Just as the story reached the brink of divorce, however, Lesley came out of hospital and the writing team had to decide whether to press on with the divorce, or save the marriage.

'What worries Mr Mason and Mr Webb – who will be meeting soon to decide – is that their last two scandals had nationwide repercussions,' the article went on. Any writer today would be far from worried by such a reaction and many court it, usually without success, so full have we supped on scandals. And I am quite sure that Ted Mason, Geoff Webb and Godfrey Baseley were not so much exercised on purely moral grounds, but because of the public reaction. The shadow of Lord Reith still fell over broadcasting: many in the BBC still applauded a viewpoint which is now dismissed as paternalistic and believed implicitly in the idea that broadcasting should be a service to the people, and should set a moral tone.

And what were the two 'scandals' that had such wide repercussions? The writer elaborated: one was the death of Grace, when 'curtains were drawn in many a home' and 'one family even set about gathering flowers for wreaths and crosses'. The second was 'only 17 months later, when a violent murder rocked the listeners back in their armchairs'. This was the accidental death of a poacher, shot by Tom Forrest, who was imprisoned but finally released. Both produced very positive reactions from listeners. What is of even greater significance perhaps is that, bowing to public feeling, the divorce never took place: Chris and Paul Johnson remain childless but devoted to this day.

As 1960 neared its close, *The Times* printed a leader on the eve of the tenth anniversary of The Archers, under the heading

'A farming *Dick Barton*'. It commented that 'the formula for "The Archers" — a farming family serial composed of ninety per cent entertainment and ten per cent information — does not on paper seem to have the promise of a great national success . . . Yet rarely can a long-running success have more naturally and more inevitably asserted itself.' It is a long and appreciative leader, whose final paragraphs deserve to be quoted here almost in full:

'The BBC, rightly having faith in the corporation's educational purpose, stresses the 10 per cent of information. The programme is always authentic. It therefore rings true to both countryman and townsman . . . There was a time when success in entertainment, whether in fiction, on the stage, or on the films, seemed to depend on getting as far away from reality as possible. So far as the radio audience is concerned the appeal of other people's ordinary lives is strong. Whether it is because of wide-spread loneliness, whether it is the satisfaction of becoming absorbed in a continuing simple human drama as an escape from a world in which so much is disjointed, complicated and inhuman, whether it is that the call of the land is heard by all, "The Archers" formula has never had to be varied. The clever and smart may be superior about it; it deals with enduring things. And they do endure.'

1961

THE YEAR IN WHICH

Sir Thomas Beecham and Ernest Hemingway died, and Dag Hammarskjöld was killed. Yuri Gagarin made the first flight into space and back. Britain's first legal betting-shops were opened. The Queen and the Duke of Edinburgh visited Pope John. Guildford Cathedral was consecrated. South Africa became a Republic and withdrew from the British Commonwealth. After a volcanic eruption on Tristan da Cunha, the whole population was evacuated to Britain. Britain's official negotiations for entering the Common Market began in Brussels.

IN AMBRIDGE

There was romance in the air: Grenville's proposal of marriage to Carol Grey was accepted, but Peggy was unhappy at the thought of Jennifer marrying Max whom she'd met on holiday in Switzerland. Teenage fire-raisers were caught on Grenville's estate. Hazel, the five-year-old daughter of Reggie and Valerie Trentham, the sporty owners of the Country Club, contracted polio in a mild form.

As the programme began its second decade, the euphoria of feeling that we had achieved things that few could possibly have imagined was tempered by a creeping shadow of doubt. The programme was as vigorous as ever; but the strain on some members of the team was beginning to show. Early in the previous December Harry Oakes once more had to leave us: 'for a few weeks' said one newspaper; 'for three months' said another. Those of us who were nearer to him wished we could be as confident.

Monte Crick again took over, endearing himself to us all by never allowing his natural delight in being called upon us to play such an important part overbalance his natural fellow-feeling and sympathy for Harry. He worked hard and long and conscientiously on his performance, trying to bring to it not an impersonation of the original, but that same warmth and geniality and feeling of reassurance which Harry's voice always gave listeners – often at the same time as Harry's own failing health and decreasing strength filled him personally with despair.

It is good to think that none of us had the least suspicion that before the next decade was over Monte too would succumb to ill-health. Like Harry he also appeared a picture of bounding vigour and good spirits. Unlike some of us, notably myself, he looked every inch the part.

So it was with mixed feelings that we entered the sixties: regret that the strains of being national – and, increasingly, international – celebrities were so severe; muted relief (cold comfort that it was) that if necessary an excellent understudy for the head of the family was available. We had, too, a sense of achievement: we had started very modestly and now we were household names around the world.

The appreciative and sensitive leader in *The Times* on 31 December 1960 was followed two days later by a generous comment in the *Daily Telegraph*. The writer was reviewing the previous year's radio and TV programmes and, having made the usual caveat that he himself did not always agree with the choice of the masses, went on to say that The Archers was 'still going strong' after ten years. Four Ministers of Agriculture, he said, had praised its usefulness to the farming community. It had been lauded in Canada and now was heard in Australia, New Zealand, Kenya, Hong Kong, Jamaica, Tanganyika, Rhodesia and Nyasaland, Trinidad, and British Forces' stations overseas. The piece ended with: 'The toast is "The Archers".'

That was among the last of such generous, unqualified tributes from the press. The world was changing: the world of journalism was changing, too.

Kitchen-sink 'realism', angry young men attacking the 'Establishment', and a new class-consciousness ('middle' was out, 'working' was in) had produced an atmosphere of shake-up, uncertainty and revaluation: the old values of public and private morality were being taken apart and scrutinized.

One simple, personal illustration will underline the point. Eighteen months before The Archers began, I, as a bright boy down from Oxford, was given some months' BBC training in the art of interviewing. Repeatedly one was told, you are less than the dust, we do not wish to know what the interviewer thinks or feels; it is your job to make the interviewee talk. We were taught how to wheedle, cajole, even to make deliberate mistakes in order to force the interviewee to rise to the bait and talk; but one should never harass, attack or be other than extremely polite.

Suddenly all that had gone. No longer were politicians allowed to make evasive 'parliamentary' answers to questions from interviewers: no longer were prepared statements accepted unchallenged: no longer was the interviewer's manner to be deferential or kid-gloved.

This new hard-hitting abrasiveness quickly ousted the quieter, more courteous and kindly manner. Following John Osborne's *Look Back in Anger* in 1956 the most favoured target was the 'Establishment'; and, in ten years The Archers, totally unsuspecting, had become in the minds of many, part of the 'Establishment'.

It naturally followed that we should before long be the subject of 'a shake-up' to our alleged smugness, complacency, unawareness of the problems of the 'real' world. The first attack came, unkindly but predictably enough, on one of our celebrations. We had marked our one thousandth episode, our second, and now, on 1 January 1961 we were to celebrate our tenth anniversary. And at last we (at least some of us) were to be seen on the telly, at home in Ambridge.

Those concerned wondered whether the fiasco created by that first attempt, already described, to show the world what the Archer family and friends really looked like, would be repeated. But no: it was all very smoothly done, without a hint of aggression or abrasion. It was not until it was all over that we realized that we had been ridiculed.

The vogue for savage television satire established by *That Was The Week That Was* had not yet arrived. But Derek Hart and the *Tonight* team arrived in the BBC television studios in Birmingham, where a mock-up of *The Bull* had been built, and selected members of the Cast (Doris, Carol, John Tregorran, Charles Grenville, Ned Larkin, and Jack and Peggy) were given a rough briefing. It was done in the way that charades are arranged at parties: I ask you this and you say that.

What viewers saw on their screens was a bland and urbane

Derek Hart chatting to 'Mrs Doris Archer' (Gwen trying not to look ill-at-ease and smiling bravely) with this sort of dialogue:

Hart: And what's that open ditch that flows through the centre of Ambridge, Mrs Archer?
Doris: Ditch? That's our river. The river Am.

Some of us, and not merely through sour grapes at not being included – indeed, those who had taken part reacted even more strongly – felt that the whole thing had been unfortunate. We old radio folk had seemed to be in collusion with bright young telly people in order to help them to knock us. But, it seems, we had the last laugh. More people seemed to have been affronted than amused. Like a mother rushing to defend a way-ward son, our faithful listeners reacted as if they too had been slurred, and their intelligence impugned.

The tenth anniversary was celebrated with more than the few minutes of television, though. Once that was over, we had a Champagne party in the studio and, as we had now grown to expect, we were joined by the whole of the top brass of the BBC, headed by the Director-General, then called Hugh Carleton Greene, now Sir Hugh Greene, to whom we were presented. Nothing memorable was said, unless I am mistaken, either to or by him. The evening seemed to have got off on the wrong foot: the tone was not only different from that on previous celebrations, it was wrong. Indeed the writer of 'Ambridge Notebook' in the *Observer* the following Sunday stated un-equivocally that 'Ambridge, the village that is more real than reality to 11 million listeners was put on trial on its tenth birthday by the bright young men of *Tonight*.'

It did seem a funny way to celebrate.

Such occasions, however, do give opportunities for the press to meet members of the Cast and the production team; and reports at this time do emphasize some of the essential points of the programme. One newspaper quoted The Archers' editor (inaccurately described as 'the bustling son of a Worcester butcher') as saying that the broad policies of Ambridge life were sketched out for the following five years, that each epi-sode contained one non-plot scene which could at short notice be replaced by a topical one, and that the formula was not as described in *The Times* only a week before, but '. . . only five per cent of the programme is educational, 30 per cent informa-tive and the rest entertainment.'

Ted Mason was also fully reported. Even then he was aware of what has now become a perennial problem in the programme: the difficulty in introducing really interesting *young* characters. His figures for the magic 'formula' are different again: 10 per cent education, 30 per cent information and the rest entertainment. He added: 'The annoyance is part of the entertainment.' Annoyance, that is, on the part of the listeners. He and his fellow writer, Geoffrey Webb, had learned the value of an irritating busybody character and of occasionally moving the story against the expressed wishes of the listeners.

The current example of this was the engagement of Carol Grey and Charles Grenville, the wealthy high-powered abrasive landowner. It was an established fact that most listeners wanted Carol to marry John Tregorran (which, of course, she eventually did: one of the great assets of a serial is that plot-lines can be laid down to extend over many months or even years).

The most significant quotation from the press reports of this time comes from Denis Morris (who had become Head of Light Programme after leaving Birmingham where, under his control as Head of Programmes, The Archers had been born). Commenting on speculations about the continued life of the programme, he said: 'It will go on as long as it remains true to itself.'

He might with equal justification say the same today.

Among the Birthday Honours in the summer of this year were at least two notable names beginning with 'S'. Only one made the headlines, though, that of Joan Sutherland.

Tucked away more modestly among the M.B.E.s, was a name we all knew, Anthony J. Shryane for services to broadcasting – Tony Shryane, in other words, producer of The Archers who had, by the time he received his award from the Queen Mother on 10 June, been producing The Archers continuously, without missing a single episode, for ten years.

Modest as ever, Tony said little to the Cast until he had in fact been to the Palace and few of us had spotted it in the newspapers. Indeed, when he received the first intimation of the award from the Prime Minister, Tony later admitted his first reaction was to dismiss it as a practical joke.

It was a reward for an astonishing record; and indeed many more years were to go by before an episode of The Archers was to be produced by anybody other than Tony Shryane. When it first happened – during Tony's three-month secondment to

Drama Department in London in 1967 – it was another Tony who deputized, Tony Cornish.

Perhaps a word should be said here about the listening figures that the press were so keen to quote at this time, which is the peak of popularity of the programme.

Some newspapers spoke of ten million, others of eleven, yet others of four or five million. The truth is that the number of listeners daily was estimated at between four and six million; and the number of listeners to the Omnibus edition, which by this time had settled into its apparently permanent time of 9.30 on Sunday mornings, was in the region of four million.

One thing was obvious: as the number of television sets increased and the coverage by new transmitters of television programmes become more complete, our figures could only fall.

I remember speaking at an informal meeting of the Cast, when pay and conditions were being hotly debated: 'We've had a wonderful run,' I heard myself saying, 'but we must be realistic. With television becoming so popular, we must gradually fade away. And what I say is, let's go quietly!'

How wrong one can be! That was fifteen years ago, and the programme, with some of us old originals, still goes on.

The threat of television wasn't the only cause for concern. The change in the attitude of what we soon were to be calling 'the media' inevitably had an effect. Nearer at hand still, there was the illness of Harry Oakes, a king-pin of the programme. If, as some of us feared, he was unable to make the complete recovery we all hoped, would the public take to his replacement, no matter how well-played? We could remember the complaints about the 'new' Walter Gabriel, Grace, and Peggy: though, on the other hand, the replacement of the original Christine had passed almost unnoticed. That, however, was in our early days before we had attracted national publicity. We tried to convince ourselves that Harry would recover. Even when scenes were recorded at his bedside, or when he was first assisted up the two flights of stairs to the studio (there was no lift) and then finally carried there, we still hoped. And Harry's twinkle and courage and endless humour helped us to deceive ourselves.

Harry became almost obsessively anxious that the public should know nothing of the seriousness of his incapacity. It must therefore have come as something like a national disaster when the news of his death was announced on radio and television and in the newspapers.

The usual things were said that people say when someone dies; but just as millions of listeners genuinely felt that they had lost a friend, the edges had already been blurred by the fact that they were already growing accustomed to hearing Harry's understudy in his place. For those of us who really knew him, though, the conventional statements of grief were all too true. We had indeed lost more than a colleague: we really had lost an old friend.

I remember working with him long before The Archers started. He was rarely angry or out of humour: he was always good company and a brilliant raconteur of Staffordshire stories. I remember especially a programme produced by Alan Burgess in London, in which both Harry and I took part, staying in the same hotel and travelling together. I found myself being a kind of straight man, egging him on to do his various party-pieces for the London cast, and enjoying them each time he repeated them. He was a born artiste: each telling differed in some slight but usually hilarious detail. On long journeys, he composed limericks prompted by the names of the places we passed through. Seconds after passing the sign at the entrance to a village, he would announce:

'There was a young lady of Lavenham . . .' or wherever it was, and within minutes a complete limerick would have emerged, always witty, sometimes bawdy but nearly always with that variety of humour that stems from delighted enjoyment of the ridiculous.

Although he found fame as a radio performer, he had a wonderfully expressive face, which was used to the full when telling stories. The necessity for quiet in a radio studio often produces an effect like that of laughing in church: a tiny unexpected remark produces gales of uncontrollable laughter.

Harry was a past-master of such remarks which, though trivial in themselves, became irresistibly funny when coupled with his mock serious expression, his diamond twinkle and the necessity for silence in the studio.

In the days when we recorded a whole episode as a single entity, he once reduced me to helpless laughter, just as the red light was flickering, signalling that the recording of a scene between the two of us was about to begin. He said, with childlike wonder and an impudently innocent expression: 'Pâté maison! . . . (PAUSE. PUZZLED EXPRESSION) . . . House Paste?'

I had the first line to deliver, without which the whole episode could not begin; and only by dint of deep breathing, muscular control – and a resultant aching abdomen, was I able to say the lines. I have often wondered why such an apparently simple four words should have had the effect they did. The answer, I now believe, lies in the fact that Harry loved to see people laughing, and was brilliantly adept at producing that effect by mime, gesture and facial expression with little or no other material.

Listeners to a radio programme probably never give a thought – why should they? – to the times the actors spend together in rehearsal. Five episodes a week, recorded in the space of two days, represent no more than seventy-five minutes. The remaining hours of those two days are spent in rehearsing at the microphone, or sitting waiting in the nearby Green Room; and far more time seems to be spent sitting waiting than appearing at the microphone, apart from those occasional episodes when one finds oneself in most of the scenes.

So, in the ordinary way, we spend a great deal of time on call together. The conditions at Broad Street, Birmingham, where the programme was recorded until the BBC opened its splendid new premises at Pebble Mill in 1971, were, to put it mildly, cramped. Many of us who were on what was called permanent contract were in nearly every episode (unlike those playing smaller parts who came in for one or two episodes). So we came to know each other extremely well, and being a member of what was officially called The Archers' Repertory Company was rather like being a member of a very congenial club. It is, to say the least, fortunate, and probably surprising that we all got on so well with each other; but I am sure that in some strange way the absence of disagreement and bad temper was mainly due to Harry's quiet assumption of the role of Head of the family. He was not a notably strong or assertive character. Indeed, he was a very gentle person, who liked a quiet life; but his tall figure and greying hair gave him a kind of presence.

After Harry's death, those of us who were left were naturally apprehensive about the changes in our 'off-stage' moments which would follow from his departure. We need not have worried: with great tact and enormous charm, his successor Monte Crick, gently but inevitably won our confidence, our co-operation and finally our deep affection.

Although there had been a few essential changes in the Cast over the years, this was the first time when a major character, possibly *the* major character, had to be replaced after some years of being high in public esteem. There were those who feared that Harry's death might mark the beginning of the end. I confess to sharing some of those anxieties myself; but once again, I was, I am glad to say, proved wrong.

Life went on in Ambridge as relentlessly as elsewhere. As I have already explained it had become an almost unwritten rule that, in order to win back the audience, a really major event had to be planned for the autumn. September was always regarded as the crucial month in Ambridge.

On 19 September 1961, we read in our newspapers gratifying headlines like 'Storm over BBC bride'. The lamentable replacement of a major character had not, it seemed, made us any less newsworthy. The item referred to the marriage of Carol to Grenville, 'despite dozens of protests from listeners' who complained 'Grenville's too old. Carol should marry John Tregorran.' It looked as if the writing team's ruse had worked: the unpopular line, the irritant, was stimulating interest in the programme yet again.

Once more the imagination of listeners was caught. The old excuse that it was 'only acting' was paraded, but somehow it never quite explained why so many people should apparently care so desperately who Carol married. But they undoubtedly did care; and we began to think that the blows which had fallen upon the programme would not, after all, be fatal.

Another member of the Cast, Peter Wilde, died in September. He played the part of the dashing Reggie Trentham whose death also took place, so that, albeit very quietly, the death of the actor led to the death of the character, as had happened with the actor Eddie Robinson, and the character Simon Cooper, Dan's right-hand man.

Our anxieties were finally dispelled – if only for a time – by a news item that appeared on 1 January 1962. We were able to begin the second year of our second decade with rising spirits.

1962

THE YEAR OF

The crisis in Cuba, when centigrade was first used in weather forecasts, the last trolley-buses ran in London and Marilyn Monroe died aged 36. A French referendum approved the Algerian peace settlement. Coventry Cathedral was consecrated. Eichman was executed in Israel. Telstar was launched, bringing live television from the US to Europe. Dr Nkrumah was made president of Ghana for life. Europe had a hard winter; the snowstorms in England were the worst since 1881.

IN AMBRIDGE

The farmers' co-operative idea was giving Dan headaches, as his partners seemed to have less go-ahead ideas than he and Phil had. Paul Johnson's sister, Sally, married Tony Stobeman, and Paul and Chris moved to Newmarket. The perennial nuisance of sheep-worrying recurred, and did nothing to improve the tempers of Dan and other local farmers. The Grenvilles' son and heir, Richard, was born.

No better New Year gift could have been received by any cast of a daily serial than the news we read on New Year's Day 1962, giving the results of the *Daily Telegraph* annual Gallup Poll: ' "The Archers" voted best on Radio.' For the fifth year in succession readers of that newspaper had voted our programme into first place, beating such programmes with vast followings as *Round the Horne, Housewives' Choice, Family Favourites* and the still-running *Any Questions?*

We were relieved and heartened. It would give a false impression, though, to say that we were smug. Every five years or so, as has already been shown Messrs Baseley, Mason and Webb would take a detailed and, as far as possible, detached look at the programme, and gently but deliberately bring it up to date.

Members of the Cast were told, sometimes at great lengths and in writing, that their performance needed to be modified in order to fit in with proposed developments; and from time to time some characters were removed and new ones brought in — on one occasion, as has already been mentioned, a whole new family.

So long as the main characters, especially the central members of the Archer family itself remained, the listening public seemed to take these changes in their stride. Even well-liked characters like the Lawson-Hopes, the Fairbrothers and Paul's sister Sally were all edged out, without offending our listeners.

The main team remained intact, though, and events had shown that the programme's momentum was such that even bitter blows like the death of Harry Oakes did no great permanent harm.

But June of this year brought a serious blow of a very different order: one of the two original scriptwriters, Geoffrey Webb, died in a road accident.

Writers of daily serials are shadowy figures to most radio listeners, even today when listeners are much more knowing than they were during the first dozen or so years of the life of The Archers. If in the early days, the writers as people made little impact on the public, while their writing made an enormous impact, it was, I believe, because secretly half the listeners didn't want to believe that anyone wrote the thing at all. They wanted to believe in it as 'real life'.

Edward J. Mason and Geoffrey Webb, known to us all as Ted and Geoff, were invited to write The Archers after their successful collaboration on *Dick Barton — Special Agent*. It was inevitable, I suppose, that we should know Ted the better of the two. Not only did he live in Birmingham where the programme was usually recorded, but a few of us had performed in some of his other radio scripts.

Geoff Webb seemed, at least geographically, more distant. Although he had both written and produced radio serials before, he was never, I felt, at his best with actors. He was a countryman and had little time for actors' shop-talk. His earthy commonsense, his slow speech, still carrying hints of his Gloucestershire origins, and his enormous frame made him at times daunting. For many years most of us saw him only occasionally, when he came to Birmingham for Scriptwriters' Quarterly Meetings or for special occasions. One or two of us met him when we were doing topical inserts into the programme from major agricultural events like the Royal Show, Smithfield, and the Dairy Show.

However, in the last year or two of his life, I got to know him very well for a reason not connected with The Archers.

From the beginning I had tried to continue my career as a writer and so, once it became clear that TV like sex was here to stay, I attended a three-month course in London on writing for television. It was organized by the British Screen Writers' Guild (which was eventually merged into the Writers' Guild of Great Britain) and Geoff Webb was one of the lecturers.

Having met him there, the ice was broken, and whenever he came to Birmingham, or whenever he happened to be in London where I was then living, he showed increasing kindness towards me and an interest in my work as a writer.

Then, early in 1962, I suddenly began to receive highly amusing and lengthy letters from him, the first of which almost casually mentioned that he was in hospital south of the river. He then telephoned me and begged me to visit him. When I did so I could see at once how starved he was of congenial company, and I stayed talking to him so long I got back to Broadcasting House for a recording with only seconds to spare.

He was in hospital 'for observation'. Although obviously far from well, it seemed that his doctors could reach no satisfactory diagnosis. They had even, to his comic indignation, sent him for a course of interviews with a psychiatrist. Now anyone – apart from his doctors – who spent more than five minutes in his company could see at once that anyone in less need of psychiatric help it would be hard to find. With great glee he recounted his adventures: how the dark-fringed Mittel-European lady with horn-rims and stopwatch would ask him silly questions to which he instantly replied with silly but witty answers. Although I was supposedly visiting a sick man, I spent some of the most entertaining hours of my life with him. It so happened that my own life was far from sunny at the time, and his high-spirits and outrageous humour were a great tonic to me.

He left hospital, after an operation, and returned to his wife and family in the country; and I for one was certain that he would soon be back in his tremendous stride in full vigour. Few people had more zest for life. I remember his picking me up one very frosty morning in London to go to a recording in Buckinghamshire. We discussed the freezing temperatures of the previous night.

'I'll tell you how I beat the cold,' he said. 'I'd got a script to write and it was getting late, so I stuck an orange with cloves, poured a bottle of port and a bottle of brandy into a saucepan, with a handy measure of brown sugar, and got it nice and hot. I soon got warm after that!'

Incredulously I double-checked. Yes, it was true. Unaided, he had drunk the whole mulling!

Sometimes his scripts seemed more artless than Ted's, occasionally crude and, at first reading, apparently less well-written. But once spoken aloud by actors in character, they came to life, as down-to-earth as a ploughshare and as authentic as a duck-pond.

Our friendship scarcely had time to grow before I had one of the worst shocks of my life when I switched on the news on 21 June 1962 and heard that Geoff had died. It was unbelievable: I had been so sure that he would make a complete recovery. Then it was revealed that he had been killed in a head-on crash with a furniture van. He had sold his old Rolls-Royce, which he loved because it was built on the same solid and expansive lines as himself, and bought a brand-new pale-blue Austin Princess. His son Kit, then a schoolboy was beside him, and survived with only slight injuries.

It all happened within a day or so of his returning home from hospital where, between treatments, he had continued to write his stint of scripts for The Archers. Many another man would have taken greater care, eased himself back into his normal routine and not, perhaps, have ventured to drive again quite so soon after leaving hospital. But Geoff, who was only forty-two when he died, wasn't like that: he enjoyed life too much to spend it like a convalescent, chair-bound and wrapped in a rug. He was a Rolls-Royce of a man, a lion of a man, a carthorse of a man. His loss to the programme was incalculable.

If playing one of the leading parts was a great strain, writing The Archers in those early days was, if anything greater. Each writer wrote, completely unhindered, twenty episodes. He then rested, or wrote other things, while his fellow-writer wrote twenty episodes. They met only occasionally, with Godfrey Baseley, often for two or three days at a stretch, visiting farms, market-gardens, estates, getting mud on their boots and ideas in their heads. After much argument they would finally agree on a line of development for the programme for the next few months and then return to their widely separated homes to write. Each writer had complete freedom to invent characters and situations as he needed them: the only proviso was that the main lines of the story should be followed. No matter how far the writer's invention took him from the agreed plan, all was forgiven if at the end of the stint of twenty episodes, the characters were back on the guide-lines.

So, for the first eleven years, only three minds had moulded the creation of the world of The Archers. The technique which Ted and Geoff had developed when writing *Dick Barton* had been adapted for The Archers. With *Barton*, every episode ended with a cliff-hanger, the three Friday nights of the twenty-episode stint with an even tenser cliff-hanger and the fourth Friday night saw Dick in an even more impossible 'impossible position' than on any of the preceding nineteen episodes. This was the point when one writer handed over to the other, who proceeded to extricate Dick Barton from the impossible situation, and then at once begin to involve him in nineteen more crises until episode twenty; then in turn, that writer could hand back to his colleague.

The disadvantages of this method are obvious: the strain of sustaining twenty episodes non-stop is considerable. In length it is the equivalent of a four-hour radio play.

There are, though, advantages. One month of intense work is followed by a month of rest. But far more importantly, a stint of twenty episodes gives the writer's imagination full rein and incidents can grow naturally and organically, so that the every-day story appears to flow, rather than run the risk of seeming to be contrived on a stop-start pattern.

Undoubtedly, writing a serial is no easy task, even when one has helped to create the characters oneself. But the idea of bringing a newcomer into the team, who was probably not nearly so well-acquainted with the material even supposing he knew it at all, was – to say the least – not conducive to main-taining the same high standard.

But another writer *had* to be found. For weeks Ted Mason nobly carried on, writing script upon script, until he, too – and unfortunately not for the first time – began to show signs of nervous and physical stress.

Some time before, a young Midland writer called David Tur-ner had written five fifteen-minute radio plays about life in the Birmingham of his childhood. They were called *Agincourt Street*.

It so happens that I had known David since we were under-graduates at Birmingham University. Indeed, ironically enough, I had given him his first acting part as Ferret, the fierce but friendly university porter in a free-treatment of the *Charley's Aunt* farce, which another undergraduate and I had written as a Degree Day play.

After graduation he turned his back on life in the theatre, and had been teaching. He began writing in order to supplement his pay, and quickly started writing for television and the stage, as well as radio. He won a £500 prize from the BBC for an original television play (*The Train Set* – still regarded by some as his best work) and wrote in succession three plays for the stage, one of which *Semi-Detached* reached the West End and made his name.

It was clear that he was unlikely to specialize in writing for radio as Geoffrey Webb had done, and although he described being a regular scriptwriter for The Archers as 'at least a fairly honest job of work', it seemed from the first to be too restricting for him. So it was decided that the writing-team should be extended to three. The decision was easy: finding a suitable and willing writer was not and could well take some months.

In the meantime, the three thousandth episode was celebrated. Among the many thousands of words written about it, were some in the *Radio Times* for 19 July 1962, headed 'Norman Painting, known to millions for his portrayal of "Philip" looks back over 3,000 episodes of THE ARCHERS'. A more surprising celebration perhaps was a six-column spread with photographs in the *Daily Worker*. The tribute was surprising – apart from one or two predictable comments, like 'Everyone works for their living in Ambridge, though some are more highly rewarded than they should be . . .' or 'Here are no evictions, no rows over overtime, no closed-down railway stations, no strikes, no real clash between the big farmer and farm labourers'. (How interesting that as recently as 1962 a Communist newspaper could refer to agricultural workers as 'farm labourers'!).

The writer seems at his most political in the short paragraph about unions: 'Trade unions are not neglected, but are kept in their place by the device of making the union secretary, shepherd Len Thomas, a moody introspective type, whose union activity can easily be explained in Freudian terms.' We rather liked that!

But far more startling is the warm tone of the whole article, beginning with the remarkable claim that while ten millions of people were listening to the three thousandth episode of The Archers, 'Television screens scowled black and neglected'.

The rest of the article is an extraordinarily generous appraisal of the programme. Here are a few of its comments:

'Townsfolk listen to it, and, contrary to the opinion of some of its detractors, so do country folk . . . Country people, their problems, their world, have never been so consistently portrayed to so many of their fellow-citizens. This is not to say that The Archers is the Truth, but it makes farming peak-listening matter for the whole nation.'

The article concludes, after admitting that 'one cannot help admiring the skill' with which topical inserts and technical material are handled, and the acting ability of the Cast, with a very fair judgement of the programme at this time:

'Its faults are plain to anyone who is socially conscious, and its virtues are clear to anyone with a taste for the little dramas of everyday life. Indeed, it is stage-craft applied to life, with an extra dab of make-up for the rough spots. It is near enough to reality to be believable – but not too close to be uncomfortable.'

From the very beginning we have at times been touched and delighted to find that we have friends and admirers in the most unlikely places!

Several of us made another TV appearance at this time, in a programme called *Twist*, compèred by that nice man David Jacobs. The 'twist' dance was all the rage, and a team of Archers vied with a team from *Z Cars* to see which was the more expert. Alas! *Z Cars* were better twisters than we were!

By September, no third writer had been found, and the editor of the series, confusingly described as Gordon Baseley in the *Daily Mail*, explained the difficulties. A new writer would have to learn the background of the characters right back three generations, their interests, their foibles, and their impact on other characters. 'That means 3,029 episodes to plod through.'

Members of the Cast reading this news item in the Green Room made rather pointed remarks in my direction. After all, I spent (at least in theory) five days a week pursuing what has always been my main line of occupation, that of a writer. I had three books in print and was producing a continuous flow of radio plays – in spite of a working week much reduced by personal appearances, photo-calls and the other inevitable distractions associated with the life of a radio 'celebrity'.

No official approach was made to me however, and I certainly didn't mention the matter myself. It seemed that I was of more use to the programme as a performer; there might well be problems if one was both writing and acting in the same programme. Apart from which – and I admit it now to my shame – I was not attracted by the prospect of writing a radio serial. With hindsight I can say that not only was I totally unaware of the extreme difficulty in writing to such a restricted form, but I also felt that I was 'not that sort of writer'.

When in October we learnt that a novelist, John Keir Cross, whose name was also very well-known through some memorable radio scripts, had agreed to join the team, there were no more nudges from my fellow-actors for a time.

John Keir Cross was an extremely experienced writer and radio producer. His adaptations of John Masefield's *Box of Delights* in *Children's Hour* were vividly remembered by many of us, and he had published several novels and written screen plays. A writer of his reputation was a valuable addition to The Archers team, and confidence was restored.

We still made headlines, often to our bewilderment. Readers of the *Sunday Citizen* on 28 October 1962 may have wondered what could possibly lie behind the heading: 'The Archers fight . . .'

It was, in fact, one more 'investigation' into 'another of Britain's favourite TV and radio series' . . . but at least we were still there at the top.

Not that the article was entirely accurate. Remarks about dialect seemed somewhat uninformed, and the assertion that there has been a Welsh and an Irishman in the programme but never a Scot is not correct. Dr MacLaren, though never very vocal, had been there for years; Angus the stockman was a very braw Scot, played among others by both Laidlaw Dalling and Andrew Faulds (before he became even better known as a Member of Parliament); not to mention Andrew Sinclair. Accurate or not, the point went home. John Keir Cross was a Scot, and Andrew Sinclair gradually became an important character.

Although the article parades various criticisms 'artificial mateyness . . . which makes you feel sick' . . . 'an impression of village life that can be too realistic', the keynote is still favourable.

More significant, though, is the list of other programmes being 'investigated'. *Emergency Ward 10*, *The Rag Trade*, *Z Cars* . . . We were still in good company.

1963

Harold Macmillan resigned and Sir Alec Douglas-Home (previously Lord Home) became Prime Minister. President John F. Kennedy was assassinated, and Harold Wilson became leader of the Labour Party on the death of Hugh Gaitskell. Unemployment figures were the highest since 1947, and it was cold: 5 March was the first frost-free night in Britain since 22 December. Pope John died and was succeeded by Pope Paul. The Christine Keeler affair, and the Great Train Robbery in which £2.5m was stolen, made sensational headlines. Dr Adenauer retired after 14 years as Chancellor of the Federal German Republic.

IN AMBRIDGE

The disappointment of Len Thomas at not being sent to manage Grenville's Welsh Hill Farm caused him to ill-treat his wife, Mary, and indulge in rabble-rousing among the farm-workers. Ambridge won the Best Kept Village competition, and the event of the year was the marriage of John Tregorran (who had overcome his despondency following Carol's marriage to Grenville), to the district nurse, Janet Sheldon. Only months later, Janet was killed in a car crash when being given a lift home by Grenville, who was badly injured, losing a leg.

The year 1963 marks for me the time when those of us who had been for so long at the centre of The Archers, began to feel slightly uneasy when giving interviews to the Press.

Since our tenth anniversary we had all begun to feel that the honeymoon was, perhaps, over; like all who climb to a high point, we developed a healthy awareness that we might easily fall.

We may even have been put on our mettle by Ellis Powell's

removal from the part of Mrs Dale – a character she had played from the outset – and the treatment which the Press gave to that story.

Criticism of both our programme and our performances had so far been muted, and on the whole favourable and constructive. But we were increasingly aware of a new approach in the treatment of the private lives of so-called celebrities and we had no reason to believe that we should be treated any differently.

It was with some trepidation that Gwen Berryman allowed herself to be interviewed by Barbara Anne Taylor for the *Daily Express*, especially when told that the idea was to see how secure the uncrowned queen of The Archers felt now that the uncrowned queen of *Mrs Dale's Diary* had been toppled from her throne.

She needn't have worried. Gwen, who is often as surprised as anyone else to hear what she is saying, was on form and the interview produced an amusing and sympathetic write-up of 'the cosy lady with the home-made apple-pie voice' who would like to have married a man like Dan Archer, but who is terrified of cows!

We were still of interest to the daily press, and gradually we were receiving the attention of weightier publications. After all, The Archers was then, as it had been from the beginning, an entertaining programme with a deadly serious intention: that of interpreting the problems of the countryman to the townsman and imparting facts and policies to the farmer in the cause of greater productivity. A long and thoughtful article in *New Society no. 29* for 18 April 1963 analysed the proportion of education, information and entertainment in The Archers and, with statistical tables, considered the impact of the serious content of the programme on different sections of the population.

The writer of the article, Peter B. Stone, recognized one of our scriptwriters' basic tricks: brevity and apparent casualness. The fact that Dan was changing his milking methods in order to save manpower was mentioned and dismissed in fifteen seconds, 'and one of the two characters present did not disguise his lack of interest'. The two characters were in fact Dan and Ned. If Ned had said: 'Ah yes, boss, Good idea. Chap down Penny Hassett way got hisself a herringbone parlour and he swears by it. Says it's saved him pounds' etc. etc., the didactic purpose would have shown through. Ned's apparent disinterest – after all it was the boss's problem, not his – was not only true to life, it turned what might have sounded like plain propaganda into an apparently conversational remark. Yet the point about milking methods was made.

Finally, in discussing the audience's belief in the reality of the programme, the writer went on to say: 'At least, it is to the BBC that the wreaths, the flowers, the bits of machinery, the packets of seed are sent, not to Ambridge. There is a limit to the imagination.'

Some of us can give the lie to that. For years we received letters addressed to our character names at our fictional addresses, at 'Ambridge near Borchester'. Some laconic postal official usually wrote 'Try BBC' on them, and it worked!

Early in June, the Chancellor of the Exchequer, Mr Reginald Maudling, opened a special exhibition at the Royal Exchange in London to highlight Britain's eighth Dairy Festival. Press reports abounded, with details of his speech, facts and figures about the dairy industry, and the problems of milk production. All serious and important stuff indeed; but the headline? It would appear that the *News of the World* was using the same technique as we were using on the air, for the report is headed not 'Chancellor Opens Dairy Exhibition' but 'Why the Archers are in town today'! And the first word was . . . Ambridge! The solid and sober facts about the dairy industry are sandwiched between the first word and the account of the chancellor's visit, which ended with a visit to a mock-up of *The Bull*, where he met Dan, Doris and Jack.

An interesting sidelight about this period in the story of The Archers is the fact that public interest in the programme seemed to be as great as ever, even though 'unpopular' events were taking place in Ambridge itself.

Most listeners, as I have said, wanted Carol to marry John, and many listeners disliked the overbearing, wealthy, high-powered landowner Grenville. So the writing-team took a calculated risk. They would do the opposite to what the public wanted – at least for the present. So Carol married Grenville and John Tregorran married Janet Sheldon (played by that fine actress and delightful person, Judy Parfitt).

We usually received our scripts on the Friday before the week's recording sessions so that we could become familiar with them; but one day in October, Judy Parfitt arrived to record an episode without having received her scripts, which must have gone astray in the post. She was given a set of scripts and sat down to study them. Suddenly she gave a smothered scream:

'My God!' she exclaimed. 'They've killed me!' Then, with an endearing mock-serious smile she added: 'Well, they might have told me!'

That was the first step towards the marriage of John and Carol. And if it came as a shock to the actress, apparently it came as even more of a shock to some of our listeners. Under the headline 'BBC kill Janet of "The Archers" ', the *Daily Telegraph* reported that 'the BBC received thirty-five telephone calls from listeners who said they were "shocked". The character Janet Tregorran was "killed" in a road accident and instead of the signature tune the programme ended in silence . . . just as it did after the death of Grace, eight years before.

But in killing Janet in a car crash, the writing-team was treading a razor's edge between contrivance and credibility, for the car was being driven by Charles Grenville himself — the only other obstacle between the marriage of John and Carol.

The *Guardian* and the *Daily Express* carried simple reports of the incident: 'Complaints over death in "Archers" ' and 'Archers row'.

The two London evening papers went further. The *Evening News* stated: 'The Archers pose a big question: What will happen to Grenville?' and went on to reveal that today's bulletin on Grenville 'was that he was "very seriously injured" '. Tony Shryane was reported as saying that the story had been planned some weeks previously and could not be influenced by public protests. The number of phone calls received was increased to thirty-eight, and then the paper declared: 'At one time Grenville's wife (*née* Carol Grey) was on very friendly terms with John Tregorran, and not a few of the programme's ardent followers were hoping for a union. But it was not to be. Now, if Grenville "dies", the possibility again presents itself.'

Note the use of quotes for the word 'dies', which contrasts oddly with the almost factual reportage of the first part of the item, as if Grenville were as real a person as 'a BBC spokesman'.

The *Evening Standard* took a different line. 'Who, I asked the BBC today, killed the pretty blue-eyed Janet Tregorran? . . . I eventually tracked down the real criminals to a private meeting in a large Victorian mansion on the outskirts of Birmingham.'

The writer's imagination is beginning to take flight: he is clearly referring to one of the regular scriptwriters' meetings which on this occasion must have taken place at Ted Mason's comfortable house in Harborne. But I interrupt his flow.

'It was there, on a rainy day earlier this year . . .' (It had to be a rainy day, I suppose. I wonder who, if anyone, remembered that?) . . . 'that the decision was taken. The ringleader was Mr Godfrey Baseley, described as an editor, who is said to control the destiny of Ambridge.

'Mr Baseley, seething with blood lust, demanded a death soon. He had already been responsible for the ritual burning of Grace Archer in 1955 and the accidental slaying of a poacher a few years later. But he was still not satisfied.

'Only one of the other men, described as scriptwriters, disagreed.

'He was tortured with cunningly designed cynicism and ridicule until he came round to the majority viewpoint.'

What is worth noting is the fact that the subject itself should be of interest. As if it mattered who was responsible for the incident! The motive for spending so many column inches does not seem immediately obvious. Even the cynical view that it was a passage inspired by a publicity-keen theatrical agent re-representing the actors and actresses involved in the espisode does not stand up: no actor's or actress's name is mentioned in the item.

The writer does refer, however, to 'that strange, meandering thing called the BBC mind' and perhaps here is the clue. The BBC as an institution still exerted an extraordinary fascination; the day was yet to come when the veils would be rent and the Corporation would begin to be called Auntie.

Readers who are unfamiliar with the facts about actors' lives may feel that the 'killing' of a character, thus depriving an actor of a job seems brutal if, as is so often the case, the actor has no other engagements booked. With actors, though, unemployment (or 'resting' as it is called) is an accepted occupational hazard. Very few members of the Cast of The Archers have been in guaranteed regular employment in the programme: the profession does not work that way. The BBC in general, however, has a very good record indeed for finding other engagements for actors who, because of the needs of the story, have been removed from long-running series; and wherever possible, the actor concerned has been given advance warning of what was about to happen.

The hard fact is, however, that actors rarely have job-security: they are aware of this when they decide to try to earn their living in this way and no one should be surprised that actors' trade unions feel justified in striving continually to improve conditions of work and rewards. An actor's success can sometimes be the reason why he is later unemployed: certainly those of us whose voices have become very well-known know that our chances of other radio work are substantially reduced. When one's timbre and inflections are so familiar, it is difficult to disguise one's voice, and to play 'character' parts without producing – with rare exceptions – an uncomfortably artificial effect.

It should also be recorded in passing that the decision to 'kill' Janet, and the timing of it, were far from arbitrary. People rarely do anything from a single motive: the writing-team were no exception. It so happened that Judy Parfitt was becoming increasingly in demand for film and TV work, and therefore not available to record the required number of scenes as the recently-married Janet Tregorran. The truth behind this 'death' lies far from 'blood-lust', but somewhere between subtle plot-making and expediency.

When, a few years later, I joined the writing-team, I was often amused by the wild imaginings of the Press over some development of the story, for which the reasons were often mundane – amused, but glad that they still took notice of us.

The apprehension which I mentioned about our treatment in the Press was heightened as the year went on. We heard that the *News of the World* was proposing to do a series of articles about us, and that their reporter, Weston Taylor, would be spending a great deal of time with the programme. In other words, it was to be what is now called 'a study in depth'.

When Mr Taylor appeared he impressed us all at once as an amiable and well-briefed journalist. He had certainly done his home-work. 'I know you all refer to the editor by the first syllable of his christian name' was his cheery opening gambit. It was curiously disarming.

Yet we felt that we couldn't afford to relax. He certainly didn't have the air of someone looking for sensational scandal, but we all had a secret; and it was that we wanted to keep, as it were, in the family.

I mention it now, at this distance, because it illustrates two points: one is the fact that life in Britain was still far from the easy-going thing it is today and criticism of the private lives of individuals could still be damaging; and the other is that it demonstrates the extraordinary loyalty of the whole team.

Our secret was a romance between two important and much-loved members of the cast. We knew that they planned to marry; and that this would mean a divorce.

Today there wouldn't be any risks, if such a divorce were publicized; in fact, it might even be considered to be 'valuable publicity'. The dictum attributed to Mae West that there is no such thing as bad publicity, and that it's better to be looked over than overlooked, was certainly not acceptable then. The lamented death of the first Dan Archer had not materially affected the programme, but for his successor to be involved in divorce proceedings might shatter the carefully nurtured image of the programme.

The hearing and the decree nisi were duly reported in the national press early in December, and the words 'The Archers' were included in the brief factual accounts. But whereas today I feel certain that the Press woud have felt themselves failing in their duty if they had not treated the whole matter in the most spectacular way, the Press for some reason gave it the minimum of attention.

We were relieved, and delighted, as much for our two friends who were touchingly and overwhelmingly in love, as for ourselves.

And when that series of articles appeared in the *News of the World* they were lively, but restrained, critical but fair, and professional without being slick. They ran for five weeks from December to January; and in the spirit of the Christmas season they were human, domestic and wholesome — just as The Archers at its best has always been.

1964

THE YEAR WHEN

Harold Wilson first became Prime Minister, and Ian Smith became Prime Minister of Southern Rhodesia. August Bank Holiday was moved to the last Monday in the month. BBC 2 opened, and the Shakespeare Quartercentenary was celebrated. Lord Beaverbrook and Mr Nehru died. Donald Campbell broke the land speed record with 403.1 mph and the water speed record with 276.33 mph. The new Forth Bridge, the largest suspension bridge in Europe, was opened. The Pope made a pilgrimage to the Holy Land. Malta became independent. Harpo Marx died. Dr Martin Luther King won the Nobel Peace Prize. Mr Krushchev was replaced by Mr Brezhnev and Mr Kosygin.

IN AMBRIDGE

P.C. Albert Bates replaced Geoff Bryden as village constable. Walter Gabriel went into partnership with Bill Sawyer and Mrs Turvey in the Pet Shop, and also became a maggot-breeder to supply bait for anglers. Sid Perks, after a scrape with the police, came to the village and was employed by Jack Woolley as chauffeur and general odd-job man at the Grey Gables Country Club. Sid, anxious to go straight, was distressed when an outing to Hollerton Fair with his new girl-friend, Polly Mead, was ruined by some of his old associates.

For five Sundays in succession, right through the Christmas season and into the New Year, the *News of the World* published what it called the 'never-before-told story of The Archers of Ambridge'. Naturally, the well-written series held few surprises for us. We had heard whispers that the doings of Ambridge were occasionally overheard in Buckingham Palace and Clarence House. We knew that high-level civil servants were consulted in formulating the future plans for Ambridge farming. Monte

158

Crick had told us himself how impressed he'd been at meeting the then Prime Minister, Harold Macmillan, who had chatted knowledgeably about farming.

The series ended ominously, with a phrase of Harold Macmillan's: 'A wind of change' it said, 'is blowing through Ambridge.'

This ostensibly referred to changes in the programme itself, including attempts at solving the perennial problem of introducing younger characters.

Behind the scenes, though, we were far from relaxed. A distinguished BBC official in London had expressed the opinion that we were sounding tired – and immediately action was taken in Birmingham. All concerned would probably now agree that it was not perhaps the most appropriate action: it was to extend by half a day the amount of time taken to rehearse and record the programme.

Like every other repertory company, we had our union representative, and soon the BBC's single proposal led to continuous discussion about fees and working conditions generally and, inevitably, an uncomfortable situation soon arose.

Most of us felt that our salaries were fair, without being generous, but not large enough for most of us to save for the time when there might be no programme to record. We had no pension and therefore no security. The so-called 'permanent' contract could be terminated at a month's notice, and from time to time we saw this happening to various members of the cast. My own contract had been ended in 1960 for example, but 'Philip' continued to appear – less frequently, of course, and on an *ad hoc* basis. All this was perfectly normal practice and some of us were a little uneasy when told by union-minded colleagues that we were being 'exploited'. The older and better-known characters after all had a limited number of perks: fees for public appearances at bazaars and fêtes and the occasional television engagement.

What we did find increasingly intolerable though were the conditions under which we worked. The only place where we could sit, while waiting to go into the studio to record, was a small studio, formerly used for broadcast talks, converted into a kind of Green Room. The floor area was less than a hundred square feet, and it had no natural light. If one person had a cold, we all caught it! When there were only a few characters in an episode, it was not too bad; but generally it was hot, crowded and stuffy.

We often thought of the contrast between our fictional lives in the open fields of Ambridge, or the airy kitchens of Brookfield or Hollowtree Farm, and the smoky debilitating airlessness of what we came to call 'The Black Hole of Calcutta'. Hardly surprising, someone suggested, if we did sound tired! We were starved of oxygen.

We realized that there was very little the BBC could do. A room with a window was made available (when it was not being used for other purposes) but, as most of us understood, conditions could hardly be expected to improve until the new premises were built.

It was a long wait, but worth it. At the splendid broadcasting centre at Pebble Mill Road we now have conditions which equal the best in the world.

There was, however, an entirely different reason why we might, on occasion, sound tired. It was not, as had been suggested, that we had become lazy and hadn't studied our scripts. That criticism could perhaps be levelled at one or two members of the Cast, but not the majority. When your contract can be ended 'a month from this moment' you cannot afford to 'free-wheel', however dull or small your part may seem to you; and most actors, like most free-lance writers, know this. The knowledge that you are as good as your last performance, and that there is no pension or golden handshake, is quite enough to send the adrenalin rushing.

But, as the programme had gone on from year to year, it was inevitable that new performers would be introduced and, as many well-known and highly experienced radio actors admitted at the time, working with The Archers was a rather hair-raising experience. The old hands knew each other's work inside out: we felt the timing of lines almost instinctively. Scenes between favourite characters were frequently punctuated with *ad lib* reactions, which were rather disconcerting to an outsider. Even more importantly, those of us who now counted the number of episodes in which we had appeared in the thousands, had enormous advantages over a newcomer. We merely had to adjust to the dialogue and situation: the character had been fixed years before. The newcomer had to find the right voice and approach for the new character as well as all the other technical problems of radio acting like waiting for cue-lights before speaking or moving nearer to or further from the microphone.

Inevitably, Tony Shryane who is a perfectionist, would rehearse and rehearse the new characters until the old hands had progressed way past the peak of their performance. Therefore often the new boys had got it right at the expense of the freshness and spontaneity which the old hands had learnt to produce in a very short time. Far from being casual and careless, we were, in fact, over-rehearsed. But, as Tony would be the first to agree, we seem throughout the life of The Archers to learn something all the time; and it is now accepted that extra rehearsal time does not necessarily produce a better product in a radio serial when dealing with a highly experienced cast.

The storm in a tea-cup – for it was no more – subsided. In spite of press reports that suggested otherwise, we never threatened to 'strike', nor was there any confrontation with the hand that fed us. In fact, after a little compromising all round, we settled down to one of the happiest periods in the life of the programme.

Changes were made, of course. Attempts were made to read significance into the termination of the contract of Bryan Kendrick (Nigel Burton) who, as it happened, had been our Equity representative. But other contracts, too – Anne Cullen's (Carol) for example – were ended at the same time, in accordance with the requirements of the impending story-line. But the termination of such a contract did not mean that the character would not appear again. Indeed both Bryan and Anne continued to appear, the former until his death six years later, at the early age of forty, and Anne's performance as Carol went on as before as a regular ingredient in the programme's mix.

Combining the ingredients of that 'mix' is one of the most taxing of the writing-team's problems. Age, sex and social status have to be balanced carefully: include too many men or women, too many 'posh' accents, too many 'rural' accents, and the final concoction is unsatisfactory.

Those listeners who in spite of all the evidence like to think of Ambridge and The Archers as real, are probably totally unaware of the many factors which influence the story they hear.

The most important of these is the programme budget. The writing-team is not, of course, told how much money they may spend: their brief comes in terms of the number of character appearances they may include in each episode. The actors are of two kinds, as indicated above: those on 'permanent' contract, who are paid a fixed salary and may, if required, be used in every episode; and the *ad hoc* artistes who are employed by the episode.

The number of artistes on 'permanent' contract has varied over the years from as many as a dozen to, for an experimental period, none at all. Considerations which govern the number are, of course, mainly financial: it is more economical to employ characters which are frequently used on the 'permanent' contract, and this weighs heavily. In fact one of Tony Shryane's greatest achievements – and one unknown to the outside world – is his iron grip on the spending of money. A writer has to make out a very good case indeed to use even one more artiste than the average budget allows.

So, if a story is going to involve, say, Nora McAuley for at least three months, then the actress concerned, Julia Mark, will be offered a 'permanent' contract for three months. If on the other hand, it looks as if fewer appearances of that character will be needed, then she is booked as and when required.

Listeners are often surprised to learn that some of their favourite characters are not employed on 'permanent' contract. Characters like Doris, Walter Gabriel, Phil, Woolley and Peggy have of course all been engaged in the past on a long-time basis; but in recent years have appeared mainly as '*ad hocs*'.

The term '*ad hoc*', especially when used as a shorthand term for 'an actor booked on an *ad hoc* basis', often seems strange to those unfamiliar with the system. Writers can be heard using the jargon quite casually: 'I've used all the permanent Cast in this episode, I'll have to get a couple of *ad hocs*!'

I only mention this because it gives me a chance to record a splendid spoonerism perpetrated by Ted Mason when casting was being considered. He meant to say, 'We'll have to get a few *ad hocs*.' What came out, to his surprise and our delight was, 'We'll have to get a few odd hacks!' – no way to talk of Archer actors who, as Ted was the first to admit, show a high level of expertise. He was in so many ways the most generous of men and, if he found a particular performance pleasing made it his business to tell the actor or actress so personally.

It will have been seen already that throughout its long run, The Archers has had its fair share of problems caused by non-availability of members of the Cast: illness, death, resignation on marriage, or for other domestic reasons like raising a family, opportunities in other fields, or even for extended holidays.

And so, as we do not live in an ideal world, the writers of The Archers, and indeed any other serial, cannot write the precise story they want: modifications have to be made to fit the budget and the availability of performers; and, on occasions, a story projected by the writers has not been approved by the 'top brass'.

The listening public, on the other hand, often criticize certain twists and turns of the plot without understanding the various pressures which have forced it to be written as it was.

From time to time, listeners who think they could write the programme better send in samples of dialogue or even whole scenes. Not all are totally without merit; but the majority, almost without exception, could never be used on grounds of cost alone.

In 1964, the newly re-formed writing-team of Mason, Keir Cross and Turner, under Baseley's watch-dog eye, were well-versed in the art of contrivance. David Turner, the junior member of the team, admitted, in a talk which he and I gave jointly at the English Club of Birmingham University, that he found the restrictions of writing for The Archers both challenging and stimulating.

The narrowness of the form did not seem to worry Ted Mason unduly; he more than readily decided to stay with The Archers, even when faced with tempting offers. The *Guardian* for 23 September 1964 under the heading 'Loyal to Archers' reported that he had declined an offer to help write a new serial being planned by Associated Television. It was to be called, *Crossroads*. Ted is quoted as saying: 'You cannot serve two masters at the same time. Apart from the disloyalty, it would drive one round the bend.'

He remained loyal to The Archers, with all its difficulties and in spite of his failing health, until he died, declining the frequent and various offers which sought to woo him away.

For years, the Press had tried to make stories out of the imagined rivalry between *The Archers* and *Mrs Dale's Diary*. It was inevitable that both 'families' met on occasions and we always found them as friendly and pleasant as any other cast of actors. It was not unknown for us to record in London for short periods, and the sight of Harry Oakes and Ellis Powell – or 'Luggie' as she was always called, the original Mary Dale – drinking happily together in the BBC Club was by no means rare.

When Jessie Matthews took over the role, it seemed only a matter of time before we should meet. It so happened that our studio in Birmingham was due for a complete overhaul and modernization, and so from November 1964 The Archers was to be recorded in London. (We always thought of Studio 2 in

Birmingham as 'our' studio, though it was in fact also used for a steady output of other radio plays and features. Studios 1, 3 and 4 had been converted for television, and Studio 2 became the only radio drama studio.)

We had expected to be in London for some months; in the event it was to be nearly two years before we returned.

Someone had the idea that the senior serial should welcome the junior serial to London, so the Dales (who had first been heard in 1949) gave The Archers a party in the Council Chamber of Broadcasting House. The Press were invited, keen for 'stories'.

The *Daily Mail* had already got in first with a piece on 25 November saying, 'Now Mrs Archer meets Mrs Dale', explaining that we had been 'evicted' from our Birmingham studios.

The new Mrs Dale, Jessie Matthews, was quoted as saying: 'I'm looking forward to meeting The Archers. I listen to their Omnibus edition every Sunday morning.'

Gwen Berryman, as frank as ever, on the other hand, had to confess that 'I'm afraid I'm not a fan of the Dales. I never remember to put their programme on when I'm at home. I'm always busy, usually with housework. But of course, I'm dying to meet them.'

Perhaps it was not surprising that after the party itself some of the papers took a different line! '*Dales* man David pops question to Polly', was the headline over an alleged proposal of marriage, with a splendid photograph of David Owen, Mrs Dale's son-in-law, to Polly Mead, then barmaid of *The Bull*. The actor, Lee Peters, said: 'I've known Hilary for some time. But with both of us working on a daily serial, we seldom get a chance to meet.'

The actress, Hilary Newcombe, said: 'It is all a bit sudden. I haven't said Yes – I need some time to think it over.'

And so far as I know, that is all that was ever heard of it.

'Said Mrs Dale, the former musical comedy star Jessie Matthews: "It has been marvellous meeting our 'country cousins'. I think we ought to get together more often." '

Oddly enough, it was five years or so before we did!

1965

THE YEAR WHEN

Great men died: W. Somerset Maugham, Albert Schweitzer and Winston Churchill. Alexei Leonov became the first man to float in space. Sir Alec Douglas-Home resigned as leader of the Conservative Party and was succeeded by Edward Heath. There was a ban on television cigarette advertising. The 'Queen's Award to Industry' was introduced. BP struck oil in the North Sea. The Pope addressed the United Nations Assembly. Parliament passed the Bill abolishing the death penalty for murder. The 70 mph speed limit on British roads came into force. Westminster Abbey celebrated its 900th anniversary and the memorial service for Richard Dimbleby was held there.

IN AMBRIDGE

The news of the death of Grenville in America rocked the village. Phil's attempts at teaching Doris to drive were unsuccessful, and Doris was unable to share the driving when she and Dan with Fred and Betty Barratt went on holiday to Ireland. Fred Barratt retired, and Ambridge Dairy Farmers Ltd became Ambridge Farmers Ltd, with Dan and Phil alone working together.

Our second decade continued its diurnal round: the usual two hundred and sixty episodes were written, edited, cast, rehearsed, recorded and transmitted. Tapes of each day's episode were flown to broadcasting stations round the world, and our writing and recording schedules were geared so that a given episode could be on tape at least one month before its date of transmission.

One of the questions we are asked repeatedly is prompted by a confusion created in the mind of the listener by learning that radio and television programmes are often recorded many

165

months in advance, and then hearing topical up-to-date material in The Archers.

Those of us who have been there from the beginning can remember occasions when scripts for the following day's transmission could not be studied by the actors because they had not yet been written! But once the programme was to be heard overseas, the programme had to exist in recorded form about one month from its broadcast date. In the most part, that situation continued from the mid-fifties throughout the programme's run to date.

There are two opportunities, though, for making really up-to-date comments: in the introductions to the Omnibus edition on Sunday morning, when Tom Forrest chats about the country scene, and the weather, about the world of Ambridge and the world in general; and in 'topical inserts' which have already been touched on earlier in this book.

Tom Forrest's introductions are normally recorded some five to ten days before they are broadcast. 'Topical inserts' are short topical scenes which can be written and recorded within a few minutes of the actual time of broadcasting.

I have already explained the hazards of making topical additions to the programme 'live', while the fifteen-minute recorded disc was actually being broadcast.

The adoption of tape instead of disc made topical inserts very much easier and virtually undetectable: the new topical 'scene' which can be as short as a few seconds or as long as required, is recorded on tape, from the same studio using the same microphone and acoustic conditions as the original. The equivalent number of minutes or seconds of tape are cut out of the programme, and the newly-recorded scene or part of a scene is inserted in its place. For all the listener can tell, the whole episode may have been recorded that very day.

The shortest topical insert I can remember making was just six words, in 1959: '... now that the rain has come ...', which were sufficient to give added immediacy to talk of plans for harvesting crops. On the other hand some topical inserts, such as the one on the day after Polling Day 1974, discussing the General Election, were three or four minutes long.

There has, from the beginning, been one other way of giving apparent topicality to a script, no matter how far ahead it was written. This involves the use of advance information. The dates of major agricultural and similar shows, for example, are often announced as much as twelve months ahead. At the very least, mention can be made of them, but in fact scenes can actually be set at such events. No reference can be made of course which will give proof positive that the episode was apparently recorded that very day – only a genuinely topical recording can do that – but the trick is one which, if carefully employed, can give a heightened sense of 'actuality'.

A slight variant of this, which was employed with great success in the early days of the programme, was the use of official 'hand-outs'. Our editor, who always kept closely in touch with the Ministry of Agriculture, National Farmers' Union and other important bodies whose work has some direct influence on the countryside and the farming scene, would be told if certain official notices were being sent out to farmers generally. These could vary, from forms needing completion and return, to important notification concerning changes in government regulations. The two factors of prime importance were that such material was being sent to most, if not all, farmers in the country and that the date of posting could be guaranteed.

It was then quite simple for a scene to be written in which Dan or Phil, like every other farmer in the country, received his copy of the official notification on the same day.

Any farmer, therefore, having received his copy that morning, and in that day's edition of The Archers hearing Dan or Phil receiving theirs, could not escape a feeling of inhabiting the same world. And so this striving for topicality became more than merely an attempt to sound 'up-to-date'. If well-handled, the sense of reality was heightened and, in addition, that essential feeling of audience identification was fostered.

The most obvious example is the Royal Show. This is timed to fall between hay-harvest and corn-harvest (sometimes, however, the weather can play tricks and ruin the theory). Most farmers tend to feel less under pressure during the first week in July, and so many of them take a day off and go to Stoneleigh.

Most years, between one hundred thousand and two hundred thousand visit the Royal Show, where they have a chance of meeting anyone who is anyone in the world of agriculture, as well as fellow-farmers of all ages and styles of farming, from the modest to the wealthy. It can therefore fairly be described as a typical activity for a farmer, and in most years some member of the Archer family has been there.

In the topical inserts that are recorded and transmitted from the showground, mention is made of facts that could only have been gleaned on that very day, and not beforehand, however trivial; and at once a new dimension is given to the programme. Not only does the farmer feel that he is doing the same thing as The Archers, but the converse is also true: The Archers are doing the same things as he is.

Not that these topical incidents have always met with unqualified praise. On Budget Day 1965 – Tuesday 6 April – Godfrey Baseley and Ted Mason were fed the Budget details as they were announced (there was no radio and television marathon programme in those days) and after brief discussion, Ted Mason, in a matter of minutes, wrote a script which was approved by Godfrey Baseley and then checked and approved by a senior BBC official. Copies were then brought to the waiting Cast, who recorded a scene giving the main points of the Budget, with typical comments and reaction – typical, that is, of the characters they played. Half an hour or so later, listeners heard, as they had done so many times before, the inhabitants of Ambridge discussing the details of the Budget, long before the economics experts began pontificating.

Most listeners probably noticed, almost sub-consciously, that here were the Archers, up to date as usual and, taking that fact for granted, paid attention to the details of the plot. But one listener, Mr David Weitzman Q.C., Member of Parliament for Stoke Newington, was far from pleased by what he heard and according to the *Sunday Express* for 11 April 'accused the BBC of a serious breach of their duty to deal impartially with controversial issues! He has sent a copy of the script to the Postmaster-General, Mr Anthony Wedgwood Benn.'

The editor of The Archers denied political bias. He said: 'The characters who were commenting were a farmer and a publican. What Dan and Jack said were the sort of things any farmer and publican would have said just after the Budget.'

And there it might have ended. But, as had been discovered years before, when Edwin Gooch, M.P., had said: 'The Archers are helping the Tories' (and by so doing caused the BBC to forbid members of the cast to appear at any political function), politics spelt trouble.

A week later the *Sunday Times* produced, in the politics column, an article called 'Umbrage over Ambridge', complete with a photograph of Godfrey Baseley, captioned: 'Baseley: a liberal at heart.'

Mr David Weitzman, Q.C.'s complaint that the Ambridge

reactions to the Budget were 'blatantly biased against the Government', is repeated, with the news that on the day after the broadcast he asked the Postmaster-General to direct the BBC, under Section 14 (4) of its Licence and Agreement, to drop 'views on public policy which have no foundation in fact in fictitious, dramatic serial programmes'.

The P.M.G.'s reply appears to have been brief and non-committal: the BBC's duty was 'to treat controversial subjects with due impartiality'.

This, as the writer of the article points out, may not be easy, when the views of characters like the Archers are more influential than those of real people.

All this discussion of politics came, I believe, as a surprise not only to most of our listeners, but also to the Cast themselves. The greatest care had always been taken in day-to-day episodes to remove or soften into ambiguity, any line which might conceivably be thought to have a political meaning. And the topical inserts were vetted with even greater care. Taking part in one of our scenes commenting on the result of a General Election was like walking a very thin tight-rope: no pause or inflection was allowed which might be interpreted as being in the least partisan.

Many must have been surprised to read the next paragraph of the article:

'Just what are the political opinions of Ambridge? Godfrey Baseley, originator and editor of the programme, admits that with a six million weekly audience, they have considerable propaganda power, but says opinions must be held if characters are to be more than cardboard cut-outs.

'They are all known: Dan Archer is a Right-wing Tory because his father was – and Doris goes along with him. Phil is a semi-intellectual Socialist. Jack would vote where his fancy took him, Ned Larkin Left, and Walter Gabriel, like Baseley himself, is a Liberal at heart.'

One can imagine quite a few raised eyebrows among readers of that newspaper on 18 April 1965. 'Well, well, well,' one could imagine them saying, 'you learn something new every day!' We certainly did!

Mercifully, the programme was not subjected to further probing of a political nature, though a headline in the *Daily Sketch* three weeks later might have given that impression: 'Dan Archer pips the BBC news', it ran. This matter, however, was not political.

At this time, the daytime repeat of the programme was from 12.40 to 12.55. But on Friday 7 May a fault developed in the transmitting equipment and the episode began five minutes late. It was followed by the time-signal, and then the weather-forecast, and finally at five-past-one the news-reader apologized before reading the *One o'clock News* by saying: 'Because of an unfortunate technical fault, everything at the moment is running five minutes late.'

There was, of course, no connection between that incident and an announcement that was made a few months later to change the pattern of lunch-time listening. But nonetheless, from 4 October, it was announced the *One o'clock News* would be incorporated in a new programme called *The World at One*, and the repeat of The Archers, instead of being heard at 12.40 would follow *The World at One* at 1.30.

Thus was established a pattern which carried the repeat of The Archers right through the ten years and more to its twenty-fifth birthday and beyond. *The World at One* made William Hardcastle a household name. When he died in 1975, The Archers lost a keen follower and a friend.

There was, in fact, a certain amount of protest about the change of time. 12.40 fitted in well with the lunch-break of most farm-workers. But the new times came into operation, as planned, on Monday, 4 October. The evening edition of the programme remained, of course, at 6.45 p.m. in the Light Programme.

Before this year was out, however, politics were to rear their heads once more, if abortively.

On 12 December 1965 the *Sunday Express* carried a head-line: 'The man the Archers shocked.' This turned out to be a prospective Labour candidate who protested both to the Post-master-General, Mr Anthony Wedgwood Benn and to the Minister of Housing, Mr Richard Crossman, against what he called, 'the most serious criticism levelled at the Government's Rent Act just before it was due to come into effect . . . The Rent Act itself was not mentioned, but the inference was that it was the source of all the misery in the particular case.'

Tony Shryane's answer seems to have been satisfactory: 'This was just a character's point of view – not propaganda.'

The Archers were still in the headlines on the very last day of 1965. 'They all copy The Archers' were the words that headed an item in the *Daily Mirror*, which recalled the summer when

Dan and Doris, together with a farmer friend and his wife, Fred and Betty Barratt, spent a holiday in Ireland as guests of the Irish Tourist Board.

These four members of the Cast really did tour Ireland, making recordings both in Eire and Northern Ireland. The producer, editor and two scriptwriters went along, too; and listeners were able to follow Dan and Doris and their friends as they visited famous beauty-spots and met local people.

This was one of those happy ideas which have several bonuses. First and foremost, the programme gained a welcome change of scene and accent: there were opportunities to compare farming in Ireland with farming in Ambridge, and in doing so to describe and evaluate both. Then again, the trip, though arduous, made a pleasant break from routine for the whole production team. And thirdly, which explains the headline 'They all copy The Archers', the Irish Tourist Board found that tourism had been stimulated by The Archers' trip, and requests had been received for details of holidays in Ireland from all over Britain and the Commonwealth.

The persuasive force of the programme was as powerful as ever.

There had been changes in the writing-team. The success of his play *Semi-Detached* with Sir Laurence Olivier and plans for further work for the stage and screen, had deprived The Archers of the services of David Turner, the previous year.

Once again the writing-team had reverted to the formula of two writers and the editor.

It soon became clear that another writer would have to be found, however, if only as a stand-by.

This seemed to be even more difficult than it was following the death of Geoffrey Webb in June 1962. There was even more back-history for a scriptwriter to study and those few years had changed the status of radio. Television was now king and sound radio was being somewhat patronizingly described as 'steam radio'. More than this, listening figures were falling; the attitude both of the press and of writers of letters to the programme was changing from laudatory to captious. Although there were only four years to the programme's twentieth birthday on 1 January 1971, there seemed reasonable cause for doubt that it might not last that long.

Apart from the inherent problems in writing for such a restricted and specialized form, a new scriptwriter could scarcely join the team at a less comfortable moment. I know, because it was me!

When David Turner left the writing-team, the inevitable rumours had started about a possible successor. This time, however, no public statements were made and it was decided not to decide on a new writer in a hurry, as both Ted Mason and John Keir Cross were expert and experienced writers and could be relied upon to keep up the supply of scripts.

The usual nudgings came from the Cast, but I was by no means certain whether I really wanted to write for a daily serial, even if I discovered that I was capable of it. For the previous fifteen years I had tended to write longish radio plays and features, several full-length stage plays and various, unsuccessful, teleplays. The shortest was thirty minutes: I had no more idea than anyone else of whether I could organize material on so small a canvas as fifteen minutes. And my being a member of the Cast was a complication.

However, no notable writer appeared anxious to offer his services and so it was decided to invite trial scripts from one or two possible writers. When asked, I agreed.

It was made clear that one was only being considered as an emergency writer and the briefing for the scripts was given exactly as it would be if for any reason one of the two script-writers were unable to write.

Weeks went by, and I continued to play Philip Archer and to pursue my career as a writer, busily making radio plays by adapting such novels as *Midwinter* by John Buchan and *The Little Girls* by Elizabeth Bowen.

Suddenly, in October 1965, the call came, and I was summoned to Godfrey Baseley's country home.

Since our argument in March 1951 over pay, Godfrey and I, while developing mutual respect, could not be said to be on very intimate terms. He had become remote as the fame of the programme had grown and had become, at least to some eyes, almost a benevolent dictator where the policy and both day to day running and long-term planning of the programme were concerned.

There was something of a feeling of entering the lion's den as I approached the cottage: but both it and Betty Baseley gave me a warm welcome. Godfrey was mowing the grass in a paddock below the house and I was sent to find him.

I remembered years before, giggling with fellow undergraduates at a Russian propaganda film in which a humble peasant stumbled upon kind fatherly Stalin busy tending his garden, with warm back-lighting and distant music. For a moment, the scene in Worcestershire reminded me of that moment in the Russian film. But on his own ground, Godfrey didn't bluster or bully, or wave his arms about or behave in anything other than a professional businesslike way.

He led me into his sunny study and at once the trial briefing began. I thought I was familiar with the past history of Ambridge and The Archers, but I could not but be impressed by the complete identification there was in the Baseley brain with every detail, not only of the farming scene, facts, figures, statistics, but also with every nuance of character.

I was required to deliver, within a week at the most, five scripts which were to be a continuation of the last week's episodes which had been recorded.

The briefing merely put me into the picture as to what had been agreed at the last scriptwriters' meeting for the long-term developments, and I was given details of how many permanent cast and how many 'ad hocs' I could use. And that was it.

The whole interview, including tea, had taken barely an hour; and as he saw me to my car, Godfrey expressed his fears for the future and the fact that, to survive, The Archers had got to be better than ever.

I motored back to London, planning episodes in my head, and began to write at once. Godfrey telephoned me six days later to say that the scripts had reached him safely and he said nothing else except that they would be considered.

It was some time before in his rumbling sort of way, Godfrey told me that my scripts had found favour, in spite of obvious faults which could easily be put right, and that I had been chosen as the emergency writer. It was to be some months before Ted Mason, generous as always, told me he thought my trial scripts were 'Bloody good, and it was a damn shame they couldn't have been broadcast.'

And there, for a while, it seemed to end.

The question of holidays is one that often seems to mystify some listeners. They hear the regular characters day in, day out, and few of them are heard to take regular or extended holidays. Tom Forrest always grudgingly takes a week off when the shooting season is over, and Dan and Doris have been on holiday in Ireland, Scotland and Jersey, among other places.

From very early on, once it was clear that The Archers appeared to be continuing indefinitely, a system was evolved whereby six episodes were recorded each week, although only five were broadcast, thus giving us one in hand. By the end of five weeks, therefore, we had five episodes in hand – a complete week's programmes. Obviously, by the end of ten weeks, we had two weeks in hand, and by the end of fifteen weeks, three weeks in hand. These episodes were then broadcast while we had a holiday.

Some members of the team have taken additional leave, however. Gwen Berryman, for example, was specially 'written out' as Doris for several weeks, so that she could visit the United States for a Soroptimist Conference on one occasion, and on another in order to visit relatives in South Africa and go on a memorable safari.

The reasons given by the writers to explain a character's absence are rarely as colourful as the actual reasons for the actor or actress's absence. The usual excuse is illness, either of the character itself or more often of a relative who needs attention. If Doris has to go away to care for a sick friend or relative, the writers make the most of the situation by showing all the preparations and the packing, arrangements for transport and for someone to look after Dan, with the inevitable delays and last-minute rushes. For a limited amount of time a character can be kept quite happily alive merely by allowing it to be talked about: eventually, though, the listeners realize that a familiar voice has not been heard for a few weeks and they write to ask what has happened. On one such occasion a listener wrote to ask why Phil had not been heard for a week or two and said: 'I hope he is not ill, but in case he is, I am praying for him every night!'

Bob Arnold, like Tom Forrest, is not given to taking long holidays; those he does take are during normal recording breaks. He has never been 'written out' of an episode, neither for health nor any other reasons. He has probably appeared in more episodes than any of us.

The system of building up reserves of one, two or three weeks of recordings continued when, later, we recorded more than five episodes a week: the same basic principle has been followed throughout the programme's run.

Before we reached our twenty-fifth birthday, however, the system and many other aspects of the programme had been altered, as will be seen in due course. Changes were inevitable and, not surprisingly, some were resented as changes almost

174

always are – whether for better or worse. What is remarkable to the impartial judge is that so much of the basic pattern of the programme, both on the air and behind the microphone, remains intact, unaltered and difficult to improve upon.

1966

THE YEAR WHEN

Dr Verwoerd was assassinated in South Africa and widespread destruction was caused by Floods in Florence. At Aberfan in Wales, 144 people, mainly children, were killed in the slag-heap disaster. Chi Chi, the London Zoo's Giant Panda, was flown to Moscow for union with An An. The Archbishop of Canterbury had an historic meeting in Rome with the Pope. The Prime Minister announced the Wage Freeze and the first British Ombudsman was appointed. S.E.T. came into force. The new Severn road bridge was opened. Harold Wilson and Ian Smith met, unsuccessfully, aboard HMS *Tiger*.

IN AMBRIDGE

Fire-raisers were at work again: this time not teenagers out for casual kicks, but a determined, methodical arsonist, who turned out to be the mentally unbalanced, Frank Mead, Polly's father. Jennifer Archer, training to become a schoolteacher, first showed her writing talent: a short story was accepted, a novel contemplated – and Jack Woolley commissioned her to write a history of Grey Gables. Grenville's estate was taken over by Jack Woolley in partnership with Ralph Bellamy, a man with strong local connections, though he had been farming in East Anglia. Valerie Trentham married Jack Woolley.

Early in 1965, an entirely fictional event had once more made the headlines: 'Squire Grenville is dead.'

The papers spoke of him as having been 'killed off', although he appeared to have recovered from the serious injuries he had sustained in the car crash when Janet Tregorran died. He had lost a leg, but had quickly mastered the use of an artificial limb.

Now, if Carol was to be free to marry John, we all knew

that sooner or later he would have to go. But in daily serials, the secret of building-up listeners' interest is to find means of extending an intention without appearing too obviously to be drawing it out.

So the writing-team sent Grenville to America on business, which was fine – for the programme. In terms of work for the actor concerned, it was, however, rather bleak.

Week after week he waited: but months went by and he was not called upon to appear. Rents have to be paid, and failing to find other work as a radio actor (being a well-known serial voice can have its drawbacks), he finally took on an appointment making films. Then, inevitably, the writing-team wanted Grenville back. Michael Shaw, who played the part, had just committed himself to a new job.

I met one of the writers in the canteen.

'I do think it's unfair of Michael,' he said to me, 'giving us another problem like this.'

I found myself pointing out that he hadn't earned a penny for some months.

'Dear me!' was the reply. 'I didn't realize that!'

And indeed, why should he? This particular writer lived some distance away, and rarely met the Cast. So events for once played into the writing-team's hands; and Grenville died in America.

Now the field was at last clear for John and Carol. But as 1966 began, it was clear that much water was to go under the bridge before Ambridge would be hearing wedding-bells again.

There would have to be regrets and recriminations: there would have to be red-herring attachments, to panic the listeners into thinking that, after all, they might each marry someone else. There even had to be declarations that they 'could never marry again'.

The listeners lapped it up. This sort of very long-term story-line always seemed to pay dividends. It was of course always a kind of running background. For the method to work, the foreground had to be filled with incident and, as always, the writers made sure that this was so.

As a diversion, the consistently controversial question of fox-hunting was introduced – not for the first time. When one of those unavoidable technical breaks occurred during the transmission of one episode, in the middle of a discussion on the subject, at least one listener was suspicious: 'Is this another instance of that obvious bias, displayed by some members of the BBC, when alluding to certain controversial problems?' she asked in a letter to the *Birmingham Post* on 10 March 1966.

In reply a 'BBC spokesman' assured her that the break in transmission really was accidental and the programme was repeated in full the next day.

As the sixties went on, the attitudes of many listeners began to change. It happened slowly, but it became apparent on an increasing number of occasions. There seemed less willingness to accept the 'propaganda' element in the programme unless it was very subtly handled; and as performers, we noted that more and more 'fan letters' were addressed to us by our real names and not the names of the characters we played.

Nonetheless, when the four thousandth episode was broadcast on 27 May 1966, there was the usual crop of analytical, and still gratifying appreciative, articles about us in the press.

'Fantasy life down on the Farm', was the promising title of one such piece in the *Guardian*, illustrated with a picture of Bob Arnold 'in character' as Tom Forrest, complete with cloth cap and authentic dog and gun.

It began: 'If you want to start worrying about your identity, or wondering if the boundary between reality and fantasy really exists, do not go to the modern playwrights, poets and painters. Go to the village of Ambridge. If you get there, you will know that for you the thin line has broken – but not more so than for millions of others.'

The writer then went on to quote the ubiquitous 'BBC spokesman' saying that listeners 'deliberately suspend their disbelief to an extraordinary degree', and continued: 'This suspension is responsible for the fact that "The Archers" has survived for its 4,000th episode today without some Campari-drinking executive getting his knife into it.'

Those of us at the centre of the programme were beginning to feel that our most likely end would be not a whimper but a bang of the sort suggested. We found ourselves ruefully agreeing with each other that anyone wanting to make a name for himself in the BBC could do so by sticking a knife into The Archers. But the kinder letters from listeners, and Press comments like this long *Guardian* article, gave one the feeling that any executive seeking fame through killing The Archers might also have to take to the hills for a while, if he wished to avoid a lynching mob of some millions of listeners.

'Listeners tend to find the characters in the programme

more engrossing than the actual people around them,' the article continued, 'which may say something about the quality of the scriptwriters or, on the other hand, about the quality of modern life.'

And once again we are back to the usual discussion of truth and fantasy, how some listeners still believe that the Archers are real people, and the actors playing the parts receive baby-clothes when fictional babies are due, cards at Christmas and on their birthdays – and even proposals of marriage.

The fourth *Borchester Echo* was published in the autumn of 1966 and the *Guardian* article previewed its appearance, descibing it as 'a thoroughly professional-looking journal that tells you in banner headlines ("Ambridge woman accused in gems case") the latest news about people that don't exist.'

Truth and fantasy were mixed in an article written by Kenneth Bird, BBC Midland's Information Officer, about this time. He revealed that he literally dreamt the idea of publishing the *Borchester Echo* as early as 1953. In his dream he was working on a weekly newspaper and found himself reading the name *Borchester Echo* printed upside-down on the plate-glass window of the reporters' room. (Could he have meant 'in reverse' rather than 'upside down'?)

Next day he told Tony Shryane of his dream, saying: 'Imagine! Working for Britain's best-known non-existent newspaper.'

But as we know, truth and fiction tend to fuse where The Archers is concerned, and five years later, in 1958, Kenneth Bird found that he was working on the paper and it did exist. At least, one edition of it did! It sold over a million copies. In December 1959 a second *Borchester Echo* was published, selling over three quarters of a million, and a third in 1961 which sold over half a million.

With these steadily declining sales (!) it was another five years before the fourth was published.

Special photographs were always taken for each edition, and this entailed finding suitable locations and then transporting the various members of the Cast there to be photographed in costume against authentic backgrounds.

For the first ever edition, a picture of Phil Archer on his motor-bike was needed. There was one small snag: the actor who played the part – myself – had never driven a motor-bike and hadn't the faintest idea how to.

'No problem,' said Tony Shryane, in a confident tone which

convinced everyone, and proceeded to explain to me how childishly simple it was. Minutes later I found myself flying across a field towards a small group made up of photographer, producer, editor, scriptwriters. I grinned at the camera and, scarf trailing in the wind behind me, shot on towards a stone wall. It was a grey misty Sunday morning, and we were on a farm deep in Worcestershire. Only then did I realize that Tony had merely shown me how to drive the thing along: the question of stopping it had been overlooked! I kept going, resolved to reduce speed somehow. Helpful advice was shouted in my direction, but I was too far away to hear. I ended up in a bed of brambles that grew near to the wall: somehow I had managed to stall the engine and leap off.

When my colleagues had managed to control their laughter, one of them said: 'Never mind. It should be a good picture. Good job it wasn't in colour, though. You looked as white as a ghost!'

The picture never appeared.

Photographs for the fourth edition of the *Borchester Echo* were to be in colour, however – at least the front and back pages were. So three days of photo-calls were arranged, starting ominously on Friday, 13 May 1966. We were all photographed in various agricultural, and other, attitudes (Jennifer was photographed in bed), but the main effort was devoted to a really splendid photograph of friends, relations and admirers at the 'wedding' of Sid and Polly.

No one had any inkling at the time those photographs were taken, that when the actual episodes dealing with the wedding itself came to be written, I was to be very much more involved with it than most people imagined.

There was an alarming headline in the *Sunday Telegraph* early in September – alarming, that is to the well over two million who still listened to the programme daily, in spite of the attractions of television: 'End of The Archers?'

Although the ostensible point of the piece was to comment on the story, then being featured in the programme, that Ambridge was threatened by large-scale development, the writer was equally speculating on the possibility of the programme being taken off the air. Gone were the days of unqualified praise: the programme was described as 'a joke to the occasional listener, mannered and contrived with its farming hints'. But he went on to concede that 'The Archers yet wields a remarkable holding power for almost anyone who tries following the story . . . if the serial is to die it will not be of monotony.'

There was no sign yet though of any great falling off in public interest. Newspapers and magazines all over the country continued to publish pieces with such titles as 'The Archers are such real people', 'The Echo is the only thing that's tangible', (the *Borchester Echo* of course), and 'The "girl" who is Lilian Archer – mother of two and 26' (a sympathetic feature on Elizabeth Marlowe).

The success of the programme brought with it attempts to imitate it; and in October, some journalists had fun writing about the possibility of a South Vietnamese version of The Archers. The head of Radio Saigon, former deputy chief of the Air Force psychological warfare department, visited the production unit, and talked to Cast, producer and writers.

He said: 'With a programme of this nature, much useful information could be put across.' Ted Mason agreed: 'When Dan Archer started his radio farm he had only two horses and a hand-plough and built up from there. I suppose the Vietnamese could build up with their own characters. But somehow I can't quite imagine old Dan discussing warble fly in the paddyfields.'

The *Observer* reported the same incident the following week with a neat back-hander: 'The Vietnamese want to find a new way of making agricultural propaganda, and they reckon that this 16-year-old steam-radio serial is the world champion at doing just that.'

Propaganda or not, the BBC did not decide to end the programme. Instead, it was transferred from the Light Programme, with its mass audience, to the more selective Home Service. Many connected with The Archers feared that this indeed might be how it would be ended.

They were, happily for many of us, proved wrong.

Back in the summer, on 6 June 1966, the *Sun* had reported considerable consternation about a complaint made by Dan Archer over what he thought was short-measure in his beer. ('Rumpus over Dan Archer's Pint.')

Polly, the barmaid, explained that his glass was not filled to the brim because it was one of the new 'line' glasses used for electric beer pumps, adding that these would become required by law in August.

The landlord of a pub called *The Cottage of Content* in Herefordshire, complained to the BBC and was dissatisfied when told that he was correct in saying that a mistake had been made and that a scene would be included at the end of the month putting things right. 'They should make a public retraction now,' he insisted, 'otherwise hundreds of pounds might be needlessly spent.'

At least one person in the country clearly felt that the influence of The Archers was undiminished! And he had a point. 'July 31', he explained, 'was the date when the new standardized optic comes into operation . . .' (the device for automatically measuring spirits from the bottle) . . . 'The point is that so many people, particularly in the country, take what they hear in The Archers as gospel. I spoke to one old country landlady and she was worried stiff about the expense she thought she would have to go to in buying the new glasses.'

The information was carefully checked and on 30 June the facts were presented correctly to, one hopes, everyone's satisfaction.

But the incident illustrated afresh the persuasive power of the programme, its continuing reputation for topicality and authenticity — and it reminded the writing-team how great their responsibility was in checking, and double-checking, their facts.

The old 'family feeling' amongst the Cast was once more clearly demonstrated when Tony Shryane married Valerie Hodgetts who had been with the production team since May 1951. Valerie has an encyclopedic knowledge of not only the 'mythology' of The Archers, but also of almost everything to do with the production of the programme. Her memory is almost photographic, recording names, addresses and telephone numbers of people in the real world and in Ambridge!

At their wedding, Ted Mason was best man and, like the groom and the bride's father, made a witty speech; while as both a founder-member of the Cast and an old friend, I made a short speech and presented Tony and Val with what has become one of their most cherished possessions — a silver salver on which the signatures of the whole team are engraved.

Most of the Cast as well as editor, writers and BBC officials were guests at the wedding, which had all the warmth and sentiment of a real 'family affair'.

Many who once formed part of the 'family' team, as actors, writers or technical staff have gone on to greater heights. David Turner the playwright, performers like Mary Wimbush, Judy Parfitt, Robert Chetwyn, John Dexter, Andrew Faulds and Alan

Rothwell, production staff like John Clarke, Michael Ford, Graham Gauld, Michael Gilliam, Barry Lankester, Richard Maddock, all now distinguished BBC producers or directors — and these names are but a random selection.

An important event occurred for me when on 8 June 1966, the telephone rang in my London flat. The caller, brusque and distant, had to repeat his name several times before I could hear who it was. It was Godfrey Baseley. 'We may want you to do a bit of writing for us. John Keir Cross is in hospital. We'll get in touch.'

A week later I found myself in Ted Mason's comfortable house in Harborne, Birmingham, ready to discuss the six scripts I was to write. By the end of the afternoon I had agreed to write nine, the first three of which would be planned and cast by Ted, who would also write a synopsis of the plot of them. After that, I was on my own.

Suddenly the telephone rang. It was Valerie Hodgetts in The Archers office at Broadcasting House saying that the billing for my scripts was required at once for *Radio Times*.

Ted's phone was in the hall just outside the sitting-room where we were having our meeting, and Ted's face appeared round the door saying: 'What name are you going to write under?'

When I looked momentarily blank, Godfrey said that it had been decided that, as I was also a performer, it would be better to write the scripts under a pen-name.

Now it so happens that I had been using a pen-name for part of my radio writing since the early fifties, but somehow I felt that I didn't want to use that. I had, however, previously registered with the Writers' Guild another name which I had concocted but so far had never used, and I found myself saying it out loud, half-apologetically.

'What?' said Ted.

I repeated it with a note of query.

Godfrey said it out loud: 'Bruno Milna. Bruno Milna. That's all right. Bit odd. But it'll do. Why not?'

'How d'you spell it?' was Ted's long-suffering question; and as I pronounced each letter, so he repeated it for the benefit of Valerie at the other end of the phone.

Throughout the winter, I had attended a course called 'Modern Farming' at an evening class in London, feeling that, as I was now an emergency writer for The Archers, I'd better try to learn more about farming. I also tried to think of a pen-name, in case it was decided (as indeed it was) that I should not use my real name. Nothing more inspiring than 'George Farmer' and 'N. P. Kay' came to mind (N, P and K are the chemical symbols for the three plant foods, nitrogen, potassium and phosphorus).

Then I remembered how I'd arrived at the name 'Bruno Milna'. I am always being asked why I chose it; numerous people have read dark things into it and many have contrived to believe that it is an anagram with outrageous possibilities! So I feel that in a book celebrating a programme with which I have been associated for over a quarter of a century as performer, and for over ten years as a writer (and for which I have written, as Bruno Milna, well over a thousand episodes) I must put on record the true, if seemingly preposterous reasons for the name.

The christian name Bruno commended itself to me in Venice; some years later I invented the surname Milna on a day-trip from France to Spain by bus.

Having known a Venetian family for many years, I have often spent holidays in that unique and magical place, and was taken to a swimming-pool run by a Venetian aquatic club and frequented mainly by local people. As I sat day-dreaming at the edge of the pool, a charming but rather over-ample girl swam towards me, and brushing the rat-tails of her dark gamine-styled hair out of her eyes mistook me for her boy-friend. 'Oh Bruno, Bruno!' she cried in a tone that was half pleading, half remonstrating, 'Bruno!' She was clearly short-sighted. Her wide round eyes attempted to focus on me. 'Sei tu, Bruno?' I murmured with some regret that I wasn't, though I should have been quite pleased if I had been. 'Oh, scusa', she cried, and before I could say another word, or offer to deputize for her errant boy-friend, she had swum away.

'What a pity I wasn't Bruno!' I thought. And then it occurred to me that one day I might be. Then the dancing *charivari* of Venice with all its opulent distractions drove the idea to the back of my mind.

Later, when taking a holiday in Port Vendres in southern France near the Spanish border, I bought on impulse a ticket for a day's excursion into Spain visiting Rosas, Figueras and Cadaques. As the coach sped along the highway we passed a continuous line of hoardings, spaced at intervals in fields along the road-side, bearing the single name 'Osborne'. I knew of course that this was the name of a famous Spanish wine house

— so well-known indeed that it didn't have to say so, but used merely the single word, just as over here we might use the word 'Guinness'. But as the names flashed past, repeating the same name, I skittishly thought 'John Osborne must have a good publicity agent!' (This was shortly after the enormous success of *Look Back in Anger*.)

Then I realized that most of the Spaniards I had heard tended to pronounce B as V in certain words. 'Hard line,' I thought, 'Osvorne isn't what the bright new playwright would expect to be called.'

So, to while away the rather tedious coach-trip (I'd quickly realized that the excursion was a mistake: I'm not a day-tripper at heart) I started to invent names which might stand some chance of being pronounced without alteration in most European languages. It was a kind of mental doodling, purely to pass the time. Several possibilities presented themselves; and then Bruno popped up from the back of my mind. So I started to choose a name that would match and chime in euphoniously with it. Undoubtedly, the combination that pleased me most was Bruno Milna.

I could see at once that it had a sort of Common Market look about it, especially ending in 'a' . . . but 'er' would have been given too much stress in some languages. Not that it really mattered! The whole thing was purely academic. I had no prospects of anyone from foreign parts ever wanting to pronounce my name, so the whole thing was of little importance; but it whiled away the journey.

Curiously enough, however, that name clicked. I have forgotten the other outlandish-sounding names I'd concocted, but that one stuck. Only half-seriously did I register it with the Writers' Guild as one of my pen-names. But suddenly, here was an occasion where a totally new name was needed, so Bruno Milna saw the light of day.

Some people, and I agreed with them, said it didn't sound particularly like the name of a writer of something as essentially English as The Archers. But, with Ted Mason on the phone wanting a decision that minute, it was done almost before its suitability was seriously considered.

What soon emerged was that not only was it a pleasant-sounding name, but it was also easy to say. More than that, it was easy to remember: it stayed in people's minds. I have been amazed how often people get it right and how rarely it's anglicized to 'Milner'.

One BBC publicity man hated it and begged me – much too late – to change the spelling. It was on the grounds, which I found hard to follow, that if spelt Milna he could guarantee me no publicity but if spelt Milner there could be many more opportunities. Luckily I was never very keen on publicity, for more than one reason and, anyway, I felt that it would be foolish to change the spelling once the name had appeared in *Radio Times*. I think that was the right decision.

1967

THE YEAR WHEN

Francis Chichester completed his global circumnavigation and came home to be knighted. Donald Campbell was killed on Coniston Water, trying to break his own waterspeed record. Harold Wilson and George Brown were in Rome for Common Market talks. Jo Grimond resigned as leader of the Liberal Party and was succeeded by Jeremy Thorpe. The Queen received Mr Kosygin at Buckingham Palace. The *Torrey Canyon* disaster caused widespread pollution of the British coast. The 6-day war broke out in the Middle East. Colour TV began on BBC2. The people of Gibraltar voted to stay with Britain. The QE2 was launched. Lord Attlee died. The Road Safety Act, dealing with drink and driving – the 'breathalyser' – came into force. Che Guevara, the Cuban revolutionary leader, was killed. Sterling was devalued. The first successful heart transplant was carried out in Capetown.

IN AMBRIDGE

Jennifer produced the first Archer out of wedlock. Ned Larkin retired and became the village's jobbing gardener. He and his wife Mabel were living in Glebe Cottage; and Ned's retirement made Doris think again, to little avail, of Dan's retirement. Bellamy, who had a growing reputation as a lady-killer, surprised the village by employing attractive Fiona Watson to be his shepherdess – or, as she insisted on being called, his shepherd. John Tregorran finally married Carol.

My first three scripts 'by Bruno Milna' were recorded in London on Tuesday 28 July 1967. The Cast were enthusiastic, finding my dialogue as speakable as Ted's, which was flattering; and Tony Shryane the producer was encouraging.

And now I will make a confession – which I do not expect

anyone to believe, and if it's dismissed as fanciful I shall not be surprised.

For the first ten years, the scripts of The Archers were always described as written jointly by Edward J. Mason and Geoffrey Webb, and many people thought that they collaborated on each episode in the same way as Norden and Muir did on *Take it from Here*. I have already explained how the writing of the scripts was alternated, and although both writers' names appeared, there was a simple way of telling who had actually written a given episode (apart from reading it! Most of us quickly learnt to recognize the differences in the two writers' styles.) The first name was the name of the writer: if the script said 'by Geoffrey Webb and Edward J. Mason' then it was one of Geoff's. If it said – and this applied to all the writing they did together – 'by Edward J. Mason and Geoffrey Webb', then it was written by Ted.

This convention had been discontinued after Geoffrey's death and Ted did not work in quite the same close collaboration when it came to writing with either David Turner or John Keir Cross.

David was an individualist: in our joint talk to the undergraduates which I have already mentioned, he went on to say that not only was writing the serial a challenge, but an opportunity to experiment, 'just as old Bill Shakespeare did with a character called "Walter Gabriel Falstaff"'.

Inevitably, the old familiar characters in David's brilliantly persuasive hands, found themselves expressing views that were different from those they had held for the previous ten years or so, and very close to those of the author. We became almost Shavian mouthpieces: not easy to do, but if writing the serial was a challenge to David, performing it was a challenge to us. This was probably no bad thing at a stage in the programme's history when accusations of tiredness or complacency might be, and indeed were, levelled at us.

John Keir Cross's scripts were even more of a challenge. Not only was he a first-rate writer of thrillers, with a great gift for touches of the macabre, he was a Scot. In spite of the fact that he now had a farm – albeit in Devon where the local dialect is very different from the basic Midland of The Archers – his dialogue, though full of quirky life, had an unmistakably Scottish flavour to it.

It is no secret to admit now that most of the Cast found his episodes the most taxing. Nonetheless, by the time we had battled with them and subdued them, the results that came out of millions of radio sets were unmistakably 'The Archers'. I was soon to discover how much the writer of serials relies on the performance he gets from the actors. A line of dialogue may look perfectly acceptable on the printed page: spoken aloud it can sometimes sound flat, or flabby, or ambiguous or even found to contain a completely unsuspected *double-entendre*. An experienced actor can so handle a line that it fits the context naturally and draws no unwanted attention to itself.

When, shortly after, eighteen more of my scripts were recorded, a few people hinted that they could see more than a suggestion or two of Geoffrey Webb in them which, to say the least, was gratifying. The truth is that when I sat down to write those five trial scripts, wondering if I could do it or not, I found, within minutes, that it was almost like taking dictation. I could hear Dan and Doris and Jack and Peggy and Walter and Jill and Phil (yes, even Phil who suddenly appeared to have a life of his own quite unconnected with me).

There was another discovery too and this is the one I expect nobody to believe. As I wrestled with the tightness of the budget, and tried to manoeuvre the performances so that I would not use more than the approved number of actors, I found, on repeated occasions, that doing so sparked off ideas for scenes and plot-development. And sure enough, when I came to write those scenes, they came 'as easily as leaves to the tree', and seemed to me lively and in many cases amusing. And as I reached out and caught and put down on paper these ideas I was suddenly aware of Geoff himself, and I heard his laugh as positively as I heard the voices of Dan and Doris and the rest.

Fanciful? Self-deception? Wishful thinking? Up to this time I had written fairly slowly. Now, suddenly, I wrote very fast, at white-hot speed, and when I came to read through what I had written I was on more than one occasion surprised to find a broadness of phrase and rumbustiousness of character that were undeniably more in keeping with Geoff's style than mine had been up until now. Geoff too had written at great speed.

Whatever the explanation, I was grateful; and when anyone in the team spoke of finding in my scripts touches of Geoffrey Webb, I smiled, and parried the compliment; which I felt I scarcely deserved.

When it became clear that I would be joining the writing-team, if only on the edge at first, as an emergency, Tony

Shryane and his wife Valerie called at my London flat one evening after a recording of *My Word!*, and left me a folder of useful material. It was a complete eye-opener. There were Minutes of recent Scriptwriters' Quarterly Meetings, with details of forthcoming story-lines, some of which seemed oddly sensational and somehow inappropriate when couched in the terms of 'minutes', together with brief accounts of the main inhabitants of Ambridge, their addresses and farm-holdings. This was dated 11.10.62 and clearly was drawn up to assist Geoffrey Webb's successor.

I was of course familiar with the past history of the programme, but the item of future plot that hit me between the eyes was 'Jennifer's pregnancy'.

Even more surprising to me was my first experience of attending the Scriptwriters' Quarterly Meeting. These meetings, held alternately in London and Birmingham, were chaired either by the Head of Programmes in Birmingham or the Head of Light Programme, London: the Assistant Programme Head and Information Officer were also present, as well as the writers, editor, producer and his assistant who acted as secretary.

The dedicated and committed seriousness with which such items as 'Jennifer's baby' were discussed was a revelation to me. We in the Cast had always taken the programme seriously, but here were senior BBC officials who seemed to be taking it even more seriously. I now realize that one of the programme's greatest strengths has been the fact that it has always sought, and always obtained, the active support and involvement of those at the top. It has never been 'just another programme': its high standards have assured that its value and importance have always won for it the eager interest of the 'top brass'.

It so happened that the first of these meetings that I attended was the last at which the chair was to be taken by the Head of Light Programme. From the beginning of 1966, The Archers was to be transferred to the Home Service. A new era was opening and I felt glad that I had seen something of the way the old regime had run the programme, before working under the new.

The Head of Light Programme, Denis Morris, regretted the change of channel. The Archers had been launched under his guidance when he had been Head of Programmes at Birmingham sixteen years before and he shared the fears that we might lose our audience. It was officially estimated that a quarter of all the radio sets in Britain were permanently tuned to the Light Programme, and, as John Woodforde wrote in the *Sunday Telegraph*, their owners used 'only the on-off switch. Many of them will dislike having to change gear to listen to a 15-minute "Archers" episode.'

The quarterly meetings were always followed by lunch and, as this particular one was something of an occasion, Head of Light Programme made a speech. Addressing himself to the Head of Home Service, the mercurial, razor-sharp and smiling Gerry Mansell, he stressed his deeply-held conviction that The Archers was one of the most valuable properties the BBC had ever possessed. Though speaking informally, his words were witty and sharp-edged, not least when he spoke of two members present who always seemed to have opposing views, which he had often been called to arbitrate over, but who now, he felt, were perhaps beginning to think more kindly of each other. I was very amused to hear both the gentlemen in question hotly deny this! It was a moment of disarming candour.

So 1967 was going to begin with change and challenge, with a distinct chance of a greatly diminishing audience because of the channel switch, and with probably the most controversial story the programme had ever carried – a member of the Archer family becoming a beatnik and having an illegitimate child.

Then, just after mid-day on Sunday 22 January, the telephone rang. It was Ted Mason to tell me that John Keir Cross had died that morning at 5 a.m. My reaction was immediately 'Poor Audrey!' Although I had not met John's wife, he had often talked about her at our informal writers' meetings, when he, Ted and I piled into Godfrey's car and went round looking at farms and 'getting mud on our boots' – an activity which is still required of writers for The Archers.

Suddenly I was no longer on the edge of things as emergency writer: I had become one of the programme's two scriptwriters on condition, as Godfrey Baseley put it, that 'there was to be no nonsense about Philip Archer. We still want him in three or four episodes a week.'

Ted wondered if I could manage this. My reply, which seemed the only one to make at the time, was that, for an experimental period, I would undertake no other writing or acting commitments but concentrate solely on the one programme. It was agreed that this was to be the policy while the search began once more for a third or standby writer.

The writing-team travelled to the West Country for John Keir Cross's funeral and when we met at our agreed rendezvous before going to John's house to meet his widow, Ted greeted me with: 'Of course, you know who the father is, don't you?'

For a moment I was completely taken aback and didn't understand the question. Then I remembered that Ted and Godfrey lived and breathed, ate and slept the programme just as, before long, I too would be doing. There was nothing in the least irreverent about Ted's question: I just wasn't expecting it.

Although John Keir Cross had written many of the episodes dealing with Jennifer's state of mind and her refusal to name the father of her unborn child, neither he nor Ted nor Godfrey had decided who the father was to be, or even if it was to be a character who had appeared in the programme. But Ted, reviewing the events of past weeks and months in his mind on the journey down from Birmingham, had realized that there was one person who *had* to be the father. He was a man who was friendly with Jennifer, who was temperamentally capable of leaving her once he knew what had happened, who had, in fact, since gone from the village and who, as Jennifer had already said, was someone not interested in marriage. This obsessive twenty-four-hour-a-day absorption in the programme, as exhibited by Ted, was infectious and stimulating. I was soon infected and stimulated.

We drove to John's home for a buffet lunch provided by his widow. Suddenly Audrey said: 'John's study is exactly as he left it . . . I don't know if you'd like to see it?' Ted eagerly said he would. For some reason, the rest of us held back.

When he returned, there was a curious note of fellow-feeling mixed with foreboding in his voice. 'Just like mine,' he said with a wry smile. 'His desk's a hell of a mess.'

There was, for a moment or two, a sudden chill silence that nobody wanted before we went on our melancholy funereal way.

As we had expected, the story of Jennifer's baby proved very controversial. The writing-team had done its homework of course, and the story hadn't been introduced lightly. Jennifer was of an age, and in a social group, which had a very high level of illegitimate births. But would our listeners, especially now we were being broadcast entirely in the Home Service (our lunch-time repeat, it will be remembered, had been in the Home Service since 1964), accept this type of story?

We received encouragement from a rather unexpected source: in a maiden speech in the House of Lords! The *Daily Telegraph* reported on 23 February 1967, a debate on illegitimacy:

'Baroness Serota, in a maiden speech, congratulated the BBC for its "sensitive and courageous" portrayal of the problem in "The Archers".

'All of us who are Archer fans were happy last week to hear Doris Archer, the grandmother of Jennifer Archer, commenting on the impact of Jennifer's pregnancy on village life in Ambridge. In her own inimitable way she summed it up by saying: "A baby is a baby and that is all that matters."'

June Spencer, who had now returned to play her original role as Peggy Archer, received several letters from listeners, which put us right back to the beginning of our 'truth versus fiction' debates.

One ran:

'Dear Mrs Archer,
    Just a few lines, did you know that your Jennifer is expecting a baby in six months time I always listen to the Archer affair every day.
    Yours Archer Fan
P.S. Theres only three people who knows about it. the Doctor, The Vicar, and your daughter Lillian.'

Luckily there was no address, (although the writer had written Ambridge at the head of the letter and then crossed it out) so no reply was needed! How do you begin to reply to such a letter?

From Hove two sisters wrote to say:

'We sincerely sympathize with you for the terrible heartbreaking news you will receive from your Daughter Jennifer sooner or later; but you poor dear you have *really* guessed! as instinctly a Mother would; dear Peggy we are *very* sympathetic to you! a great Sorrow! maybe will lay you low! your parents the Archers will rally round you & Jack your Husband you will find hidden depths of love & kindness in him, as to Jennifer! I do not know what his *hidden* depth of character will do about her!! he may punish her beat her or lock her up in her room & she will have to accept it!! no good in brazenly not being ashamed! (if one is *not* ashamed

of *that*! there is nothing else worth being ashamed of! ..
find the father & *make* him marry her, is the only way to
peace & Happiness again in the Archer Family. deep Sympathy to you all.'

As if all this was not enough in itself, the actress who played
Jennifer, Angela Piper (her stage name) announced that she,
too, was pregnant.

When her son was born, the *Sun* printed a picture of her
with two-day-old baby Benjamin under the ambiguous heading: 'Fact catching up with fiction'. It also reported the confusion that had been caused in the village where Angela and
her husband, Peter Bolgar, lived, as the story of illegitimacy
became embarrassingly mixed with fact. The incident illustrated afresh the hazards of being an Archer.

The situation wasn't helped when one newspaper reported
that 'Jennifer's baby was conceived over a cup of coffee in the
BBC canteen by Godfrey Baseley and Ted Mason.'

June Spencer, whose son David was at the Rambert Ballet
School, was specially singled out by Dame Marie Rambert on
one occasion. Wondering what was coming, June was delighted,
amused and somewhat nonplussed when Dame Marie's first
words concerned the father of Peggy Archer's daughter's child,
rather than June Spencer's son's dancing career!

Not all our listeners reacted uncharitably or in a disapprov-
ing way about Jennifer's baby.

Angela Piper received more than one letter from people offering her a home 'if Jennifer should be turned out by her parents'.
One East End couple wrote most sympathetically, saying that
though they were poor, they would at least give her a roof over
her head and help her all they could.

Condemned or approved, the story certainly aroused considerable public interest.

Over the years, certain incidents in the life of The Archers
stand out as high spots: the birth of Anthony William Daniel,
the sheep-worrying incident, the death of Grace (which was
surely the peak), the murder charge against Tom Forrest, the
threat of building development which could ruin the face of
Ambridge, and then Jennifer's baby.

Great interest was aroused by major stories like these both
among listeners and in the Press.

'Back-stage' stories, while receiving a measure of coverage, never seemed to arouse nearly so much interest. There was, though, one sad exception.

Something happened on the morning of Monday 11 December 1967 that was reported in all the papers and on radio and television: one of the most popular characters ever to appear in The Archers suddenly died.

The word 'character' is apt: Bill Payne was a character, on mike and off. Once the character of Ned Larkin was established on the air, Bill Payne and Ned Larkin became one and the same. His authentic Cotswold accent had brought him early to the microphone, and he had quickly developed technical skill in reading from script. Never formally trained as an actor, his native intelligence which was of a high order, his mother-wit and his natural histrionic sense soon commended him to Midland regional radio producers.

He was a clown, a leg-puller, a joker, apparently contemptuous of authority while carefully conforming, his smile was broad and his laughter loud. It was of the 'he-he-he' variety, in which the shoulders shook until the eyes watered, rather than the 'ha-ha-ha' sort in which the joke seems to rumble in the stomach. His poker face was classic; he could, and did, tell wildly improbable stories with a look of such sober seriousness that even those who knew him would find themselves taken in, if only for a moment or two. Then the broad smile and the laughter would take over, and no one enjoyed the joke more than he did.

He was the darling of the scriptwriters. He was of course very easy to write for: Ned Larkin was a broad, credible character, a countryman with a fund of stories which were told in so digressive a style that at intervals he had to stop and say: 'Where wuzz I?'

His yarns nearly always concerned the mythical Coppy Treadwell, who became the vehicle for broader country humour and slightly larger-than-life anecdotes than it was otherwise possible to fit easily into the basic authentic atmosphere of Ambridge. Dramatically, of course, this broad folksy humour was invaluable: a couple of hilarious Ned Larkin scenes could lighten the toughest texture.

Throughout the whole world of the arts, contrast, it seems to me, is a fundamental quality: light, dark; fast, slow; long, short; funny, sad. A work of art, whether poem, play or novel, drawing or painting, musical work or photograph needs contrast to avoid monotony. And plastic arts like sculpture and architecture are themselves the embodiment of contrast: a created shape contrasted with the space around it.

A daily serial, if expertly written, needs the same basic rules as any other work of art, and high among them is contrast: of scene-length, subject-matter, pace, mood, character. Ned Larkin, both as himself, or yarning about Coppy Treadwell, was an invaluable means of achieving that essential contrast that gave life to any episode. His loss seemed irreparable: the character was, and remains, inimitable.

Some of us had known Bill Payne since the late nineteen-forties, and we had seen how the strain of being Ned Larkin twenty-four hours a day gradually wore him down. I occasionally caught him wincing with obviously agonizing chest pain; but the moment the spasm was over, he'd say, 'Don't you say a word about that to anyone.' The more his popularity grew, the greater his problems became. There were times at rehearsal when he almost seemed to be sweating blood, when coping with apparently interminable tales of Coppy Treadwell – long complicated speeches, which would tax the technical skill of an Olivier or a Richardson. It need no longer be any secret that he begged Bruno Milna to write him shorter speeches, or that the writer tried to oblige.

Bill died, as we all felt he would have wished, on his way to the studio. He was that day to have recorded some hilarious scenes of Ned and his wife Mabel moving into Woodbine Cottage on the Green. As they were scripts that I had written I was quickly telephoned; and by the time I reached Birmingham at lunch-time (I had now moved to the country mid-way between London and Birmingham) I had re-written the scripts, removing Ned from them, but using the other members of the Cast who had been booked and who were waiting in the studio. Here a curious numb stunned atmosphere lay like low cloud-cover over all. Kay Hudson, who had played Ned's harridan wife, Mabel, was red-eyed and bewildered: she was not the only one who had been overcome by tears.

No-one would expect to have anything but unhappy memories of a beloved colleague's funeral, but Bill's was among the most harrowing I have ever attended. I could not suppress the anxiety that this, perhaps, was at last the blow from which the programme might not recover. Bill Payne was unforgettable: Ned Larkin irreplaceable.

But the programme went on.

1968

THE YEAR THAT

Martin Luther King was assassinated and Vietnam peace talks began in Paris. British Standard Time was introduced. Senator Robert Kennedy was shot and died. Britain had the worst floods for fifteen years. Princess Marina, Duchess of Kent, died. The two-tier postal system began. The Theatres Act abolishing censorship came into force. France again vetoed British entry into the Common Market. The US successfully launched Apollo 7, the 3-man moon rocket. Richard Nixon won the US Presidential Elections.

IN AMBRIDGE

Most people were relieved when the Woolley-Bellamy housing development scheme was rejected. Peggy accepted the fact that Jack was becoming an alcoholic. Mrs P.'s second Perkins, Arthur, died. Jennifer and Roger Travers-Macy were married. Paul, after the failure of his feed-milling project, ran the local garage, with Sid working for him, but bad debts threatened his solvency. Nora McAuley and Gregory Salt were married.

The world, as always, went on and of course the world of The Archers went on, too. As in real life, we all felt in some way diminished by one man's death, in another the mere continuity of things was by its nature reassuring.

Our lives were to go on, changed and changing, and pleasant things, and some not so pleasant, inevitably lay ahead.

Anxious enquiries from my colleagues when I was wearing my actor's hat (I took great care from the start to make it quite clear which role I was playing at any given time) seemed to reflect the anxiety we all shared about the future. And yet I found myself repeating, whatever hat I was wearing, two simple facts which I believed implicitly. One was that if we survived the next couple of years or so, we might stand a chance of going on, as Ted Mason often said, 'for ever'. The other was, quite simply, that gimmicks and panic were useless. Our only weapon was quality: of conception, editing, writing, performance and production.

Late one Saturday night at the beginning of 1968 (it was in fact nearly eleven o'clock on 27 January) the telephone rang in my old country rectory home. No one normally rings so late in the country, unless there is some emergency. But this was no emergency, though there was a certain amount of cloak-and-dagger about the call. Having assured himself that I was Norman Painting, who writes under the name of Bruno Milna, the caller then announced his name and swore me to secrecy. I was fascinated, but mystified. It was John Lemont giving me advance notice, later confirmed in writing, that Ted Mason and I had been jointly awarded a Merit Scroll by the Writers' Guild of Great Britain for our scripts for The Archers written during the past year.

This was a much-needed boost to our morale. If our fellow-writers, who presumably knew the problems involved in writing a daily radio serial, had voted in sufficiently large numbers that our work was to be thus honoured, it could not after all be too bad.

Many, particularly those who do not win awards, are sometimes cynical about them: certainly both Ted and I were not swept off our feet by the honour.

But it would be less than honest to deny that it was a proud moment when at the Awards Ball in the Dorchester Hotel, Kenneth Horne called out our names, and we walked, in company with such writers as Harold Pinter, David Mercer, N. J. Crisp and Robert Bolt to the dais to receive our award. We allowed ourselves to feel that we had perhaps in the last year changed a situation of doubtful confidence into a more euphoric one. The tone of each succeeding quarterly meeting had become more optimistic, letters and official audience research results showed a renewed warmth on the part of listeners.

Even technical faults were of sufficient interest to merit headlines. 'Arr! It be a rare old clanger' said the *Sketch* on 29 November, using what is thought to be typical 'Archer' language, which is in fact so untypical of most of our dialogue. The *Guardian*'s paragraph headline was more surrealist or nightmarish: ' "The Archers" – backwards'!

What had happened was that on the Thursday in question, two reels of tape were put out ready: one contained the repeat of Wednesday night's episode, the other the Thursday night's episode. Unfortunately the wrong reel of tape was laced into the machine, and instead of 'last night's repeat', listeners heard 'tonight's episode'.

The presentation announcer made an apology over the air and 'an official at Birmingham' said 'This was human error.'

What some of us found interesting was that it was regarded as important enough to be noticed by the Press after all these years. It was, in a way, another 'first' for The Archers!

Just for the record, though, the Thursday episode was repeated that same evening and, confusingly enough, instead of hearing a repeat of Thursday episode on Friday lunchtime, our devoted listeners heard Wednesday's episode repeated.

The story gives a glimpse into the complexities of organizing the writing, editing, booking of artistes, rehearsal, recording, timing, cataloguing, storing and actually transmitting a serial like The Archers. Every year two hundred and sixty episodes are broadcast, each one repeated in full the following lunchtime and a slightly shortened edited Omnibus is prepared for Sunday morning. It seems remarkable that only once in a quarter of a century has the wrong episode been transmitted.

The feeling that being a member of The Archers' team was rather like belonging to an exclusive club was emphasized when, early in the programme's run, the cast banded together and commissioned the production of an 'Archers' tie.

Its simple design – a bow and arrow, with the letter 'A' in gold on a dark blue background – made it popular among the Cast. Soon, many other male members of the BBC staff saw it and wanted one; but it was decided to preserve its exclusiveness by making it a rule that only those who had been directly involved with the programme should qualify to wear it. Controllers and Heads of Programmes were presented with one and, of course, the Director-General: one Minister of Agriculture, when given his at the Royal Show, tore off the tie he was wearing and instantly sported the Archers tie for the rest of the day! There have been exceptions to the rule, of course, and one or two favoured listeners have been presented with an Archers tie; but it still remains that most desirable thing, something that money cannot buy. Now the stocks have exhausted it has become a collector's item.

There have over the years, however, been various articles connected with The Archers that have been available for purchase by the public.

There was a tea-set for example, with a map of Ambridge and views of village landmarks painted on each saucer and plate, and with cups of bright red colour. A colourful tea-towel showed Ambridge scenes. There was a boxed game, brought out in time for Christmas one year; and there have been various publications. The first of these was a 36-page booklet of biographies and photographs called *Meet the Archers*. Then came two novels by Edward J. Mason and Geoffrey Webb: *The Archers of Ambridge* and *The Archers Intervene*. Gwen Berryman published *Doris Archer's Farm Cookery Book* in 1958; and ten years later BBC Publications brought out *Peggy Archer's Book of Recipes*. Succeeding years have brought other publications which are dealt with in later pages of this book.

The appearance of books or other articles connected with The Archers added in some ways to the confusion of fact and fiction. When 'Doris Archer's home-made fudge' was marketed, a leading woman journalist asked the BBC who was being paid – the actress or the character? To her credit she is reported to have blushed when the absurdity of the question was pointed out. The fudge bore the 'signature' of Doris Archer commending her product and there was some anxious discussion for a time as to whether the handwriting should be that of Gwen Berryman or some anonymous artist!

Fact and fiction became blurred, too, when real-life celebrities were heard in the programme talking to the Archers: Humphrey Lyttleton, Gilbert Harding, Ann Sidney (Miss World), Richard Todd, Alan Oliver and Ann Moore as well as leading figures from the world of agriculture like Sir Richard Trehane, Chairman of the Milk Marketing Board.

It is always a pleasure to receive letters from listeners, especially if they are not too critical, but appreciative letters from distinguished figures in the 'showbiz' world give an added fillip. We were all thrilled to read a letter which began 'Cleo and I', and which was something of a tribute from the great John Dankworth.

One of the most rewarding aspects of the programme is the knowledge that it is listened to and liked – in many cases loved – by people in every walk of life. Later, when Princess Anne was opening the new Broadcasting Centre, she confessed that while not claiming to be an avid listener herself, she had heard the programme since her grandmother had been known to follow some of the events of Ambridge life.

One peer insists that his butler keeps him fully informed of

Tony Shryane at the controls while Dan and Doris Archer (Harry Oakes and Gwen Berryman) record

Dan Archer (Harry Oakes) and Doris (Gwen Berryman) looking at a copy of *The Borchester Echo*, 1958

Valerie Fidler, Assistant The Archers, who joined the team in 1965

A family picture, taken shortly after the birth of the twins, Shula and Kenton: with their parents Jill and Philip Archer (Patricia Greene and Norman Painting) and their grandparents Doris and Dan (Gwen Berryman and Harry Oakes)

Christine Johnson (Lesley Saweard) with her horse Midnight

A sing-song round the piano with Walter Gabriel (Chris Gittins) in charge. *L to R:* Ned Larkin (Bill Payne), Tom Forrest (Bob Arnold), Jack Archer (Denis Folwell), Doris Archer (Gwen Berryman), Dan Archer (Monte Crick), Carol Grenville (Anne Cullen) and Philip Archer (Norman Painting)

Monte Crick as Dan Archer found Harold Macmillan as Prime Minister very knowledgeable about farming at the 1963 Dairy Festival

Ned Larkin (Bill Payne) busy at lambing time. In real life, Bill was a true countryman at heart

Carol Grey (Anne Cullen) and Charles Grenville (Michael Shaw) on their engagement day

Simon Cooper (Eddie Robinson) with Dan Archer (Harry Oakes) and Tom Forrest (Bob Arnold) in front of 'Brookfield Farm'

Harvest Festival in Hanbury Church, 1974. *L to R:* Tom Forrest (Bob Arnold), Dan Archer (Edgar Harrison), Walter Gabriel, with specs (Chris Gittins), Jack Woolley (Philip Garston-Jones), Gregory Salt (Gerald Turner), John Tregorran, with beard (Philip Morant), Nora Salt, behind rod (Julia Mark), Ralph Bellamy, with goatee beard (Jack Holloway), Carol Tregorran (Anne Cullen), Sid Perks (Alan Devereux), Lilian Archer (Elizabeth Marlowe), Christine Johnson (Lesley Saweard), Peggy Archer, with fur hat (June Spencer) and Tony Archer (Colin Skipp)

Delighted as many listeners were when Carol at last married John Tregorran (Philip Morant), they were even more pleased when baby Anna Louise was born in 1969

When Princess Anne opened the new Pebble Mill studios in 1971, she met the whole Cast and this picture shows her chatting with three Archers – Phil (Norman Painting), Peggy (June Spencer) and Doris (Gwen Berryman). Tony Shryane, the producer, is just hidden

This picture of the entire Cast was taken in December 1971 on the occasion of the programme's twenty-first birthday

our activities whenever he is out of the country; and an industrialist who has for many years been a close follower of the programme, used at one time to give instructions for his secretary to take down in shorthand and then type out the whole of each Sunday's omnibus when he was abroad! A BBC official recalls a conference held at one of our leading industrial concerns where senior executives and directors spent ten minutes discussing serious matters of export and trade and economic problems, and the rest of the three-hour session considering the problems of Ambridge, especially the current mystery of the fatherhood of Jennifer's baby!

Just as The Archers has never been either a man's programme or one directed exclusively towards women, so too has it appealed to town and country, rich and poor, unlettered and intellectual. Several universities have established 'Ambridge Appreciation Societies' – the most recent one, at Leeds University, appealed for autographs of the Cast as this book was being written.

From the time when The Archers began to command a mass audience, listeners, both when we met them while doing personal appearances and in their letters, seemed to be worried lest 'they' should 'take it off'. We must have been told hundreds of thousands of times: 'That's my favourite programme, that is. I hope they'll never take it off.'

Naturally we agreed, and tried to sound optimistic.

But when in 1968 the BBC announced that Mrs Dale's Diary was to end we were given a vivid enactment of what could easily happen to us. It was in a way cathartic: seeing it happen to someone else, purged away the horror of the unknown. 'So that is what it will be like', we found ourselves saying. 'It will be announced; hundreds of listeners will complain; and three months later it will all be over.'

At one time it seemed that a day's radio programmes without Mrs Dale was incomplete. But now, here it was. Life went on and those who'd earned a steady living in the programme seemed to survive. So it would be with us.

Strange as it may seem, the demise of Mrs Dale's Diary lessened much of our tension. Like the man in the trenches seeing his best friend killed, we were almost ashamed of feeling, 'Thank God it wasn't us!', and we developed a kind of fatalism. If the lightning were to strike twice in the same place, at least we hoped there might be a decent interval between the two occasions.

1969

THE YEAR OF

Concorde's maiden flight. Mrs Golda Meir became Israel's Prime Minister. M. Pompidou was elected President of France when General de Gaulle resigned. The Victoria Line was opened in London. Prince Charles was invested as Prince of Wales at Caernarvon Castle. The Church of England rejected the scheme for Unity with the Methodists, who approved it. Armstrong and Aldrin became the first men to land on the moon. Prince Juan Carlos was named as the future King of Spain by General Franco. Halfpennies ceased to be legal tender. Increasing violence led to British troops being on duty in Ulster. TV colour programmes began on BBC1 and ITV. Both Houses of Parliament voted for permanent abolition of the death penalty.

IN AMBRIDGE

Polly took over the village stores and Post Office, and Sid gave up his job to join her. Dan and Phil joined a shooting syndicate with Woolley, Bellamy and Brigadier Winstanley. Lilian married Lester Nicolson.

So throughout 1968 we continued to attract and even increase the large audience that had followed us to the Home Service. In spite of set-backs, the programme seemed to be on an even keel again, and in full sail.

However, there were sadnesses and disappointments ahead, some unsuspected, some long awaited and one which was already casting its unwelcome shadow before it.

Since 1959 the programme had been taken by the BBC Transcription Service, a commercial section of the BBC which sold programmes in the form of recordings to overseas radio stations. For some years there had at intervals been gloomy talk that the Transcription Service would no longer take the programme and thus reduce our world-wide audience by millions; and early in 1969 the talk became action.

The Director of External Broadcasting, Oliver Whitley, told the House of Commons' Committee of Broadcasting Estimates on 11 February that radio stations in the Old Dominions which had taken the programme for years had now decided against taking it any more. Without the certainty of a firm booking by these old customers it no longer made financial sense to keep the programme in the catalogue of available programmes, and it was dropped.

The financial loss to the members of the Cast was almost equivalent to a third of what they had been earning. There was no complaint, no demonstrations or representations. Perhaps they realized that such things could be a waste of effort. But this was a time when much was heard of unofficial strikes and demonstrations in other parts of the national life. I can think of few other bodies of employees who would have accepted a net reduction in income of thirty-three and a third per cent without a murmur.

Monte Crick perhaps voiced the feelings of most of us. He had known the bright lights as a young man; but his middle years had been unmarked by continued success or by affluence. He spoke movingly of the years of loneliness, when work was hard to find and cash was short. We were, he said, fortunate to be part of a continuing success, however tedious or irritating it could be at times – what job isn't? After all, many members of our profession had no work at all.

The tone and temper of the Cast has always depended on the character of the man playing Dan Archer. Monte loved every minute of it and his years as Dan were among the happiest of his life.

They were not, alas, destined to last very long. At first we were as mystified as Monte and his wife Anne, when he developed symptoms of acute laryngitis. At times he lost his voice or it became so strained as to be unrecognizable, and lines were written into the programme to explain it. Undaunted, he continued working and even insisted on making a 'live' appearance on Christmas Day with Charlie Chester. Those few minutes on the air cost him and Anne a Christmas by the fireside of their delightful country cottage which Monte regarded as the next thing to Paradise.

The symptoms persisted, the voice became more strained. A meeting of writers, editor and producer was called to discuss what should be done. We had been told that after X-rays, the prognosis was good. Before the meeting proper, Ted Mason, Godfrey Baseley and I met to discuss story-line, and the decision to integrate our new third writer, Brian Hayles who was to be guaranteed at least thirty episodes in the next year or so. Ted and I were to write a slightly reduced number of one hundred and fifteen each!

The three of us joined Tony Shryane in Studio Two, prepared for a light-hearted discussion. Brian Hayles arrived, and pleasantries were exchanged. Then Tony dropped his bombshell. Anne had been told that Monte was a very sick man. 'But how sick?' we all asked, aghast. Then the slow realization came. He had no hope of recovery.

With heavy hearts and a sudden feeling of unreality, we had to make contingency plans. Auditions would have to be held, reasons found for Dan's absence for a week or two.

Then came another complication, which in a harsher less humane organization might not have been allowed to arise. Monte had no inkling that he was as ill as he was; Anne begged us, through Tony, to do nothing immediately which would make him in the least suspicious. Their days together had been all too short: their delight in each other and in the programme were disarmingly obvious. We agreed to do what we could to avoid cutting short the happiness that was now, so suddenly, doomed.

The next weeks were among the most unforgettable of any in the whole twenty-five years of The Archers. We all found ourselves part of a kind of benign conspiracy with Monte. Even when he could no longer climb those merciless two flights of steep stairs to Studio Two which had defeated his predecessor eight years before, he remained bland and smiling. His scenes were recorded separately in a small new studio, recently made as part of the recording suite. Once he had been comfortably settled in there, we would go down and greet him, and rehearse and record carefully written short scenes. 'Hello, old boy!' was the invariable cheery greeting. 'How are you?'

We all found it a testing period of realistic acting. Just as Harry Oakes had become obsessed with the idea that none of the listeners should know how ill he was, now we were engaged in a similar deception, but this time it was we who were deceiving the man playing Dan Archer himself.

The courage and self-sacrificing devotion of Anne won the admiration of all of us. She confessed to me later, on an occasion I shall return to in succeeding paragraphs, that he never appeared to have the remotest idea that he was so ill. Each week she motored him to Oxford for treatment, knowing that the following day would see him sick and wretched with the after-effects. All the effort they could both summon was needed to drive him to the studio on Monday or Tuesday of the next week, before the same relentless pattern was repeated. They were inseparable, as always; now there was never a moment in which Anne could relax, or find relief in tears. Apart from looking after Monte, she had her own performance to give as Carol Tregorran. True professional that she was, and is, no sign of her personal agony ever filtered into her portrayal of Carol, who was now, ironically, enjoying the long-deferred married bliss and indeed was delighted at the prospect of bearing John's child.

There was, of course, a conspiracy of silence where Anne was concerned, too. For the few minutes when she was away from Monty, rehearsing and recording her own performance, were too short for anyone to discuss the unspeakable burden she was bearing.

Then, one day, at the top of the stairs, in a voice that was level and controlled, she made it clear that she had everything in order in her mind: 'When Monte dies,' she said, 'would you play the organ at his funeral?'

Soon it was all too obvious that time was running out. The auditions were held and out of some half dozen excellent performances, we chose Edgar Harrison.

Remembering Harry Oakes's distress at the thought of an understudy playing his part, I managed to persuade the team to refer to Edgar in all press hand-outs as a 'temporary' understudy. If Monte had read the papers, or even had a remission from the somnolent state into which he was slowly drifting, at least we would have done nothing to give him additional stress at the end.

On Easter Sunday evening, Tony Shryane telephoned me to say that Anne had been called to Monte's bedside at the nursing home where he had been for nearly a month, and that clearly she would not be in the studio for recording the following day. We discussed simple ways of writing Carol out of my scripts which were to be recorded, and in bed that night I revised the scripts until long past midnight.

Next morning Valerie Fidler, Tony's assistant, telephoned for the re-written scenes for the day's first episode which I dictated to her, and then spent the morning typing the rest of the scenes, which I took with me when I went to the studio to record an episode as Phil.

That evening Tony telephoned to say that Monte had died a few hours earlier. Anne had been with him all day. The most he had been able to say for some time was 'Oh Annie!' She was alone with him when he died, with instructions to ring for help if needed. She knew the moment of his death; there was no need to ring for any help. She looked at her watch. It was 6.45. Time for the evening episode of The Archers. For the full quarter-hour she stayed alone with him. Not until seven o'clock did she ring the bell.

Monte was a musician. I was determined that the music at his memorial service should be such that he would have enjoyed. I chose Tallis, Byrd, Bull and Charles Wesley. Only in one heavily disguised modulation did I make any musical reference to The Archers' signature tune, 'Barwick Green'. No one there, I believe, recognized it; but I liked to think it pleased him by being there.

It was a 'thanksgiving for the life of' type of service, with no mournful hymns and ending on a note of triumph.

I had discussed the details, of course, with the Rector of the village where Anne and Monte lived, calling in first to see Anne. She was bearing up remarkably well, too well in fact. She left me for a moment, only to return clutching an enormous pile of letters. 'They keep coming,' she said. 'Most of them from strangers!'

This is not the place to quote any of those letters which so touched Anne, even if I had them before me. But the point is that fantasy or not, the love and sympathy expressed by complete strangers who felt that they had lost a dear friend, sustained Anne then and for a long time afterwards. Like the rest of us, she too was finding how impossible it was to separate fact from fiction. And was glad of it.

Monte died without knowing that an understudy had been appointed. Our innocent conspiracy had worked. But Fate was on our side. We knew that there had been a remote possibility that he might by chance hear the voice of the new Dan Archer, if he had happened to be well enough to listen to the programme when Edgar Harrison's first appearance was broadcast. And that, as we had agreed, could only beg questions in his mind.

We need not have worried. Monte died three weeks before

the voice of the 'temporary understudy' was heard. And so close was the tone, so similar the manner, that it was soon clear that we should have to fix it in our minds that the name of the actor playing Dan was now Edgar Harrison.

The scenes of course had to be recorded while Monte was still alive. Dan was supposed to have gone away for treatment and Edgar's first lines were spoken over the telephone. He had the unenviable task of making his voice sound slightly hoarse, to match up vocally with Dan's last appearance.

It was perhaps more traumatic for those of us who knew and were so fond of Monte, than it was for Edgar. Artistically, though, the match was almost perfect, the continuity complete. Monte, like Harry, had left us. But Dan Archer went on.

Just as the death of Harry Oakes had led to Monte Crick's taking over the part of Dan at what was to become one of the happiest – probably – *the* happiest periods of his life, so Monte's death marked the beginning of a particularly happy time for Edgar Harrison.

Within months of taking over the part – after, incidentally, a stringent medical examination – Edgar entered a competition, for fun, and found himself the winner of a Hillman Hunter car. After a lifetime with its share of good and bad luck, it seemed to Edgar that Fortune was suddenly smiling upon him with a broad grin.

Just as his predecessor had done, Edgar inherited a whole series of public appearances, and requests for photographs – all the paraphernalia of being one of the leading people in a still very popular radio serial.

We knew from what happened after Harry Oakes died that the public would, with a little help, eventually take the new Dan Archer to their hearts. For Edgar, though, this meant hard work in the studio, and a succession of interviews and photograph calls outside it. The rest of us knew each other so well that it would take a time for him to feel like the 'head of the family' and, above all, the husband of Doris Archer. But Edgar and his real wife Kay soon became friends of us all.

The fact we had a very new Dan Archer presented a problem to a London television producer who was planning a new quiz programme called *I give you my word*. He had wanted one of the series of half-hours to be a contest between the Archers and the Dales – even though the Dales were no longer on the air. I was about to leave for a holiday in Malta, but agreed before I left that, the day after my return I would appear with Patricia

Greene (Jill) in a half-hour contest against Dr and Mrs Dale (Jessie Matthews and Charles Simon). This duly took place. It was a close thing, but we won.

One of the questions directed at me was the identification of a sound heard on the farm. Under television studio conditions all I could discern was a kind of squawk: clearly some young creature, but for all I could tell it might have been a baby kangaroo! I guessed that it was a day-old calf. It was in fact a new-born lamb. The fact I got it wrong seemed to go down well in the studio; but not all the viewers were pleased.

An irate farmer wrote to one of the farming magazines, declaring that it was intolerable that those who purported to be experts in farming in The Archers couldn't tell the difference between a calf and a lamb! The BBC should sack the lot and get some farmers to do the job properly.

I mentioned the holiday in Malta, because of a strange experience I had there. There was piped radio in the hotel bedrooms, and one evening I happened to switch on in time to hear The Archers signature tune. Then followed an Omnibus edition, introduced by the familiar voice of John Hogarth, the popular Midland Region announcer. Although the date was in fact 29 April 1969, the Omnibus was the edition as broadcast on 22 December 1968 and in it, with only slight hints of throat trouble, was Monte Crick playing Dan Archer with all his verve and warmth and charm. Ambridge was preparing for Christmas and the New Year, which itself seemed odd when heard during a Maltese spring. But the talk of plans for the 'New Year' was almost unbearably poignant, knowing as I did then, with hindsight, that within a few months of making that recording, Monte had died.

1970

THE YEAR WHEN

Edward Heath became Prime Minister. There was continued violence in Ulster. General de Gaulle, President Nasser, Sir John Barbirolli, Iain Macleod and Bertrand Russell all died. The complete New English Bible was published. June 11 was the warmest night in Britain for a century. Britain made her third application to join the Common Market. Damages were awarded to 28 thalidomide children and their parents.

IN AMBRIDGE

Dan and Doris left Brookfield for Glebe Cottage and alleged 'semi-retirement'. Lilian's husband died. Chris and Paul Johnson adopted a little boy, Peter. The facilities for serving food at *The Bull* were again re-organized. Adam Archer, aged three, was kidnapped and a ransom demanded. He was recovered by the police unharmed after a week.

The start of a new decade was, as happens so often, a time of change. The much-debated blueprint for 'Broadcasting in the Seventies' was being put into effect within the BBC. But for the early part of the year, we in The Archers had other matters on our mind. We were approaching yet another milestone, our five thousandth episode, and our thoughts were concentrated on how to mark the occasion both within the programme and socially, by doing something different. We did! We – Cast, writers, editor and producer – turned the tables on the BBC and we threw a party for the Corporation.

To our delight, most of the top executives accepted our invitation including the Director-General, Charles Curran, and the new Managing Director of Radio, Ian Trethowan.

It was a far better party than readers of the *Morning Star* might have believed. That newspaper's report was headed:

'Scythes out at Archers party'. The story suggested that it was 'more like a night of the long scythes than a convivial occasion'. It spoke of those present being 'more concerned with contracts than compost and combine harvesters' and said that on all sides were reflected 'disillusion, lack of security, general dissatisfaction with new programmes and scarcity of knowledge as to what the future held – attitudes so rife throughout the BBC structure today'.

To me, that reference to *new programmes* (which were scarcely in the minds of most of us who were celebrating the continued success of our own long-running programme) gives the game away. The writer was simply using our party as a peg on which to hang a discussion of a policy outlined in the official BBC publication 'Broadcasting in the Seventies'. This was a controversial document and regarded by many as changing the BBC quite radically.

But ours was a celebration, not a conference. The *Morning Star*, determined to make a story, concluded: 'Throughout the evening a seemingly benign Mr Ian Trethowan, managing director BBC, moved from group to group. One would hardly think that he had that day signed 134 letters to restive members of his staff, who were opposing 1970 broadcasting plans, threatening them with the big stick.'

What really happened is that it was one of the best celebrations of an Archer anniversary in a long series.

Godfrey Baseley made a speech, so full of hope that the *Daily Telegraph* headlined their report. '"Archers" set for another ten years', and accurately reported Godfrey as saying: 'Farming and the countryside are entering a very exciting decade with intensive methods of farming and increasing use of the country for leisure purposes. We hope to reflect this in the series.'

He then invited the Director-General, Mr (now Sir) Charles Curran, to cut our birthday cake which was in the shape of a large reel of recording tape. Mr Curran made an amusing, informal and charming speech, in the course of which he said: 'The longer I stay, the longer the series stays. I have been involved with "The Archers" almost since its beginning.'

The *Morning Star* on the other hand saw things differently, reporting Godfrey Baseley as telling of the trials and tribulations of the programme in a speech liberally laced with the hope that 'they would continue to maintain the 6.45 p.m. bucolic suspense that held a four to five million audience' while the Director-General in his reply 'gave no indication that Mr Baseley's hope for the future was founded in fact.'

It is a pity that the *Morning Star* reporter had such a miserable time. Most of us enjoyed playing host to old and new friends and to meeting people like Ian Trethowan, already known to us of course as a television face, and Mr and Mrs Curran (as they were then) whose knowledge of and enthusiasm for the programme were extremely encouraging.

This party also gave us the opportunity to meet for the first time, Tony Whitby. As Controller of Radio Four, it was he who would be making any future decisions about The Archers. Meeting him was to find a new confidence for he at once expressed his enthusiasm for the programme and a determination to keep it going for as long as the audience wanted it. With him was his Chief Assistant, Clare Lawson Dick, whose interest in the programme was also evident. Cool, elegant, with a wide-eyed modesty that belied a penetrating mind, and an enviable wit, Clare quickly won the respect and then the affection of Tony Whitby. Indeed, from that time until Tony Whitby's tragically early death in February 1975, when she became the first woman Controller of Radio Four, they each took it in turn to come to Birmingham for our quarterly script and policy meetings.

The five thousandth episode inevitably brought with it a fair quota of press comments and features. Long-running as we were, The Archers were still good copy for the newspapers. The *Observer*, for example, devoted a lot of space to a pen portrait of Ted Mason and even *The Times* found us worthy of comment. It referred to our 'vast listenership' and said we brought 'a whiff of unpolluted air to people who don't know a pig from a potato and for whom Spring is three daffodils in a window-box.'

It was particularly bad luck that Gwen should return from a cruise having developed Bell's Palsy which completely distorted her face, although only temporarily. Its sad presence is recorded in the many photographs that were inevitably taken at this time.

It took great determination on her part to appear at the party, to act as hostess to the Director-General and be the centre of family groups, when the mere physical act of both speech making and eating was far from easy.

The celebrations over, we returned once more to our weekly routines. But by now there was no escaping the feeling that the changes going on all round us in the Corporation would sooner or later catch up even with The Archers.

The changes in Birmingham had included the programme management and in August the production team – producer, editor and writers – were called to a meeting by Alan Rees, newly-designated Head of Network Production Centre (as the Birmingham regional headquarters had now become). He explained the intentions behind 'Broadcasting in the Seventies' and estimated that, in fact, we would hardly be affected at all.

He also introduced us to the new Network Editor, Radio: Jock Gallagher who was then to take over direct managerial responsibility for all radio programmes produced in Birmingham, including, of course, The Archers.

He was almost totally unknown to us. He had worked for a short time in the regional newsroom and had previously been a television correspondent in newspapers. Our first associations were nervous and it didn't help very much when he said he'd always resented The Archers for knocking off the air his schoolboy hero, Dick Barton.

Still, The Archers had seen programme heads come and go and was still thriving.

It was around this time that we did find things changing. We were encouraged to try to bring the programme more up to date. There's no doubt that life outside Ambridge had undergone a dramatic metamorphosis. London had taken us swinging through the sixties and the Permissive Age was all around us. There were hints that 'Ambridge was perhaps just a bit too cosy and that it wouldn't hurt to reflect current behaviour a little more.' Not all of us agreed.

Dan went into semi-retirement and he and Doris moved out of Brookfield and into Glebe Cottage. They were being gently eased a little off-centre of the stage to make way for the younger characters.

At the same time, any element of propaganda – however good the cause – was positively discouraged. With the new style of Radio Four, there was an abundance of news and information programmes and it was felt that there was no longer any need for straightforward farming information in the programme.

Meanwhile, members of the Cast continued as before to receive fan mail and to be invited to make personal appearances.

Alan Devereux, who plays Sid Perks, remembers one such occasion. He was opening a church fête and during the intro-

212

ductions, the vicar's wife arrived late and sat down beside him. 'Why does everybody keep going on about The Archers?' she asked. 'I can't bear them myself!'

One wonders how she felt as Alan rose seconds later to make his speech declaring the function open as 'Sid Perks of The Archers'!

Alan also remembers another occasion when, with his wife and little daughter eagerly waiting, he was checking a map for directions to the village whose fête he was about to leave home to open. The name seemed strangely familiar and, hearing it spoken aloud, his wife Chris asked if he hadn't opened a fête there before? His mother arrived and took over. She rang the organizers, said she was from the Press and wanted to know when their fête was, and who was to open it. She was told a different date from that day and a different name from Alan's. Her enquiry as to who opened it the previous year was met with an immediate: 'Alan Devereux: Sid Perks of The Archers!' Alan had somehow filed a previous year's letter with his current invitations.

There have been fêtes we might have preferred not to open: there have been occasions when the introducer has got carried away and opened the fête himself; but this was the only occasion I am aware of when one member of the cast of The Archers nearly opened the same annual fête twice!

1971

THE YEAR WHEN

Decimal coinage was introduced to Britain. There were many casualties when crowd barriers collapsed at Ibrox Park Football Ground. The Open University began. The highest ever January temperatures were recorded in London. Further troop reinforcements were sent to Belfast. The financial collapse of Rolls Royce Limited was widely discussed. There was a one-day strike by 1.5m engineers against the Industrial Relations Bill. Mrs Ghandi had a landslide victory in the Indian general election. The Soviet Union agreed to outlaw germ warfare. Igor Stravinsky died. Three Russian spacemen were killed just before touch-down after 24 days in space. Louis Armstrong and Nikita Krushchev died. Prime Ministers Heath, Lynch and Faulkner met at Chequers to discuss the Irish Question. Both Houses of Parliament voted in favour of joining the Common Market.

IN AMBRIDGE

A large tract of land was dedicated as a Country Park through the generosity of Jack Woolley. Greg Salt left Brookfield to work for Borchester Dairies. A local campaign was started to keep the village school open. Lucy Perks was born, Lilian made a controversial marriage to Ralph Bellamy, and Dan and Doris celebrated their Golden Wedding. Brigadier Winstanley had a fatal fall in the hunting-field. Jack, whose instability of character had led to unpredictable behaviour, like attempting to become a farmworker at Brookfield and then leaving through ill-health, was suddenly taken ill again, and went to a sanatorium in Scotland.

The longer a programme runs, the greater the speculation about when it's going to end. When it was decided not to mark our twentieth birthday with any particular celebration, there was a great deal of anxious discussion. Was this the beginning of the end? Were we going to be phased out quietly with the minimum of fuss?

Then Jock Gallagher came into the Green Room during rehearsals one Monday morning. This, most of us thought, was it. Here was the announcement that we had all feared for so many years. But no. Instead we were told that the twentieth anniversary was being played quietly so that we could really go to town for the twenty-first the following year! The relief was something of a celebration in itself.

He also took that opportunity to tell us that Princess Anne would be opening the new Broadcasting Centre at Pebble Mill and that he hoped she would visit our studio while we were recording.

Although we had had our critics from the beginning, the number of people who appeared to dislike us never seemed very great. However, it was understandable that as we passed our various milestones those who thought little of the programme should renew their attacks. To those of us who had lived through the time when it was first 'non-U' to listen to The Archers (or at least to admit it) and then became trendy to do so, it seemed inevitable that taste would change again, and it would become fashionable to 'knock the Archers'. By this time, of course, we had become inured to unfair and unkind criticism, though, as always, very receptive to comments that were just and informed.

Few of us however would have expected quite so much support as we received when, early in January, following, no doubt, some discussion of long-running programmes like ours, and the even longer-running *Desert Island Discs*, the *Sunday Times* published a letter by 'J. A. Smith of London N.6'. (There were some cynics among us who wondered how authentic Mr Smith of such a vague address was, but we were grateful to him, whoever he was.) Under the heading 'The Archers: a nasty dream?' was a photograph of Harry Oakes and Ysanne Churchman which was captioned: 'Those were the days: Dan and Grace Archer (Harry Oaks [*sic*] and Ysanne Churchman) when Grace "died" in 1955.' Mr Smith's views were sure to be noticed.

He wrote that while he could just understand how Roy Plomley's programme had lasted so long he considered three and a half hours of The Archers every week a nasty dream. He was filled with horror at the thought that anyone listened to a serial that demonstrated to an astounding degree every out-of-date concept of ham acting, superficial human relationships, and keeping up with the Joneses, plus a habit of facile analysis.

He went on: 'I fear that Britain will never get on top of its present difficulties until The Archers are abolished – I mean the programme not the actors. They should all be given the OBE and a pension by Equity in recognition of the dreadful experiences they have undergone merely in order to make a living.'

Could the effect of listening to a soap opera really have such dire results for the country? Was Mr Smith being ironic?

Apparently not. A selection of replies from listeners was prefaced in the following Sunday's edition of the paper with the remark that 'those wonderful heart-warming Ambridge folk have a weekly audience of millions – the majority of whom appear to have written to us indignantly in the past week'!

One reply described Mr Smith as a small-minded snob with pseudo-intellectual pretensions; another writer agreed with all he said but still listened to the programme; others were uncritically in favour of the programme; one declared that Mr Smith had expressed what thousands of listeners had abstained from saying by sheer inertia; and one, the shortest, whose words have been referred to elsewhere in this book, suggested in a single sentence that 'There is no proven evidence that listening to The Archers is injurious to health'.

All of this would have been good fun, splendid knock-about stuff, if Mr Smith had not accepted an invitation the following week, to have what the paper called the last 'unrepentant word'. He would have done well to have declined, saying, 'What I have said, I have said.' In his long and self-indulgent reply he revealed the superficiality of his listening, and the charges he made are just not true. The material to which he objected, or rather about which he chose to be so superior, was in fact very carefully researched. The examples he quoted about an incident where a character (it was Doris in fact) makes a claim – which Mr Smith declares unconvincing – against the Criminal Compensation Board, and which he suggested, must encourage false pretences, was in fact written with the close collaboration and approval of the Criminal Compensation Board. We had chosen the very type of claim which the know-alls would regard as 'unconvincing'!

A few weeks into its twenty-first year, the programme received one of the most serious body-blows of its entire lifetime. On 3 February, Ted Mason died in an Edgbaston Nursing-Home.

Ted's output was prodigious. Many of us produced what can fairly be called a continuous flow of scripts: Ted gave birth to an unending torrent. When he died he was writing over a hundred episodes a year of The Archers, together with two highly successful series *My Word* and *My Music* which, with their producer Tony Shryane, he had devised. Before that were films, thriller serials, television plays, stories, novels, children's programmes and occasional articles. He never seemed to be in a hurry. He was a very sociable man: easy-going, friendly and apparently relaxed.

He was a family man who cared for and worked for and worried about his wife and family. His parents were ill and incapacitated, and this was enough to make him decide to stay in Birmingham within reach of them, rather than go to London. He thus ran the risk, as we all do who find life in the Great Wen no longer attractive, of being labelled provincial. This, in the self-deluding language of some olympian metropolitans, means second-rate and not quite good enough for Town. Yet among his peers Ted was much loved and very highly regarded: a professional among professionals. At a time when some held that radio was fast dying, three programmes in which he was heavily involved, were attracting audiences counted in millions.

Until the last minute of his life he was working. I was due to visit him in the nursing-home, to discuss story-lines, the day before he died. Only the day before that, he had sent a message to say he was looking forward to our meeting. Shortly before I was preparing for the visit, came the message that he was no longer well enough. At 7.45 the next morning, Tony Shryane rang to tell me that Ted had died earlier that day.

It was only then that I fully realized with what an eager and light-hearted air Ted had performed superhuman labours to keep the programme going, when his original collaborator, Geoff Webb, had died ten years before. Brian Hayles was still at this time contracted to write only a small number of episodes and so was committed elsewhere. Just as Ted had done, all those years before, now I was called upon to do the same. Writing more or less continuously, I completed fifty episodes of the programme in eighty-odd days.

At Ted's funeral, which was thronged by numerous friends and colleagues, the conviction in my mind would not be suppressed that his obsession with work in general and dedication to The Archers in particular, had induced Ted to drive himself too hard. I found myself silently vowing not to do the same. Scarcely was the thought formed, than the realization dawned: I was in danger of doing just that. Soon, though, Brian Hayles could make himself available to write half of the scripts, and the programme would have two scriptwriters as before.

In view of the criticisms of people like Mr Smith of N.6, it might have been feared that the death of Ted Mason, coupled with the fact that the programme was now over twenty years old, might have a more serious effect than any of our previous misfortunes. But Ted had done his work well. He and Geoffrey Webb had together clothed Godfrey Baseley's original idea with its first flesh. Now the body was alive, growing and continuing. A few months later, Tony Shryane called me into the producer's control-room after a recording. He had just been looking at recent listening figures. Far from showing any decline, they were holding their own and, on occasion, even climbing above recent averages. 'There's nothing to worry about if we can maintain those figures,' he said.

I snatched two weeks holiday in Rome; but the moment I returned home, another shock awaited. Denis Folwell, one of the original members of the Cast, who had played Jack Archer continuously since the trial run had died.

Yet again we found ourselves attending funeral services. Once more, in funeral orations, we heard how much pleasure The Archers had given over the years to so many people.

Denis Folwell was one of those people you couldn't help liking. The more he tried to appear worldly-wise and dignified, the more he seemed, endearingly, like a naughty little boy. He was invariably cheerful; often when, in fact, he was far from well. He rarely took as much care of himself as he might have done; but any friendly attempts to suggest otherwise were greeted with an impish smile and some such remarks as, 'I've stopped taking the quack's tablets. They were interfering with my social life!' We assumed that he was joking. He usually was.

Apart from the personal loss, Denis's death caused us great problems in the programme itself. Before our quarterly meeting, the editor and two scriptwriters met and decided on a storyline in which Peggy would find Jack apparently asleep in his chair. Only slowly would she realize that he had died in his sleep. We felt that – if carefully written – this would offend no one; we were quite certain in our minds that the character should not be re-cast and played by somebody else.

But the powers that be had other views; while it was agreed that we should not try to replace Denis, they overruled our storyline – a very unusual occurrence. Their feeling was that with our twenty-first anniversary coming up, we should avoid for the time being the depressing effect that the death of Jack would have on listeners.

So it was decided that in the programme Jack Archer would stay alive. This explains the story that was contrived of Jack going away to a sanatorium for treatment; of Peggy visiting him; and of his eventual death 'off-stage' in mid-January – after the anniversary.

As part of the attempt to keep the character alive, another long precedent was broken: a member of the Cast was allowed in two brief scenes to impersonate a dead colleague. Tony Shryane and I listened carefully to Edgar Harrison speaking some lines which I had written for Jack. The similarity was chilling. In spite of our personal feelings, though, we felt that in this macabre business of keeping a character alive, casual references were insufficient. He had to be heard. And so Jack became first seriously ill; then better; and finally well enough to be heard on the telephone talking to Peggy.

The scenes were recorded separately on Monday, 9 November 1971 after the rest of the Cast had broken for lunch. The following day, however, Tony played over the recording to the Cast. It was very short: the final scene for transmission on the night of Friday, 17 December, Jack's birthday and also Dan and Doris's Golden Wedding. We had restricted Jack's lines to a minimum; but when Edgar's icily lifelike impersonation was heard saying 'Hello Peg!', with just that half-apologetic warmth that had endeared the character to millions, there was a loud gasp from the assembled Cast. One of them, a man who had been a colleague of Denis's for half a lifetime, burst into tears.

The Cast's reaction made us wonder whether we had been wise in letting Jack be heard. But as always, the interests of the programme had to over-ride our personal feelings.

The reaction of the Cast to another situation that same day surprised both Tony Shryane and me. For the date was 10 November 1971 and the official opening by Princess Anne of the splendid new Broadcasting Centre in Pebble Mill Road, Birmingham – soon so quickly to be known affectionately as merely Pebble Mill.

The Cast were assembled for lunch on the seventh floor of

the building from which it was possible to see the helicopter bearing the Princess land on a sports field about a mile away, and to follow the procession most of the way into the building.

I had assumed that we should all have watched the descent of the helicopter, the presentations on the field and the rest of the procession with a kind of detached interest. Not a bit of it. As the helicopter touched down, everyone cheered. And when the Princess stepped out, the Cast cheered louder still. The magic of royalty could be effective over quite long distances, it seemed.

It had been decided that as part of her tour of the building Princess Anne should visit Studio Three and find The Archers busily recording an episode – one I had written, as it happened. We had contrived that this episode should deal with a village concert. This had several advantages. Most important of all, it meant that every member of the Cast, whether working that day or not, could be present in the studio to form the 'audience' in the village hall. Secondly, and far more practically, it meant that we could rehearse the song which Bob Arnold as Tom Forrest would be discovered singing when Her Royal Highness reached us.

The actual recording had in fact been safely made that very morning, and I had some slight disagreement with my producer on the question of what to say if asked. Remembering stories of the Queen's reaction to things obviously staged for her benefit, we decided that the truth was always safest. The truth was that our concert was a mixture of a recording in a real village hall, made some years previously, and some items recorded in that very studio, with Bob and Chris Gittins (Walter Gabriel) singing while I accompanied them on the piano.

Messages were relayed by Jungle Telegraph of the Princess's progress through the building. When she was within minutes of reaching us, Bob Arnold took his position on a rostrum, Gwen Berryman and June Spencer stood in front of the rest of the Cast, I sat at the piano while Tony Shryane hovered, ready to be presented and then to present us. It all went like a dream. The Cast, as 'audience' clapped like mad, and their 'acting' applause as if from the audience in the village hall became a spontaneous and warm greeting to the Princess.

'Twenty-one years,' said the Princess. 'Same age as me.'

We suddenly felt very old; and she seemed so young.

'And who was playing the piano?' she asked.

June Spencer said, 'He was!'

'It's an amalgam of two recordings made on different occasions,' I heard myself saying.

'So long as the finished result is convincing, what's it matter?'

She looked at one of my two names.

'Ah! Philip Archer,' she said. 'Father of that ghastly child!'

'That ghastly child, ma'am,' I said, talking too much as usual, 'is a talented actress called Judy Bennett who is older than she sounds and has children of her own.'

Then it was time for a very nervous Gwen Berryman to say her piece and make our presentation. To commemorate our twenty-one years a medallion had been struck (showing Dan and Doris on one side, and Ambridge village street on the other). One had been struck in solid gold and Gwen offered it to the Princess, who was clearly delighted with it. Rumour had it that, on a less formal occasion, she had declared herself 'right chuffed with it'.

As she said goodbye, I issued an informal invitation: 'Come and see us again in another twenty-one years.'

She was by now much more relaxed. We are usually a jolly crowd. She turned her eyes up to Heaven, made a marvellously comic gesture, as if to say: 'Oh my Gawd!', and reduced us all to the broadest of unceremonial grins. Then, with another spontaneous burst of applause from the crowded studio she left, with the rest of the Royal Party, led by the then Chairman of the BBC, Lord Hill, and a small army of photographers.

There was euphoria all round, slightly heightened by our sense of relief in the fact that it had all gone off well. Only Gwen was wondering if it mattered that she'd said 'Horsewoman of the Year' instead of 'Sportswoman of the Year' when referring to Princess Anne's recent award. We assured her that, as always, she'd been her natural self, informal and unassuming.

Our relief was more than justified. Not long before it seemed as if Gwen might have done her own version of the three old ladies and got herself locked in a studio, and not been presented to Princess Anne at all.

The reason for this was that the new doorknobs fitted throughout the building were handsome but not very easy for anyone to use, and for someone like Gwen with arthritic hands impossible. She literally could not grip them sufficiently to turn them. If the door happened to shut, Gwen was a prisoner until someone came to rescue her. Now more orthodox lever-type handles are fitted; but relief was enormous when the Royal visit had come and gone, without a hue and cry to find where Doris Archer was inadvertently held in captivity.

The gold medallion presented to the Princess was also struck in bronze for general distribution. The idea for the issue came from two ladies closely associated with the programme for many years – Tony Shryane's wife, Valerie, and actress Julia Mark, who plays Nora McAuley, the barmaid at *The Bull*. They talked to Alan Rees about it, he liked the idea and it was only a matter of time – and dozens of visits to a little Birmingham factory – before thousands of Archer fans were able to add to their growing collection of souvenirs.

As well as the medallions, it was decided to mark the forthcoming twenty-first anniversary with a special publication. This was in the form of extracts from twenty-one years of Doris's diary, written and edited by Jock Gallagher. Since 1951, we had been telling the story of life in the countryside. But as a daily serial, we have been telling it piecemeal, like a jigsaw.

By publishing Doris's diary, an attempt was being made to put the pieces together to create a more complete picture of life in the English countryside. How successful it was only the readers of *Doris Archer's Diary* can say, but it did sell many thousands and it was followed next year by a twelve-month diary. It did contain something that had never before been attempted, for reasons already explained; a visual description of Ambridge.

Much of the success of radio – and The Archers – is due to the scope it leaves for one's own imagination. Some of us still prefer the imagined to the visual.

Something of imagination that should be dispelled at this stage, perhaps, is the thought that life for the real-life actors, actresses and writers was just as secure and comfortable as life in Ambridge. It never has been. Such has been the professional organization behind the programme, that only the writers had any degree of security of employment. Even then, their contracts were for only a year at a time. The members of the Cast could never – nor can they today – be sure of staying for more than three months, for that is the longest contract offered to them. This tends to keep us all in touch with reality because we're all aware that whatever the past, we're only as good as our last performance.

Another factor in this is, of course, the continuing presence of our critics. Around this time, their manner changed and we were subjected to much harsher comment than we were used to. As the character of Radio Four became established, it was clear that it was different in many respects from the old Home Service from which it evolved. In particular, news and current affairs programmes, informational magazines like *You and Yours* and the remarkable 'phone-ins' greatly increased the amount of more or less plain fact which was put out. It was therefore decided that The Archers should be changed so that the overtly didactic and factual aspect of the programme should be reduced and spread more thinly. Facts about farming and the country scene were only to be introduced where essential to the plot. Tony Whitby suggested that anyone listening to Radio Four from its first minutes in the early morning until close-down around midnight would be at the receiving end of a formidable body of facts: he wanted The Archers to be an island in this sea of information, a respite for the listener, an escape almost.

Godfrey Basely was not at all happy with this change. The rest of us, on the other hand, whatever our personal misgivings about the new policy, knuckled down to attempt to carry it out. The Press weren't too happy either.

The two writers in particular were accused of initiating changes and allowing Ambridge, as Sean Day-Lewis wrote in the *Daily Telegraph*, 'to become uniformly insipid. The successful citizens [*sic*] sound and think like a grey variety of Birmingham business people, the more humble are goody-goody, and many of the bit parts are frankly embarrassing in both their writing and their acting.' This sort of criticism was particularly hard to bear when one felt oneself substantially in agreement. One could only applaud, for example, Day-Lewis's final words, even though their meaning seems somewhat convoluted:

'When inconsequential chat gives way to talk it is no longer informative on farming and country life, but almost invariably concerned with business affairs.

'Only if "The Archers" return to the land, its wonders, and its problems, will a 22nd birthday be justified.'

But it is true that for some of us, keeping the programme going was becoming far from easy, not from any lack of invention or imagination from the writing-team, but because of this change of policy. There was also another reason which may not be quite so obvious.

The editor had always worked closely with bodies like the

National Farmers' Union, and the agricultural workers' union, the Country Landowners' Association and any appropriate government department. We visited the Ministry of Pensions to be sure we got Ned Larkin's 'retirement' right: we went to the Ministry of Housing to be briefed on forthcoming changes of government policy as they might affect characters like Sid and Polly, Woolley and Bellamy. And on more than one memorable occasion we went to the Ministry of Agriculture.

One occasion stays vividly in the memory. The Minister, Fred Peart, received us with more than courtesy and gave us an hour of his time. The talk was all of high productivity, the growth and efficiency of this country's agriculture and plans for the future. Geoffrey Webb when faced with such discussion, no matter how impressive, would listen patiently and then, searching for the human interest, ask: 'Yes, but where's the torn drawers?' I phrased my question differently, remarking that many of our listeners wanted a rural story, of Brookfield as a farmhouse with roses round the door.

The Minister's Number One fixed me with an iron look and said: 'Agriculture in this country is not a matter of roses round the door, but efficiency and productivity. It is a growing and major industry.'

Here, then, was another of our problems clearly emerging. Country cottages with roses round the door; happy countryfolk in harvest-fields; Blossom and Boxer pulling the plough, and merry milkmaids singing at their work – these were no longer real or valid images of country life. Farming was becoming very big business with vast capital investment and enormous mechanization. The Archers had always been authentic, and the picture which it had painted in earlier years had been very attractive, coloured as it was with sentiment and nostalgia. Now the authentic picture of life in the English countryside was far less attractive: vast combine-harvesters and machine-milked dairy herds had much less romance and farmers who talked about overdrafts, capital depreciation and food-conversion rates had not the same folksy appeal as those who talked about tupping, muckspreading and larks in the hayfield.

Secretly some of us wondered how long the programme could survive in its traditional, or indeed in any other, form. The early years of the seventies were probably the times of greatest anxiety in the whole life of the programme. It did survive though, and survives still; but not without even greater changes than many of us thought it capable of withstanding.

In the autumn of 1971, Godfrey Baseley's book *The Archers: a slice of my life* was published, and the occasion was marked by a series of reviews not only of it but of the whole story of the programme so far, with much speculation about the future. Such headlines as 'Will the Archers be there in 1992?', 'The Archers down the years', and 'Life with The Archers', were typical.

It is the greatest pity that in order to get the book written in time for the 21st Birthday celebrations on 1 January 1972, so many small mistakes and one or two major errors of fact, were allowed to creep in. For this was a story which, mainly auto-biographical as it was, only Godfrey Baseley himself could tell; and if the extrovert gusto and breathlessly enthusiastic style with which it is told are typical of the man, the inaccuracies are not.

In his haste to put on record the facts of the genesis and achievement of The Archers, in which it is undeniable that he played a major and essential part, Godfrey only managed to do himself less than justice. This is very much to be regretted, especially in view of subsequent events of which it now seems, looking back, Godfrey himself had more than an inkling long before they happened.

1972

THE YEAR THAT

Saw queues outside the Tutankhamen exhibition, with 1.6 million people visiting it. Thirteen civilians were killed on 'Bloody Sunday' in Londonderry. Britain recognized Bangladesh. Maurice Chevalier died. A state of emergency was declared because of large-scale power cuts, when 1.5 million workers were laid off. The Berlin Wall was opened for the first time in six years. Direct Rule came into force in Northern Ireland, with William Whitelaw appointed Secretary of State. Cecil Day Lewis, the Poet Laureate, died, and was succeeded by Sir John Betjeman. The Watergate Affair began. President Amin ordered the expulsion of forty thousand British Asians from Uganda. President Nixon was re-elected. The Queen and the Duke of Edinburgh celebrated their silver wedding. President Thieu rejected the Vietnam peace terms.

IN AMBRIDGE

Tony celebrated his 21st birthday and Peggy, after Jack died, became manageress at Grey Gables. Walter had to say goodbye to his bulldog, Butch; and Greg Salt and Nora agreed to part. Woolley bought the village shop, and Sid and Polly Perks left it to run *The Bull*. Elizabeth Archer had a successful heart operation and Haydn Evans arrived in the village. On Christmas Day, Martha Lily married Joby Woodford.

By the time it was twenty-one years old, The Archers had achieved all that it had been set up to do – to establish an information service for the working farmer and to foster better understanding between the urban dweller and the countryman. Despite the ever-growing competition from television, it was still counting its regular listeners in millions. It has become an accepted tradition that each one of the programme's milestones is marked by some major event in the imaginary life of the Archer family. For the twenty-first birthday of the show itself, the Golden Wedding of Dan and Doris was celebrated.

There are, however, dangers in this practice. People who celebrate their golden weddings must be of a certain age; and yet, wherever possible, the clever writer of a long-running daily serial avoids mentioning the passage of time.

The problems don't arise with the younger characters. Anthony William Daniel Archer, for example, is slightly younger than the programme – he was born on 16 February 1951. Now that he has grown into a young farmer and the more familiar Tony, who is in his twenties, there is no likelihood of any difficulty for some fifty years or so!

But it is quite difficult with characters like Dan and Doris and Walter Gabriel. Once grandchildren and then great-grandchildren are born, it becomes increasingly difficult to provide activities for them which are in keeping with their age.

The fact that many country people are still energetic in their late seventies isn't quite enough to satisfy the sort of critic who is determined to find the characters' activities 'unlikely at their age'. Anyone starting a daily serial should be warned: benefit from the experience of The Archers, and realize that success can mean longevity, and major characters should start off as young as possible.

Milestones also bring with them another phenomenon: pulse-taking and prognosis. Will 'they' take the programme off when it is twenty-one or twenty-five or what-have-you? There is, in fact, a very simple answer to this question. 'They' are concerned with providing programmes that find favour with the listening public. So long as a programme continues to attract a steady and sizeable audience, 'they' are very unlikely to remove it. If, on the other hand, the size of the audience and its degree of appreciation fall to a low level, then 'they' would be failing in their duty to allow it to continue.

Although the audience for The Archers is now far below the twenty million who listened to the programme on 23 November 1955, the day after Grace died, it still continues to attract millions every week – a sufficiently high audience to merit its continuance.

A question we are continually asked is how the BBC estimates the size of its audience. In spite of much-repeated explanations, this is still a predictable question after any talk or after-dinner speech given by a member of the team. One extraordinary old wives' tale refuses to die: it is based on the odd belief that the BBC can physically measure the number of sets in use at any given time. This persistent piece of mythology recurs as regularly as hay-fever. The idea seems to have arisen from stories told by wired relay organizations who pipe programmes direct along their own network in places where normal reception is poor. These rediffusion services quickly knew how much power was needed to give a satisfactory reception at any given time.

The BBC, though, have their own system of estimating the number of listeners or viewers, based mainly on two sources: a panel of selected listeners who regularly return information on their own listening habits and their comments on programmes; and a series of spot-checks, carried out like opinion polls by stopping people in the street or other public places and recording their answers to a series of questions.

There are many secondary factors which affect listening figures: programmes competing at the same time on other channels; and the programmes which precede or follow the programme under discussion. But the results do give a solid basis of information.

At the moment of writing, the information we're receiving allows us to assume The Archers will not end on its twenty-fifth birthday.

The splendid Board Room in the new broadcasting centre at Pebble Mill was the setting for the party at which the twenty-first anniversary of The Archers was celebrated. Tony Whitby made a witty and optimistic speech, to which Tony Shryane replied; whereupon, with a greater or lesser degree of self-consciousness the whole team took a bow.

The film about us made for *Nationwide* was given a second showing for the benefit of our guests, and three veterans, June Spencer, Tony Shryane and myself were presented with silver replicas of the medallion presented to Princess Anne. (Gwen Berryman, Edgar Harrison and Godfrey Baseley had received theirs earlier in order to launch the sale of the mass-produced version, which became a favoured memento among devoted listeners.)

Sadly the one man more than any other who should have been there, taking the plaudits with Tony Shryane wasn't at the party. Instead, Godfrey Baseley, originator and editor for twenty-one years, had sent a simple telegram of good wishes. We were naturally surprised and disappointed, but what we didn't know at the time was that his association with the programme was coming to an end. Jock Gallagher commented later, 'In fact it could have been the perfect opportunity for us to say a glorious farewell to the man who had done so much, not only in creating The Archers but in sustaining its vitality over so many years.

'The termination of his contract left Godfrey very disillusioned and understandably bitter. He didn't want to join in any celebrations at that particular time. As he saw it, he was being unceremoniously sacked. He expressed his feelings to the national press.'

The Times, for example, carried the following item: 'Mr Godfrey Baseley, creator of The Archers, the BBC's longest-running radio serial, complained yesterday that he had been dismissed without warning or consultation. News of his departure had become public before he had been officially informed, he said.

'Mr Baseley, aged 67, said the network editor had told him in a letter that a transfusion was necessary and it had been decided to invite a leading dramatist to head the writing team.'

The BBC denied ever making any public statement about Godfrey's contract and it is a fact that nothing appeared in the press until Godfrey himself quoted that letter from Jock Gallagher.

Of the incident, Jock Gallagher recalls: 'Godfrey and I had several long discussions over the preceding eighteen months about the way the programme should go. He, understandably, was adamant that things had gone extremely well for more than twenty years and that there was therefore no need for change. Tony Whitby and I thought differently.

'Godfrey was a tremendously forceful personality and it soon became clear that we couldn't cajole him towards our way of thinking. We were looking in different directions and the final decision to part company was, to my mind, mutual.

'No one was happy about the situation because Godfrey had undoubtedly played the vital role in creating the programme and his contribution over the years was immeasurable.'

It would be unjust to Godfrey simply to leave the matter there as just an item on public record. It would be wrong of me, having been associated with him for the entire life of the programme to that time, not to express my personal feelings.

Godfrey not only created The Archers, but for many of us working on the programme he virtually *was* The Archers. In the history of British radio, his niche is assured. But for his seizing upon a suggestion at which others laughed – the idea of a farming *Dick Barton* – many of us would have earned our livings in quite a different way, and the BBC would never have possessed such a valuable property. Like most really creative people, Godfrey was not always easy: his enthusiasm sometimes seemed like brusqueness. He had a forthrightness that was not always very comfortable. Ironically, his abrasive manner at times was more in keeping with the alleged mood of the seventies than the fifties when he virtually bull-dozed his programme through the jungle of red tape into life. He enjoyed, and always freely acknowledged, the support and encouragement of John Dunkerley and Denis Morris, Controller and Programme Head of Midland Region respectively.

After his dismissal, the *Telegraph* reported him as being angry at the abrupt way it was done. This is scarcely surprising and from the sidelines it did seem that a farewell party and a golden handshake might have been a preferable way of removing him.

The possibility of who would be brought in to replace him caused endless speculation. While we anxiously awaited an announcement, Jock Gallagher himself acted as caretaker script-editor and then nearly three months later, the waiting was over. The new appointment could hardly have come as a bigger shock. One of the national newspaper headlines summed up our feelings: 'It's a long way from Coronation Street to Ambridge.'

The new editor was Malcolm Lynch who had been editor of Granada's *Coronation Street* – highly successful as a television soap opera but as different from The Archers as chalk is from cheese. How, we wondered, was a man who's been so closely involved with the urban life of the northern terraced houses cope with the fresh air and wide open spaces of rural England.

When he arrived, we soon found his ideas were certainly different from anything that had gone before in The Archers. Under Malcolm's editorship, every aspect of the writing of the programme was considered afresh: dialogue, scene-length, characterization, moral tone, mood, atmosphere, episode construction and content. We were, in fact, taken apart and re-examined. It was a salutary experience and, for me, an uncomfortable one. Although, as I have explained, the programme had been analysed and brought up-to-date every five years or so, there had never been anything quite so radical before. The programme was like a patient undergoing a complete physical and mental investigation, not always under an anaesthetic, and with a certain amount of surgery thrown in.

The programme heads described it merely as a change of gear and they were satisfied with the long-term effects, although they too now confess to an initial feeling of shock.

As for Malcolm, the tremendous effort of trying to change the course of direction of a programme that had ploughed the same furrow for so many years, began to affect his health. After several spells of serious illness, he eventually had to resign and move to the South Coast for a more peaceful existence.

1973

THE YEAR THAT

Britain first entered the Common Market. The Vietnam cease-fire agreement was signed. VAT was introduced into Britain. President Nixon denied all knowledge of Watergate, Vice-President Spiro Agnew resigned, and the Senate Select Committee hearings on Watergate opened. The Skylab space station was launched. Fifty people died in the Summerland fire disaster in Douglas, I.O.M. There were bomb attacks in London. Sir Noël Coward, Pablo Picasso and Prof. J. R. R. Tolkien died. Dr Henry Kissinger became US Secretary of State. Len Murray succeeded Vic Feather as T.U.C. General Secretary. Britain's first commercial radio station opened. Princess Anne married Captain Mark Phillips. A 50 mph speed limit and 3-day working week were announced to conserve fuel. Gerald Ford became Vice-President of the USA.

IN AMBRIDGE

The Festival of Ambridge was not an unqualified success. Ambridge Farmers took on young Neil Carter, and Trina Muir came to manage Lilian's riding stables following the birth of James Bellamy. With Valerie and Hazel Woolley away most of the time, Woolley sold Ambridge Hall to Laura and moved into Grey Gables, where, shortly after, he was attacked and robbed. Doris gave a memorable Wine and Cheese Party, which was more convivial than planned, and Tony left Brookfield to go into partnership with Haydn Evans at Willow Farm. Early in the year the vicar died and the new vicar took over in October. At Christmas Zebedee Tring was found dead.

When Malcolm Lynch left, there was another gap of months before Charles Lefeaux was appointed script editor. He was as different from Malcolm Lynch as Malcolm had been from God-frey Baseley.

Charles lived in Hampstead and had for many years been a radio drama producer. Although not a countryman, he brought to the programme a long and wide experience of a BBC radio production department and he quickly turned his organizing abilities to the greatest advantage. New writing schedules were drawn up, and the whole system of planning, researching, writing and editing scripts was rationalized and codified. Charles had also been an actor both in the provinces and on the West End stage, and so had an understanding of a performer's problems.

Another new face appeared on the scene at this time, that of Tony Parkin, the BBC's radio agricultural editor. With the growing importance and complexity of agriculture, he was brought in to act as expert adviser and to feed the writers with workable story-lines on farming. His arrival was both personally and professionally welcomed by everyone.

Tony is one of the most likeable and apparently indefatigable people in the BBC today. He not only has a first-hand knowledge of farming in this country but, seeking material for his weekly programme *On Your Farm*, he is constantly travelling round the world. He has a mischievous and devastating dry wit, and those who do not catch the twinkle in his eye occasionally find him enigmatical. He rarely raises his voice or appears to turn a hair, and his no-nonsense statements are often examined for hidden meanings that are rarely there. He is forthright but rather brusque: he just happens, quite simply, to say what he means and to mean what he says. Such plain unvarnished honesty is rare and refreshing. He is fearless in defending the views he hold and far from joining the 'Let's-knock-Auntie' brigade, he is unashamedly a loyal BBC man.

His task is to ensure that the writers do not allow their characters to move too far away from genuine country activities; that any farming process mentioned is seasonally appropriate and accurately portrayed; and from time to time to take the editor and scriptwriters into the country in order to get mud on their boots and the authentic smell of farms into their nostrils. Picking a path between overt farming propaganda on the one hand, and just enough farming colour to give an air of authenticity to the programme is not easy, but Tony pilots us with a surefooted confidence.

When he took over, Tony continued the visits of the writing

teams to farms; and he also contrived one of the most useful tools the scriptwriters have ever had – *The Archers' Agricultural Calendar* which shows at a glance the normal farming activities at any given time on efficient West Midland farms.

So with his help we were by now re-establishing The Archers as pure entertainment in an authentic and contemporary country setting, centred as always on Brookfield Farm, described by the journalist Linda Blandford as 'Warm Comfort Farm'.

Linda, an ardent fan of the programme, used the title to head a long piece in the *Observer* on 13 May 1973, in which she previewed the latest edition of the *Borchester Echo* which was to appear that week. She quoted Jock Gallagher, who produced the mock newspaper as saying: 'You may not credit it but we'll have hundreds of replies to the fictitious small ad for a cottage for sale near Ambridge. There are actually people who still believe the Archers exist.'

She went on to say that the programme was still, after twenty-three years, as much a part of people's lives as fishfingers 'which *are* made from fish, though some trawlermen might not recognize them and Ambridge *is* fashioned from everyday life. Life became a little strained there, however, about a year ago when the scriptwriter from *Coronation Street* took over. In one week alone Ambridge suffered a plane-crash, a quasi-rape and the church bells fell down. "I went through a terrible patch then," says June Spencer who plays Peggy Archer. "I was going through my change-of-script-editor."

'The script editor had a heart attack. The village settled down – more Ambridge again than 'Ampstead.' Ironic, since the new editor came from 'Ampstead!

Linda Blandford went on to write that so far the village has been spared a lot: abortion, homosexuality, drug addiction. She described it as a haberdasher's shop still peacefully stocking bed socks and knicker elastic as if the three-lane speedsters didn't exist. For lonely people in towns, Doris Archer is a symbol of the way people ought to care for each other. Finally she quoted Tony Shryane as saying that one of the programme's secrets is that it 'doesn't change too much'.

In fact, attempts had been made to change it completely. The lesson of 1973 was, as Tony Shryane expressed it, that listeners don't like change any more than people like Doris Archer do.

The edition of the *Borchester Echo* published in 1973 seemed to me easily the best of the whole series. A *Borchester Echo Colour Supplement* published in October 1970 was well done.

too, but like its predecessors it fell between the two stools of fact and fantasy. The cover picture of Phil and Jill outside Brookfield with the caption 'The fourth generation takes over', with, below, 'Twenty years of The Archers' refers to a well-known radio serial, if only by implication, and thus shatters the illusion that this is a colour supplement of a small-town weekly paper.

The 1973 *Echo*, however, kept entirely within the convention. Apart from the essential imprint in tiny type at the very bottom of the last page, declaring that the publishers were the BBC, every word, every photograph and every advertisement might easily have appeared in the weekly paper of many a small English country market-town. The style of journalism, the type-faces, the lay-out of the advertisements were as authentic as the picture of country life projected by the programme itself, when at its best. It even had small inaccuracies which are not unknown in such publications, and in many larger ones: getting wrong the name of the saint to whom Ambridge Parish Church is dedicated, for example. Editor Jock Gallagher claims that some of the misprints were deliberate but confesses that the wrong name for the church was a real clanger!

Michael Watts, writing in the *Sunday Express* on 3 June 1973, told of the embarrassment the BBC caused him as he traipsed around newsagents trying to find a copy of the *Borchester Echo*: '. . . one feels a bit of a chump asking for a mythical newspaper published in a mythical town and featuring in particular the mythical Archers of mythical Ambridge.

'It presents no problems for Dan, Doris, Phil, Peggy, old Uncle Tom Forrest and all. But for the rest of us . . .

' "Have you a copy of (and here one lowers the voice) the *Borchester Echo*?"

' "*What's that, love?*"

' "Er – the *Borchester Echo*. It's published in connection with The Archers – you know, the radio programme."

' "The *Borchester Echo*?"

'(Wince, wince. Why does she have to shout? She's got all the blessed customers looking at me now.) "Any *Borchester Echos*, Frank? No? Sorry – don't stock that sort of thing.'

'It's worse than trying to buy a confiscated copy of *Men Only*.'

Luckily not all would-be purchasers had the same problems. The sales ran into hundreds of thousands.

June Spencer, who plays Peggy Archer, had an experience which begged the perennial question. When the programme *Any Questions?* visited her part of the world, June was part of the audience and submitted a question. To her surprise and mild embarrassment it was chosen. Using her married name, and with no hint about her being an actress, or associated with The Archers, she asked her question. Shortly after a listener wrote to her: 'Dear Peggy Archer. What were you doing in "Any Questions?" You're not real, are you?'

'Some of the Ambridge folk occasionally travel around the world and listeners often hear about their adventures. The actors rarely travel, however, and the recordings of their exploits are usually recorded in the Birmingham studios. Britain's entry into the EEC changed that, however, as Jock Gallagher explains:

'During the controversy prior to our entry to the Common Market, we'd had to more or less overlook the great debate that went on particularly in agricultural circles. The problem of maintaining a delicate balance on such an explosive subject was just too much for us. If Dan had come down on one side, we'd have been torn to pieces by the others. It wouldn't have been any use trying to balance it with another character having opposite views. "Dan is a much more important and influential character than anyone else," we would have been told. Even trying it with lesser individuals was ruled out because no one would have agreed that the case had been fairly dealt with.

'Now the controversy was over (or so it was at that time) and Britain firmly "in", it was decided that we should catch up on events. We too would go into Europe and this time the fact and the fiction came close together.

'In the story-line, Sid Perkins was to arrange a coach trip to Holland for the Ambridge football team to play a return match with a Dutch village side. Apart from the players, other villagers were to join the trip and some of them, including Dan, were going to have a first-hand look at farming within another Common Market country.

'In reality, the coach trip also took place. One Friday morning, the Cast and production team and I piled into a luxury coach outside Pebble Mill and set off for Holland and our first actual visit abroad.

'Just as the Ambridge coach would have done, we drove up to Hull and there joined the ferry that would take us – not without incident – to Rotterdam.'

Cabins had been booked, but as they were only reached by descending two long flights of very steep stairs, they were virtually out of reach for Gwen Berryman. In the end, she passed the night in the ship's hospital which involved taking fewer steps. Recordings were made with the captain as we pulled away into the North Sea and these, with the others that were to be made during the next four days, were inserted into the daily programmes that week.

In the programme, Tony and Phil had to stay behind to keep the farming going, so I was wearing my 'Bruno Milna' hat while actually in Holland. Brian Hayles had written the scripts to be broadcast that week, and so it fell to his lot to write scenes on the spot, which were recorded in the studios at Hilversum. My work was to be done when the trip was over; for, although we had not planned it, we found it worth while to re-record scenes in the following week's scripts which I had written, so that those who'd been to Holland could look back on the trip with greater wealth of detail.

So Dan and Doris, Laura, Chris and Paul, Carol and the rest of them all mentioned some authentic detail which stayed in their memory, which could only have been the case if we really had been to Holland and seen those things for ourselves.

The trip was a success both in programme story terms and in reality as an excellent publicity and public relations exercise. We found, for example, that we have something like 10,000 regular listeners in Holland and the programme is listed in the Dutch equivalent of *Radio Times*. Everywhere we went we were asked for autographs and photographs. It was very good for morale.

It was also good for our press coverage. Three journalists had joined us for the trip – Pat Healy, whose long and considered articles made the front page in *The Times*; Phil Phillips who featured us in the *Sun*; and Martin Jackson (now the *Daily Mail*'s television editor) who got us splash coverage in the *Daily Express* for which he then wrote.

While we were in Holland, another issue arose that also brought us again into the forefront of the national news.

An information officer of the Community Relations Commission was reported to have complained to the BBC that The Archers was out of date because immigrants were not featured in it and overlooked the fact that 'Britain is a multi-cultural and multi-racial society.'

The usual anonymous 'BBC spokesman' was quoted as saying, quite rightly, that there are few immigrants in country areas; that the BBC had no policy either way; and if authenticity required a coloured person, then one would be introduced.

This story made the popular Sunday newspapers but it was all a storm in a teacup, much enjoyed by us all as we read the English papers in Holland; and indeed, the officer who was alleged to have made the original complaint wrote to the *Telegraph* on 28 September explaining that what she had in fact done was to write a letter to the fictitious *Borchester Echo* making a lighthearted suggestion that immigrants *might* be included in the programme, and she was in no way complaining. Few could doubt the truth of her last sentence: 'We are, of course, delighted that the idea is being discussed.'

Three days later Barry Norman enjoyed himself in the *Guardian* in a long consideration of the idea, beginning: 'I can't really believe that the Community Relations Commission had given very deep thought before they complained to the BBC that "The Archers" showed bias because there were no coloured people in its cast.' And ending: 'Better to leave "The Archers" alone. Let them carry on with their caricatures of indigenous country folks, and far from clamouring to have coloured people represented, offer a fervent prayer that no immigrant should ever be so unfortunate as to end up in Ambridge.'

Over the years we have become used to such barbs. To my mind, they mainly spring from a feeling that we are part of the Establishment and therefore are fair game for anyone who wants to knock.

One of the snags of being the oldest inhabitant is the feeling which seems to recur more frequently each year, that one's heard it all before. Listeners hear what they want to hear, and are deaf to what displeases or disinterests them. We rarely say or do in The Archers what we are indignantly accused of saying or doing; and our glaring omissions are few. When people say they are amazed that we've never had this or that in the programme, with, what I hope is a kind smile, I find myself saying more often than not we have; and then quote chapter and verse.

Just for the record, we had dealt with the problem of the coloured immigrant in December 1972, when Hazel Woolley, who with other girls had been doing social work at the Borchester Settlement, brought a coloured girl, Rita, home for Christmas.

A series of letters appeared in the Press, which must have gladdened the hearts of the Community Relations Commission, but the issue soon disappeared. There was, however, a curious tail-piece just over a month later, in *The Times* of 8 November 1973:

'Next time the Gurkhas do a spell of guard duty outside Buckingham Palace,' it began, 'engage one in conversation. If he replies in the bucolic accents of Walter Gabriel, it will be because the British Forces Broadcasting Service in Hong Kong has just started broadcasting The Archers there, to teach the Gurkhas English!'

1974

A YEAR OF

Two general elections in Britain, with a change of government. In the USA Gerald Ford succeeded Richard Nixon as President. In Israel Mrs Golda Meir and her cabinet resigned. President Pompidou of France died. Direct rule by the British Government in Northern Ireland was ended. An attempt was made to kidnap Princess Anne. The Achbishop of Canterbury retired and became Lord Ramsay, being succeeded by the Archbishop of York, Dr Coggan. Richard Crossman died.

IN AMBRIDGE

Tony celebrated his engagement to one girl in January and his marriage to another in December. An outbreak of Swine Vesicular disease meant the slaughter of all Phil's pigs. Following the divorce of Jack and Valerie Woolley, Hazel seemed loth to return to the village, preferring life in London. Lilian's Indoor Riding School was built and the Post Office bus service began. Robin Freeman, the Warden of the Arkwright Hall Field Centre, left to take up an academic post, and John Tregorran went on a long lecture-tour of America. Good farming land came on the market following Ralph's heart attack, when a great deal of the Bellamy Estate was sold up.

The beginning of 1974 brought another milestone. Once again I found myself writing an episode whose number ended in three noughts: this time it was the 6,000th.

The special event to be the cause for celebration was easily decided upon: Tony Archer's long-awaited engagement.

Long-running serials present their creators with difficulties when dealing with weddings. Listeners love them. The enormous interest aroused by Phil Archer's extended courtship has already been described. Listeners of all ages, and not only the women, seem to identify with the process of discovery, court-ship, wedding and living happily ever after (or not).

The problem arises once the characters are married. The interest engendered during the courtship stage seems to evap-orate the moment the honeymoon is over, returning to some extent when the patter of tiny feet is expected. This, as I have suggested, was one of the reasons behind the death of Grace Archer: the courtship was prolonged almost to breaking point. The marriage was short but idyllic, with only one small shadow: Grace was not keen on having a family. Suddenly she changed her mind, and then the listeners' interest was revived. In a short time she was dead.

This was a formula that could not be repeated without modi-fication; but certainly the early stages had to be prolonged. After all, Tony Archer was almost as well-known to our most devoted listeners as any member of their own families. He had been born during the lifetime of the programme: many of them had been there, and had overheard what Jack had said to Peggy. (And those who weren't listeners then had heard Peggy re-membering it on Tony's twenty-first birthday!)

So Tony's love-life became of as much interest to many listeners as if he were their son. Anxious to avoid too early a marriage we showed him having what we hoped was, for a young farmer in the 1970s, a typical series of romances with a variety of girls, few of whom appeared to his mother as de-sirable daughters-in-law. That we were not entirely successful was indicated by a letter we received from a Gay Liberation type writing from South Kensington. He suggested that we had delayed too long before revealing that Tony was not the marry-ing king. I was astonished to find the same view repeated by a journalist who interviewed me later in the year and who clearly followed the programme closely!

However, Tony met Mary Weston at a Young Farmers' Club Dance, and was bowled over. This was the one, he said. And we meant him to mean it. The part was written and cast with the intention that Mary Weston would become the future Mrs Tony Archer.

Once again, though, difficulties over which we had no control altered the story-line. It will be remembered that the actors and actresses who play the parts are, in the main, booked by the episode, often a month or more in advance. It is often diffi-cult for performers, or their agents, to be sure whether or not they will be free so far ahead. After all, many of them cannot live on what they earn from occasional radio appearances and are naturally loth to commit themselves to a recording session which may last only a few hours, but which would preclude their acceptance of a part in films or TV or possibly a long engagement in the theatre.

Difficulties of this sort arose with Catherine Crutchly, the actress who played Mary Weston. There was nothing unusual about them: they are one of the commonplaces that make writing a radio serial less simple than some imagine. Since the fifties, attempts have been made to offer block bookings to artists wherever possible, but this is not always desirable. Major characters have to be introduced gradually: new arrivals who swamp the scene almost invariably antagonize listeners. And that initial period, when the character appears at long intervals, is invariably the difficult one. No one expects actors to sit by their telephones, refusing all other work, while they wait to be invited to play a small part in one episode, with only a verbal assurance that the character may well become a major one within six months or a year.

So, even while the listeners were hearing the engagement party, the writers had to begin to think of excuses for Mary's very rare appearances: she was busy, she had been taken out for a meal by Tony 'off-stage'; she had gone to Majorca with her parents. Soon it was felt that the illusion could no longer be kept up without straining credulity beyond reason, and Tony and Mary parted.

People do marry on the re-bound, just as engagements are sometimes quickly broken, and the task of the writing team was to find someone who really would sweep Tony off his feet. That was how Haydn Evans's niece, Pat Lewis, came to be invented.

The value of using the Archers as a means of drawing public attention to an extremely wide range of subjects was illustrated yet again by a letter to *The Times* on 1 July 1974 headed 'The Archers and archaeology'. We were running a story dealing with the discovery of a corner of a small Roman house beneath a field which Ralph Bellamy intended to plough. We wanted to show how conflict between progressive farmer and archaeologist might easily arise; and, having exploited the dramatic possibilities, to demonstrate how a little compromise and common sense could reconcile apparently opposing views. The story would reflect a situation that was arising more and more, as so many different interested parties were anxious to use the

countryside. Ths speculator and the conservationist; the culti-
vator and the naturalist; the juggernaut-mechanized farmer
and the traditionalist: all these confrontations provide us with
material which echoes similar conflicts all over the British
countryside in the mid-seventies.

The writer of the letter, Dr Ian Blake, was only following
precedent in using The Archers as a mounting-block for his own
hobby-horse: Roman remains were common enough, but Iron
Age remains tend to be discarded unrecorded. Could not Iron
Age settlements be found 'beneath the relics of an invasive sub-
urbia'. Then, breaking from jog-trot into gallop, Dr Blake concluded: 'We must educate Ralph Bellamy and others of his
like. Although wall-stubs of a Roman villa may well halt his
subsoiling, it is essential that he should realize that, unless he
is prepared to accept archaeological investigation *before*
ploughing, he may rapidly, irretrievably and ignorantly destroy
invaluable archaeological remains.'

It so happens that as the scriptwriter mainly concerned with
this story, having once been President of Oxford University
Archaeological Society and having excavated on sites for some
years, I was entirely in agreement with Dr Blake. What does
seem encouraging is the fact that in spite of snide comments
about 'caricatures' of country types, our characters in the main
continue to have life in them. Dr Blake refers to Bellamy 'and
others of his like', suggesting, surely, that there are enough of
them about to justify a busy man, which I am sure he is, in
spending time and energy writing to *The Times* about him.

What Linda Blandford of the *Observer* had referred to as the
more 'Ambridge than 'Ampstead' quality in The Archers is difficult to explain to those who insist that Ambridge should be
their own idea of a country village, and not the true one. All
the scriptwriters live in the country and write of what they see
around them. This does not always coincide with that rural
Never-never land which many townsmen, especially those who
write to us in letters or about us in newspapers, would wish it
to be.

In spite of motorways and two-car families, of colour television and deep-freezes, in spite of the pill, the pop festival and
permissiveness, Ambridge and 'Ampstead are still worlds apart.
We think differently in the country and speak to each other
differently. One is as likely to be addressed as 'Sir' as by one's
christian name, and not always predictably. Our critics love to
label us feudal and hierarchical because, for example, Tom

Forrest never addresses his boss by his first name; and we are called 'old hat' and 'stick-in-the-mud' because titles of family relationship are still widely used. Things are changing, of course, and those changes will be reflected, but our role remains to reflect and not to fore-shadow.

We are sometimes accused, as the writer of a long article in the *Guardian* did on 18 October 1974, of having dialogue which, while being straightforward, does not communicate the way people really talk – with grunts, pauses and unanswered questions. One is tempted to reply that grunts and pauses are clearly indicated in every script and duly performed by the actors. But one of the snags of radio dialogue is that whereas an occasional pause is tremendously effective, repeated pauses sound like holes and have people quickly adjusting their sets.

From the time the tape-recorder became almost a household gadget, most of us have recorded real conversation and some of us have analysed it. To reproduce that sort of thing, or even an artful imitation, would irritate more than it would convince.

There is one further consideration: dialect. The original brief given in 1950 to both actors and writers – I remember it well – was 'character not dialect': the inability to comply with this explains why some of the original performers in May 1950 were not asked back for January 1951. Yet the rule was almost immediately broken. But your Tom Forrests and Ned and Jethro Larkins are really the exceptions that prove the rule. The programme was designed to be heard all over the British Isles. It had to be not merely intelligible, but easily understood from the Hebrides to Land's End, from Ulster, through the whole of Wales to the Wash. Even the Forrests and the Larkins had to tone down their dialect. The dialogue is in fact a kind of Standard Rural, whose basic structure and vocabulary, like the countryside as a whole, is that of the simpler parts of the Authorized version. And not always the simpler parts.

Years ago when writing the scripts for the popular *Country Magazine* programme, where non-actors were called upon to read a script, I found that many people seemed incapable of reading their own precise words, no matter how carefully written down by themselves. The most they could deal with were simple statements in short sentences, stripped of all the parenthesis and qualifications and irrelevant reminiscences with which their normal speech was decorated. But this spare muscular dialogue, pared down and lean, still sounded, from their lips, authentic. Those who speak the dialogue of The Archers are of course experienced actors; but the bare-bones style still works. There are amazingly few 'aaarhs' and 'orrhs' in an Archer script; very little of Rambling Sid Rumpold; and not a great deal of 'come next muck-spreadin'' or 'three months since last tupping-time'.

The people called 'vocal impressionists' have had singularly little success in imitating The Archers. Making a few guttural sounds and saying: 'Me ole pal, me ole beauty' does not add up to an impersonation of Walter Gabriel. The reason for the inimitability of The Archers lies, I believe, in the fact that it is writen (at its best) in Standard Rural: no single line or small group of lines gives the flavour. It is structured in units of short scenes, from ninety seconds or less to a maximum of five or six minutes. Monologue is rare, duologue common, and the whole is writen to its own lilting rhythm.

My greatest advantage when I came to write the programme was not merely that I had been around from the time when the programme was being created, nor that I had actually appeared as a performer in the majority of the episodes broadcast to that date, nor even the fact that when I sat down to write I heard the characters talking, so that writing The Archers was almost like taking dictation. No, it was something more than that and something simpler. What I wrote was immediately accepted as genuine 'Archers' for one reason: I knew the tune.

A good example of listeners hearing what they want to hear came in a letter in December 1974. The writer, who described herself as an ardent fan and admirer almost from the first broadcast felt that she had to protest at hearing Helen Fairbrother referred to as Jill Archer's stepmother. 'Helen Farebrother [sic] was Phil Archer's *Mother-in-Law* and surely is of no connection with his second wife.'

What the script, and the actress concerned, actually said was: 'Grace Archer's step-mother, you mean?' And although the writer mentioned both the mid-day repeat and the Omnibus edition she had on each occasion heard something that was never said! (For the record, Helen Fairbrother was Grace's step-mother, and Philip Archer's mother-in-law.)

Another amusing incident which revealed how vividly people hear what they want to hear was illustrated when someone wrote complaining of the inaccuracy of our facts concerning marriage by licence. The facts had of course been carefully checked and were perfectly accurate. We were therefore quite amused to receive a second message from the same complaining listener saying: 'We think you're marvellous! We've just heard today's repeat of last evening's episode and are amazed how quickly you managed to put things right!' They were never wrong of course; and the listener had heard exactly the same words on each occasion.

One of the most enjoyable events many of us can remember took place in 1974: the celebration of Tony Shryane's forty years with the BBC. Apart from a brief interview with Tom Coyne on television early in the evening, Tony spent the day at Pebble Mill quietly celebrating the occasion with old friends and colleagues. In a quarter of a century those of us concerned with the programme have experienced almost every kind of BBC function: official lunch or dinner, reception, cocktail party, Champagne party: functions where the guest list ran into hundreds, and smaller occasions where those present numbered a mere handful. Few, if any, were as pleasant as Tony's 'Forty Years with the BBC' lunch. An excellent meal was served in the airy Board Room at Pebble Mill, with its wide vistas over a surprisingly green and tree-planted area of Birmingham, and the atmosphere was as calm and unassertive as Tony himself. The speeches were brief, informal and amusing, following the mood set by the first speaker, Phil Sidey, the dynamic Head of Network Productions Centre.

After a brief interval, an even more informal party was held at which representatives of every level of BBC programme activity were represented, from John Grist, the Controller of English Regions, to Janey, the most junior secretary. All of The Archers office staff were there, of course – Valerie Fidler the Archers Assistant, and Christine Hardman and Jane Barton. Jock Gallagher presented Tony with the original disc of Episode One of The Archers, which had been specially sprayed gold for the occasion, and in a short informal tribute John Pierce, who has for many years built up a unique library of authentic recordings of countryside and farming sound effects, gave a vivid picture of what life is like working for a perfectionist.

In the early days, Tony himself went on location to record the sounds of Ambridge, first on disc, later on tape. Then in turn the mantle fell upon John Pierce, who having made an extensive series of tape-recordings of every sound likely to be needed, found that he would have to start all over again making recordings in stereo. The story he told went down very well among a friendly audience who knew how painstaking Tony was.

The programme needed the sound of treatment being given to a cow suffering from an attack of warble-fly. John suggested that the sound of the cow's hide being scrubbed could be produced by attacking a coconut mat with a household scrubbing-brush. Tony was not satisfied. He wanted the real thing. John must go to a farm, find a real cow and record the effect. Returning in triumph, John reported that he now had an excellent recording of the sound of a cow's hide being scrubbed. 'Ah yes,' Tony replied, 'but is it a cow with warble-fly?'

Although he has spent forty years in direct contact with BBC studios and microphones (apart from his army service throughout the 1939–45 war) Tony is not easily persuaded to use the microphone as a performer. Although he was heard in *Woman's Hour* talking about his experiences over forty years, the recording was in fact made surreptitiously by Jock Gallagher. Tony is not the speechmaking type and doing so seems to have all the attraction for him of a long session at the dentist.

He began working for the BBC on 12 February 1934 and by 1936 he was a studio manager at the age of seventeen. In this capacity he worked on a wide range of drama and documentary programmes, both in Birmingham and London, including – significantly – serial programmes like *The Robinson Family, Dick Barton* and the early stages of *Mrs Dale's Diary*. Few people have a wider or more intimate knowledge of the daily workings of the BBC, especially in its essential function, that of producing programmes.

He seems to thrive on crises – which is fortunate, because, as this book clearly shows, The Archers has had its fair share of disasters. When some of us become frustrated by the difficulty of avoiding giving offence to at least some of our listeners, no matter how carefully we treat controversial (or even apparently non-controversial) matters, we tend to say: 'You can't win!' It often seems like that, especially to the writers. By straining every muscle to avoid giving one wrong impression, the result is often that another occurs. Tony, however, expresses the thought less desperately. He often shrugs, smiles, and says: 'You can't win 'em all!'

The year 1974 brought a typical example of this. One writer introduced a story in which a fly-by-night character arrived in Ambridge trying to find customers for a certain industrial process which had a domestic application. The rest of the writing-team naturally continued the story through several weeks of scripts. At this date, the scripts were written at least two months before they were broadcast, so by the time it was discovered that the process described was in a monopoly situation there were many scripts to alter. Urgently the editor, producer, three writers and network editor met in Jock Gallagher's office to decide what should be done. The BBC was being accused of giving publicity to a commercial firm and the impression had to be corrected as quickly as possible. It was decided to change the story, by giving the fly-by-night character a far wider range of services offered to the householders of Ambridge, and not the specific one which had caused offence. We chose a name which sounded almost as innocent as, say 'Smith's General Design Service', and felt that the problem was solved. Within days a letter was received bearing the very heading we thought we had invented, from a firm that was delighted to hear itself mentioned!

I still feel that the scriptwriter's motto should be 'You can't win!'

One memorable occasion was a Harvest Evensong that took place during this year in the church where Archer weddings and carol concerts had been recorded: Hanbury Parish Church near Bromsgrove in Worcestershire. 'Worship with "The Archers"' said the handbills that were distributed, and which attracted a large crowd. Most of the Cast were present, and Gwen and Edgar remember with a mixture of humility and affection that when they entered to take their places at the front of the church, the whole crowded congregation rose to their feet and did the same when they left.

Dan and Tom, the churchwardens at Ambridge, were photographed taking the collection – the event was organized to raise money for the church.

Among those characters present were Walter, Jack Woolley, Greg Salt, Nora, John and Carol Tregorran, Ralph Bellamy, Peggy, Tony, Lilian, Christine and Sid Perks.

1975

THE YEAR OF

Britain's first Referendum which brought problems for the Prime Minister, Harold Wilson, both before it and afterwards. Edward Heath bowed out as Leader of the Conservative Party in favour of Margaret Thatcher. Vietnam, and neighbouring countries, and American foreign policy still filled the headlines. John Stonehouse, M.P., presumed drowned in Miami, turned up with a false passport in Australia. The controversial *Crossman Diaries* were made public in the face of official objections. Economic problems – inflation, rising prices, the value of the pound – dominated the headlines.

IN AMBRIDGE

Lilian and Ralph Bellamy left to live abroad after making a handsome gift to the church, which ended the year in good repair and with its bells re-hung. Jennifer, whose detective novel, *It's Murder!*, was published in June, decided to part from Roger. Following an accident to Jethro Larkin, Phil was in danger of being sued for negligence at Brookfield. The Vicarage was sold and part of its extensive grounds used for building – with a new bungalow vicarage included. Pat and Tony announced that there would be an addition to the Archer family in the New Year. Carol Tregorran was charged with shoplifting.

We entered 1975 with the feeling that we were approaching what Sir Winston Churchill described so vividly during the later stages of the 1939–45 war as a 'Grand climacteric'. We were in our twenty-fifth year and within twelve months we should complete our quarter-century. As when we were approaching our twenty-first birthday, the euphoria was tempered with anxiety. Once again the question was asked: 'Will it be so far, and no further?'

Yet the very repetition of arguments that had been rehearsed many years before seemed to carry an answer with it: what applied then could equally apply now, and may quite possibly still apply after five, even ten years hence. One writer in the *Guardian* had spoken, only a few months before, of the 'apparently eternal' Archers.

Yet, nearer at home, there seemed to be more positive reasons for alarm. Two major characters in the programme appeared to have been removed: Lilian and Ralph Bellamy. Inevitably, in a tight little community like the Cast of the Archers, the whisper went around, 'Who'll be next?' Once this sort of uncertainty creeps into a group of actors, the wildest imagination is given full rein. Even those who had been there longest, or those who had once been among the most popular characters with listeners, even those without whom the Archers would not seem like The Archers at all, were in their own minds candidates for speculative guillotining.

But the departure of Ralph and Lilian in the story brought us once again into the headlines. First, the Press reported a great public outcry from listeners who didn't want to see them go and then came reports that we had succumbed to public opinion and that they'd soon come back. It was comforting to see that even after so many years, the national Press were covering our every move.

The same incident also attracted a great deal of press coverage but from a very different angle.

A letter from Mr Roger Horne of Lincoln's Inn, London, was published by *The Times*. In the programme, we had had Ralph Bellamy breaking up his estate, selling most of it but keeping 1,000 acres for his son, James. Mr Horne's letter contended that we had been very careless and that under existing tax laws, Bellamy would have had to pay out nearly £1m to the Exchequer.

Mr Horne, in a long analysis of Ralph Bellamy's finances, as deduced from listening to the programme, suggested that the scriptwriters had not been correctly briefed. It was a detailed and, in some places, a very technical letter written, one suspects, as a kind of *jeu d'esprit* by a lawyer specializing in tax affairs, and ending: 'Mr Bellamy's total tax liability will therefore be £883,857 plus any capital gains tax that may be payable in respect of the sale of the Ambridge Garage.'

Jock Gallagher wrote the following reply to *The Times*:

'Mr Ralph Bellamy asks me to say that he is honoured that his tax problems should merit the attention of our very well-qualified correspondent Mr Horne (January 15). Sadly, however, I have to tell him that he makes at least two false assumptions:

(a) That being a country yokel Mr Bellamy did not get expert advice and

(b) that he intended settling 1,000 acres on his son, James.

'Mr Bellamy's advice from an excellent country accountant has allowed him to nett over £1m (after paying capital gains tax of £225,000) from the sale of 2,500 acres . . . Mr Bellamy intends retaining ownership of the 1,000 acres for the time being, and this will be managed by the very able Mr Andrew Sinclair. At some stage, he hopes to pass this on to his son but had accepted advice not to do so at present because of the new capital transfer tax.

'Like other land owners, he hopes the present economic climate will not continue for ever.'

This exchange prompted several thoughts. One was to marvel afresh at the interest aroused by a topic touched upon in The Archers. The *Daily Mail*, for example, quoted the facts from Mr Horne's letter to *The Times*, with full acknowledgement. Rarely does one newspaper quote another.

Another was the way the incident underlined one of the harsh facts of being a member of The Archers' writing-team: people remember. Wherever possible we avoid mentioning actual prices for almost anything, as they vary so much all over the country, and from time to time. Even before days of rapid inflation, when prices can alter enormously between the writing of a script and its recording four or five weeks later, it was always regarded as politic to avoid precise prices and amounts if at all possible. Keith Miles, a comparative newcomer to the writing-team, had included a few figures. He also appeared on *Nationwide* and had to justify his figures, such was the interest that the matter aroused. It wasn't, of course, just a coincidence that the politicians were at that time still debating new tax proposals.

The last words of Mr Horne's letter struck me with particular force, '. . . plus any capital gains tax that may be payable in respect of the Ambridge Garage.' Innocent enough words, but they reveal that the writer is an attentive listener to the programme, who has clearly followed, over a number of episodes, the details of the story.

As Jock Gallagher was reported as saying in the *Daily Mail*: 'From experience we know that listeners pick up errors, whether they concern milk yields or the profitability of pigs.' 'Or indeed,' one might continue, 'any detail, however small.'

If the bowling green at *The Bull* is altered, people in other villages where there is a bowling green remember. If a character expresses a dislike for Gorgonzola, he is stuck with that dislike forever, unless and until a scriptwriter allows his taste to change in full view of the audience. If a character is referred to as Charles, then much ingenuity is needed to explain why he returns after an absence as Oliver (this is how Oliver Charles Grenville was named). The list is endless. It is not merely that listeners have good memories: their identification with the characters fixes the details of those characters in their minds. We have all been told, on occasions: 'I always remember that. I'll tell you why. Our Ethel was having her baby at the time, and we all said . . .'

For this reason, not only is the greatest care taken to ascertain the facts and to present them unambiguously, but a detailed list of 'continuity' points is kept regularly up-to-date.

A copy of every script is, of course, preserved. One wall of The Archers office in Pebble Mill is occupied by shelving full of the 6,504 scripts from 1 January 1951 to 1 January 1976, and every week their number is added to.

I remember how I started by keeping all of the early scripts. When they began to take up more shelf space than was convenient it was clear that a stop would have to be made. Then by chance I heard that the BBC's own set of scripts had been damaged by water and so several car-loads went from my country cottage to Broadcasting House in Carpenter Road, Edgbaston. Now I merely keep all the current scripts together with all those written by Bruno Milna: well over one thousand of them, occupying many feet of shelf space.

Apart from the actual scripts, an abstract of the salient points of each script is made into a 'continuity' list, which is circulated to writers and editor. In addition, a card index records every fact about every character, location and incident that has ever been mentioned. This work is done by The Archers' 'Assistant'. For many years this was Valerie Hodgetts, now Mrs Tony Shryane, who, like him, contributed enormously to the early success of the programme with an enthusiasm and dedication which placed the programme first and almost everything else second. This obsessive concern for the programme – as I know from personal experience – is not necessarily a good thing. Godfrey Baseley had it in great measure, as did Geoff Webb and Ted Mason. And the present 'Assistant', Valerie Fidler continues the same tradition, and has a motto: 'It matters that we get it right.' Newcomers have been mildly surprised that anyone can take so seriously the importance of knowing Pru Forrest's maiden name for example, or the date when Bellamy bought the garage. But if our ignorance of these matters appears in the programme then its authenticity is immediately impaired in the eyes of those many listeners who remember the true facts.

My own amazement at the earnestness with which Jennifer's illegitimate baby was discussed by senior BBC officials around an impressive board-room table, as part of the serious business of the first quarterly meeting I attended, quickly changed to admiration; such enthusiasm is infectious. Our worst critics are those who have never really listened to the programme: people with closed minds full of pre-packed ideas. Patronizing condescension is quickly changed, first to mild interest and then, in many cases, to a state of being 'hooked' – unless the listener happened to begin at one of our intermittent low points. It would be foolish and arrogant to pretend that we do not occasionally have 'off' periods. But by and large the standard maintained must have been fairly high for the programme to have outlived so many of its rivals and contemporaries and to have held on to its sizeable hard core of listeners.

One of its secrets – it has many! – is that, despite what some uninformed critics believe, it has never been afraid of change. The changes in characters and characterization, location, life-style and farm-style have already been mentioned. There have been considerable changes too in the way the programme has been physically produced.

Episodes have always been recorded in batches for simple reasons of logistics. The batch for many years was six. Now the programme is recorded in groups of ten. In order to avoid solid booking of the studios. The Archers is recorded on Monday, Tuesday and Wednesday morning for two consecutive weeks, during which time twenty episodes are produced. The Cast are then free to do other work for the next two weeks.

The physical conditions are rather more comfortable than in the dear dead days in Broad Street. There are airy concourses with comfortable chairs or sofas outside the suite of studios: within there are a small 'narrator's' studio, a large one divided into smaller areas by curtains and acoustic screens, and adjacent rooms for technical control and recording processes.

The main studio, Studio Three, is fitted with a vast staircase leading nowhere, but with a part of each tread surfaced in a different material, so that the effect of feet on different sorts of stairs can be produced: wood, carpet or metal. There is a sink with a tap for 'washing-up' and other effects: there are electricity and gas points, so that kettles may boil and cooking noises may sound authentic. These effects, which are done in the studio as the performers act out the script, are called 'spot' effects.

Many effects, though, are obviously impossible to achieve in this way: a herd of sheep, a flight of birds, a tractor in motion, a milking machine. All these are recorded. For many years, the radio actor, for technical reasons, never heard the sound of the car he was driving or the river in which he was swimming or drowning! Now it is usually possible for the effects to be played over a loudspeaker into the studio which makes the act of imagination, which is so much part of the actor's work, much easier.

The Archers is produced exactly as any other radio drama is produced. The actors arrive, wearing whatever clothes they feel most comfortable in, and gather in the concourse outside the studio. Each scene is rehearsed with the assistant, so that inconsistencies or irregularities in the dialogue may be ironed out – unnoticed *double-entendres* or occasional typing errors. Then, scene by scene, the actual recording is made under the direction of the producer who sits in the control room behind a glass panel. He hears the actors' performances through a loudspeaker, just as listeners eventually will at home. He talks to the actors by means of a microphone and loudspeaker.

Usually the last scene of each episode is repeated, but without the signature tune, for all except the Friday episode, so that the scenes can be joined together to make the Omnibus edition which is heard on Sunday mornings. As five fourteen-minute episodes have to be condensed to under one hour, at least ten minutes has to be cut out for the Omnibus and this fact has to be borne in mind by the scriptwriters. The preparation of the Omnibus edition is the responsibility of the Assistant, who also has two other important functions in the studio, in addition to her work in the field of 'continuity', already

254

described: to supervise the recording of the daily introductions, and the Omnibus narration.

The brief introductions to each daily episode are recorded at a single session by announcer John Hogarth, who has been introducing The Archers for many years. Before him Christopher Stagg, Philip Donnellan, Richard Maddock and Tony Raymont, who are all still in the BBC but in other capacities, took their turn. These introductions are written by the scriptwriters, but the introductions to the Omnibus are normally written by a specialist country writer. Godfrey Baseley himself wrote them every week for over twenty years: then the scriptwriters wrote them in turn, until C. Gordon Glover took over. On his death, that first-rate naturalist and best-selling author Phil Drabble began to write them, ensuring that the breath of country air that Tom Forrest brings to our Sunday audience is authentic and unsentimental: rural life as it is, not as those ignorant of it would wish it to be.

Bob Arnold usually records these Omnibus narrations before, or sometimes after, the main recording session.

A much-repeated question is: 'Do you read it off a script? If so how do you make it sound so real?'

The answer has already been given: The Archers is produced in the same way as any radio drama. The combination of script, actors and producers has one aim: to produce a credible illusion. The actors have to sound like real people in real situations. And so, a well-dressed actor holding a clean white script can, with the combined skill of his own talent and that of the producer and technicians, sound as if he's wearing old farming clothes and gumboots, and is up to his neck in mud in a thunder-storm trying to rescue a stray calf.

The script is undoubtedly present: but any actor who sounded as if he were reading the words would not last long. The technique of radio acting is a specialized one, as different from acting in the theatre is from acting for the screen. A good radio actor can make you feel the coldness of a January wind, or taste the pastry on one of Doris Archer's pies, or smell the steamy atmosphere of a stable – all by concentrating his imagination into his voice, whilst at the same time concerning himself with essential technical problems like not speaking until a green cue-light tells him to, or delivering his lines faster or slower according to the demands of the scene.

Let no one imagine that it takes less technical skill to perform in The Archers than it does in any other form of radio drama, whatever our detractors may say. It should surprise no fair-minded person to learn that distinguished performers like Sir Ralph Richardson and Irene Worth have been heard to say that they listen to performances in The Archers with pleasure.

Less knowledgeable listeners, a group which includes some professional journalists and critics, often mistakenly describe as a bad performance a characterization which does not please them. Even devoted listeners will admit that they 'never miss an episode' but 'can't bear Walter Gabriel' or some other favourite character! The Archer family is indeed like most other families, not least in the fact that some people like one member of it, and some another; but everybody is somebody's favourite.

If those early attempts at creating a 'family atmosphere' by making us all eat together in the BBC restaurant failed, the passage of time has succeeded. Perhaps it would be hard to find a kind of sentimental family feeling in The Archers team; but there is a very strong *esprit de corps*. It should be stressed, yet again, that The Archers is a team job. Under the guidance of Jock Gallagher, the producer Tony Shryane, the scriptwriters Bruno Milna, Brian Hayles, Keith Miles and William Smethurst, with Charles Lefeaux as script editor, produce the material which the Cast perform. It is checked for agricultural accuracy by the BBC's Agricultural Editor in Birmingham, Anthony Parkin.

Meeting each other so often, even though our homes are spread widely over the Midlands – and some live in Surrey, Devon, Lancashire and Essex – we members of the Cast have become in many ways like a family.

The older members cannot help feeling that Tony Archer is a child of the programme: he was born on 16 February 1951 shortly after the programme began. At first he was merely a recording on disc of somebody's baby. Then when he began to say the odd word or two, that versatile actress June Spencer spoke his first words, as well as playing the young Lilian and, of course, Rita Flynn.

Children's performances are always difficult to produce in radio serials, which is why, once they cease to be heard as recorded childish babble, they tend to be heard very sparingly until they can be played by an actor or actress whose range starts with early teens and can be extended indefinitely as the character ages. This has been the case with Colin Skipp who took over at the point when Anthony-William-Daniel's voice broke, and he insisted on being called Tony. As the programme enters its second quarter-century the arrival of Tony Archer's own child is awaited and a new era, long or short, will begin.

Colin's own child, his daughter Nova, was born while her father was in the studio rehearsing and recording The Archers.

It was a Tuesday and Budget Day. Colin commuted from studio to hospital, and in between times from studio to phone. As the Cast were informed of the Budget announcements, they all asked about 'the Baby'. At 3.20 a daughter was born, to the relief and delight not only of her parents but to the whole Cast of The Archers.

It is on occasions like this that the real family feeling of the team is demonstrated. If one of us is just too ill to get to the studio, but well enough to speak, the recording is made at the invalid's bedside: Harry Oakes, Eddie Robinson and Gwen Berryman have all recorded scenes in this manner, with the rest of us leaning over the pillows or bed-head. Bill Payne was allowed out of hospital just long enough to record as Ned Larkin before being driven back to hospital by Bob Arnold. On occasions of severe weather, rail strikes or other emergencies, Tony Shryane always marvels at the way the Cast never fail to reach the studio.

Apart from the four people who are on permanent contract, the rest of the Cast, having been booked for separate episodes, may have to travel many miles to record one episode. Yet they get there somehow: the old showbiz tradition that 'the show must go on' operates at least as strongly with the Cast of The Archers as with any other company.

Sudden incapacity is the most difficult thing to deal with, though on more than one occasion, scripts have been re-written at a moment's notice when a member of the Cast has been whipped into hospital. Normally, though, any member of the team who is unlikely to be available for whatever reason, makes it a point of honour to give the longest possible notice.

Unavailability of actors, through illness or other professional commitments, often strains the inventiveness of the writing team. In order to introduce the Welsh girl, Pat, whom we intended should quickly become Mrs Tony Archer, we decided that Haydn Evans should strain his back (something that is very easily done on a farm) and that his niece should come from Wales to look after him.

This all went well and according to plan. Then, just when we were congratulating ourselves on having got Pat and Tony safely married, and we had decided on several more story-lines involving that excellent character Haydn, the equally excellent actor Charles Williams suddenly found himself much in demand for appearance on radio and TV. So, the injury to Haydn's back plus his wilful carelessness caused the back trouble to recur. This, we thought, worked well. Whenever Charles Williams couldn't be with us, Haydn's back took a turn for the worse. It couldn't be better. But engraved on the heart of every Archers scriptwriter are the words: 'You can't win!'

In April a card arrived at Pebble Mill addressed to Bruno Milna saying: 'For God's sake get an Osteopath to Haydn Evans! We are all getting sick of that back! From a Registered Osteopath.' The writer, whose osteopathy, it is hoped, was better than his or her typing, went on to give the address of the General Council & Register of Osteopaths. Well-intentioned, no doubt. But if we took a risk and sent Haydn to an osteopath, successfully, and then we needed a reason for the absence of Haydn once again, what then? A recurrence of the injury might provoke the ire of all the osteopaths, and no doubt many orthopaedic specialists too, in the country. There are times when making even a casual throw-away remark in The Archers is like stepping into rapidly-drying concrete: the least impression is fixed there forever.

The last year has brought a typical crop of examples. We wrote a scene involving Sid and Polly and a tea-making machine that went wrong: the biggest manufacturers of the machines were quick off the mark to ensure that we got our facts right and that it was only Sid's hamfistedness that caused the problem, not the machine.

Even Walter Gabriel's home-brewing got us into trouble. As comic relief, the beer caused a minor explosion and immediately brought the wrath of home-brewers everywhere down on our heads. *Guardian* columnist Richard Boston even launched a campaign for a safe brew by Walter Gabriel – though thankfully he did so goodnaturedly.

Forever Ambridge? Eternal Archers? In one way, perhaps, we have already achieved a kind of immortality by finding our way into the social histories and the record books.

Even now in its twenty-fifth year, the programme is still unique. On 6 June 1975, the votes were being counted after the Common Market Referendum the day before. The way the votes were counted around the country meant that results were coming in almost continuously from mid-day onwards and so Radio Four planned a marathon results and commentary programme that knocked all other programmes off the air . . . all other programmes, that is, but The Archers.

The planners obviously still felt that, to its many faithful listeners, the programme was just as important as the result of the Referendum.

We did in fact end that night's episode with reference to the Referendum. We were all delighted to find that the experimental broadcasting of Parliament was reported in some newspapers as likely to rival The Archers. Richard Last wrote in the *Daily Telegraph*: 'Like that evergreen daily report from Ambridge, it had pace, a large and diverse cast, and a slight air of being not quite real.' Life is often like that.

The secrets of The Archers are many: the reasons for its success equally numerous. At its best, which has been for the greater part of its long history, the programme has been a true reflection of life in the country, even though that picture has not always harmonized with the townsman's idea of what country life ought to be. It has constantly been updated, but rarely tried to be trendy for fashion's sake. It has, in Huw Wheldon's phrase, been made, not merely manufactured: if it had ever been mechanically 'churned out' it would have disappeared long ago. It has rarely been simple 'soap opera': its characters, situations and stories have usually been true. At the very least it has, at its best, been 'soap opera plus'. Those of us who have been associated with it from the beginning react very sharply to the idea, stated or implied and no matter from what source, that a script, a performance, an effect 'will do, because it's only The Archers'. We take the opposite view: only the best is good enough for The Archers.

We have, after all, created a whole mythology in the world of Ambridge and the Archers. And as with mythology, not everyone's notion of it is the same.

Whilst this book was being written, someone rang up Tony Shryane and asked: 'It's true that the village of Inkberrow in Worcestershire is the real-life village on which Ambridge is modelled, isn't it?'

'No!' he replied.

'Then that kills a story I'm writing!'

The story was published all the same in the following Sunday's *News of the World*, and very sensational it was too. It told of 'wife-swapping parties' in this rural community. But sensational as the story was, it needed a very big peg to hang it on. So Ambridge was used, even though Inkberrow had merely provided occasional locations for photographs – as several other villages have. This did not deter the journalist, who began his piece: 'Listen, me old pals, me old beauties, you'll never guess what's really been going on in Ambridge' – and proceeded to give the tedious facts. Without the connection with The Archers, tenuous though it is, the story would have had little general interest. But Ambridge is now an accepted prototype and must expect to be used as a yardstick for both the worthy and the scurrilous.

Those of us who have been concerned with helping to make Ambridge a living reality in the minds of so many remember the pains and delights of bringing it to birth.

We remember that, at a time when the programme was most committed to being informative and factual, we won the highest available award for the most entertaining programme. So long as the programme keeps its feet in the soil it has as good a chance as any of surviving.

The editor and scriptwriters who originally created the programme have gone: an experienced editor and an enlarged writing team have taken over. Bruno Milna and Brian Hayles have been joined by Keith Miles and William Smethurst.

Brian Hayles first joined as a standby writer during the last years of Ted Mason's life and became one of the two scriptwriters when Ted died. Born in 1931, he became a full-time writer in 1965. He wrote an 'Archer' novel set in 1919–20.

Keith Miles, who was born in 1940, became a staff writer with ATV for one year in 1966 before turning free-lance. His 'Archer' novel – *Ambridge Summer* – set in 1971, was published in 1975.

William Smethurst, the latest recruit, was born in 1945. He became a TV drama script editor and joined The Archers' team in 1974.

The writer of this book, having formed a human link between the original writers and the present team, finds his thoughts turning to the idea of a long sabbatical, having written well over a thousand episodes in under nine years.

For the programme, the future awaits, though few can say how short or long that future may be.

As Denis Morris said, so many years ago: 'It will go on as long as it remains true to itself.' And, to quote again that leader in *The Times* in 1960: 'The clever and the smart may be superior about it; it deals with enduring things. And they do endure.'

So long as the programme continues to avoid the trivial and the trendy, the insincere and the unconvincing, the cheap and the unworthy; so long as it continues to concern itself with the yearly round of country life; so long as it continues to reflect the enduring things of human life and love and death, The Archers itself will endure.

And we will continue to see things like this item in a very recent West Country newspaper: 'Wood for sale. Call anytime (*except* during The Archers).'

The time may come, sooner or very much later, when broadcasts of the daily life of Ambridge may be a thing of the past. Yet 'Forever Ambridge' will not even then be an empty boast. The phenomenon that is The Archers has made itself a permanent place not only in the record books and the social histories, but in the memories and in the hearts of millions of grateful people.

Index

All Sphere Books are available at your bookshop or newsagent, or can be ordered from the following address: Sphere Books, Cash Sales Department, P.O. Box 11, Falmouth, Cornwall.

Please send cheque or postal order (no currency), and allow 19p for postage and packing for the first book plus 9p per copy for each additional book ordered up to a maximum charge of 73p in U.K.

Customers in Eire and B.F.P.O. please allow 19p for postage and packing for the first book plus 9p per copy for the next 6 books, thereafter 3p per book.

Overseas customers please allow 20p for postage and packing for the first book and 10p per copy for each additional book.